C000256638

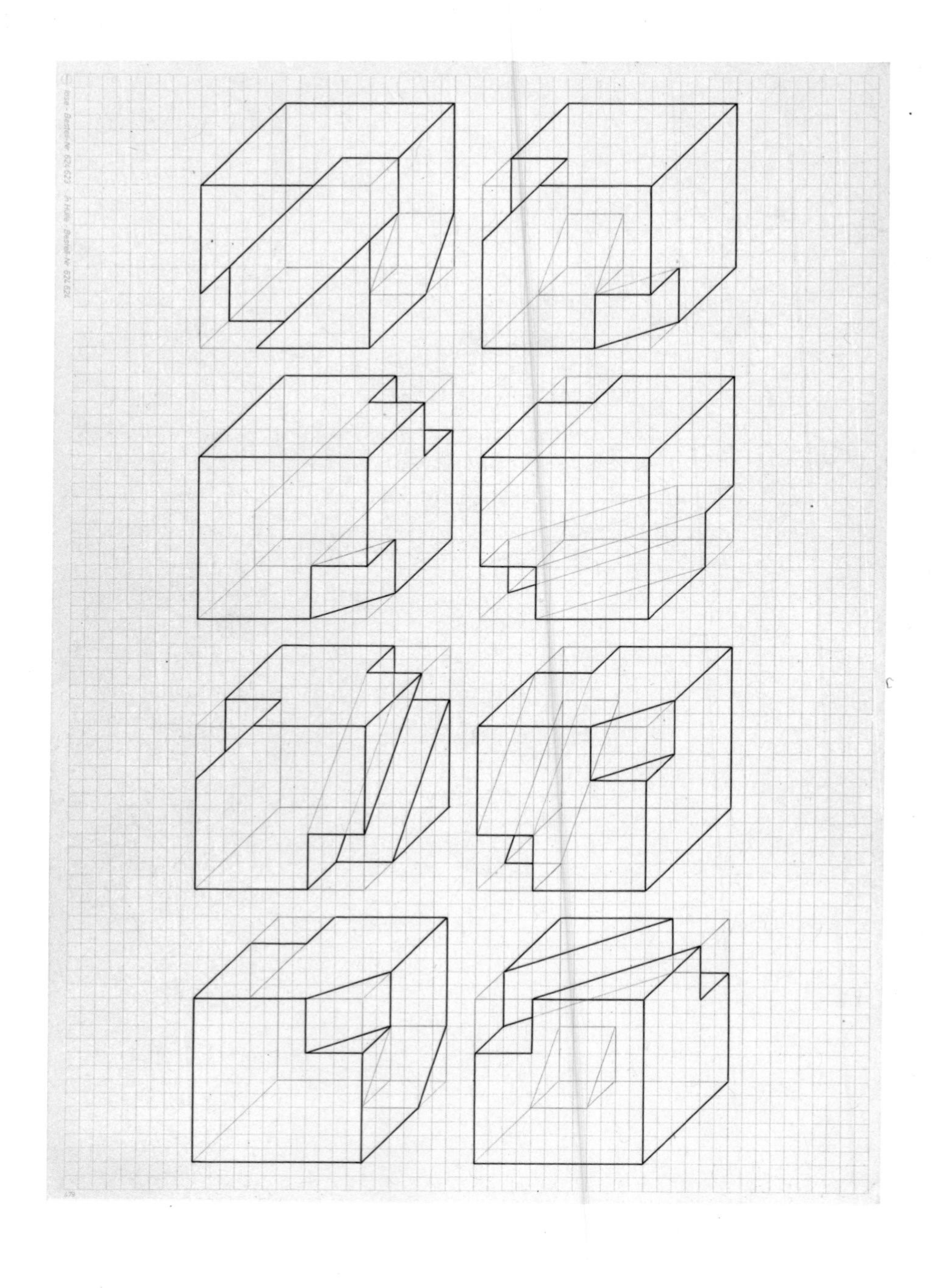

HO
RE 29-71

THE
GRAND BUDAPEST HOTEL
F. MURRAY ABRAHAM
MATHIEU AMALRIC
ADRIEN BRODY
SAOIRSE RONAN
LÉA SEYDOUX
JASON SCHWARTZMAN
TILDA SWINTON
TOM WILKINSON
OWEN WILSON
TONY REVOLORI
GRAND BUDAPEST
WES ANDERSON
2014
GRANDBUDAPESTHOTEL.COM

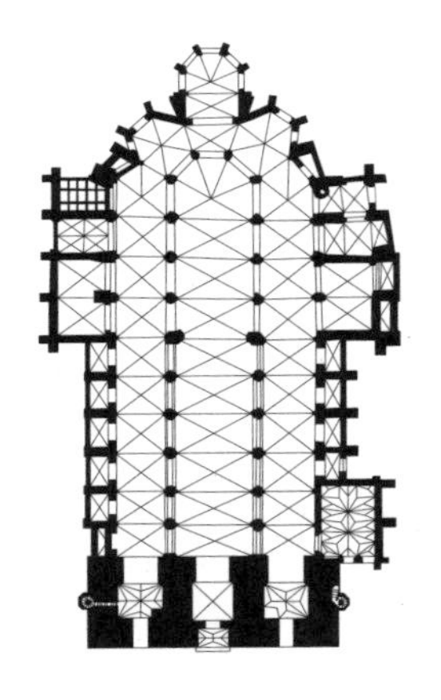

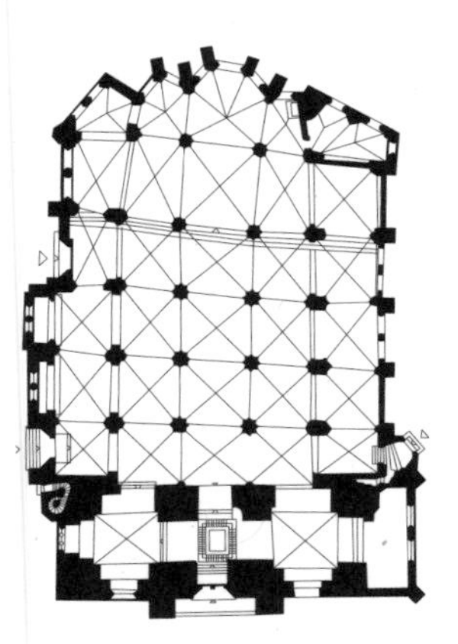

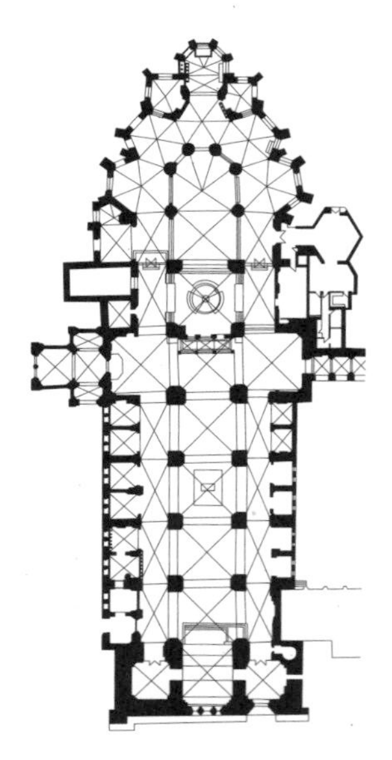

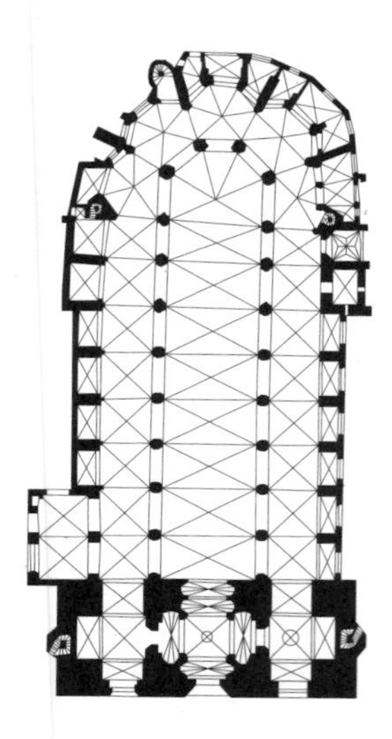

ALTO ADIGE
2160 m
SPORTHOTEL VALMARTELLO
PARADISO DEL CEVEDALE - ORTLERGEBIET

Zickzack

William Firebrace

THE MIT PRESS
Cambridge, Massachusetts · London, England

Preface

One summer's day in the late 1950s, when my family was living, for reasons never quite explained, in Vienna, we went on a trip to an area beside the border to the east. Once merely a line of demarcation between parts of the same empire, this border was now the dividing line between the Western and the Soviet zones. We children knew and cared nothing about such things, about these countries and zones, for us it was just a place to have fun. We picnicked by a small river. The other side of the river seemed deserted, apart from a tall tower. We swam in the shallow water and wanted to cross over to the other side. A man on our bank called out that we should be careful not to go more than halfway, that the other side was another country where different people lived, that they were dangerous, that they might snatch us and not allow us to return. Quick, come back now, called our anxious parents. All this frightened us, but it also made the other side appear rather attractive. What went on there? Was it really so different to our side? Who were these other people? Might it even be better to be snatched away than stay with our parents?

The exact location of such borders is often rather arbitrary, drawn up by competing nation-states to settle, even if only for a period, longstanding disputes about who controls what. A definite line is drawn on what may be an area of gradual transition. One side may be much like the other, plants and creatures and weather are all much the same, even the people may be hardly different. Then, over time, the border hardens, laws, customs, currency, language change, the colour of the shirts worn by the football team and other issues become drawn into the sphere of the home nation and differences become more distinct, even antagonistic.

Both within and also around the German-speaking world—as opposed to merely the German state—there are many such uncertain zones. This large and rather undefined area of Europe was for many centuries divided into empires, mini-states, baronies, counties, free cities, city leagues, speaking different versions of German, with varying loyalties, coming in and out of existence. The various cultures of this zone cross over into the Lowlands,

Scandinavia, France, Italy, Poland and various other countries of Eastern Europe. The German-speaking world is thus not monolithic, but diverse and sometimes contradictory, shading into differences, and still evolving. In spite of the standardisation of written German, there still are many spoken German languages, often mutually incomprehensible. Culture and language do not of course always align, nor is either confined to national borders. They cross over and intermingle with other cultures and languages, a condition that remains in spite of the violent and destructive pursuit of a reductive nationalism throughout the twentieth century. The borders of European nation-states have recently softened as a result of membership of the European Union and the Schengen treaty. Inhabitants of signatory states can travel and live where they wish, allowing something of the feel of the old multi-ethnic empires which once controlled much of Western and Central Europe. These states have also in turn been changed by immigration from locations outside Europe, so one can no longer speak of any fixed national cultures.

It is primarily in the edge zones—the places that are not quite certain, that are difficult to pin down—that different cultures and languages mix. The locations in this book are not the big well-known cities, such as Berlin, Vienna, Zurich or Munich, but rather areas that lie along or beyond the edges and are often dismissed as provincial. Two lie within the borders of contemporary Germany: the towns of the Baltic coast, with Scandinavian influences, and an area west of Düsseldorf, between the Rhine and the Netherlands. Another lies on, and also over, the border with Poland, just north of the border with the Czech Republic, on the edge of the large Eastern territories lost by Germany after the two world wars. And then there are three locations that were once within this loose German-speaking cultural zone but are now in other countries: to the east, Kaliningrad, formerly Königsberg, in Russia; to the west, Strasbourg and Alsace in France; to the south, Südtirol–Alto Adige, formerly in the Austro-Hungarian empire, but part of Italy since 1920.

In some of these locations the original culture survives, in others it has been deliberately destroyed; sometimes it merges with other cultures or, if submerged, resurfaces in a different form. Some continue to be marked—overtly, or almost invisibly—by the violent struggles and mass displacement of population they endured in the twentieth century. It is not the intention of these texts to be revisionist, to suggest that history or geography should run any other way, rather, simply to observe and comment, in a variety of ways.

These six locations are not definitive and their inclusion has evolved gradually, like pieces added to a game, rather than being planned in advance. They range East–West–North–South. Large and tempting holes are left in the pattern—it would also be interesting to include, for instance, the areas which had very mixed populations such as Ukraine, Romania and Hungary, other Baltic cities like Gdansk–Danzig, the former Sudetenland, or Trieste with its Austro-Italian-Slovene heritage. Such questions of ethnic and linguistic mix are sensitive. Some of these communities vanished or went underground after the wars of the first half of the last century. If the investigation started, unconsciously enough, on that childhood borderline, then there is always another potential move, every revelation suggests a slightly different angle from which to look at a complicated and sometimes controversial subject.

Zickzack is the German for zigzag, for an erratic movement, hopping around, unpredictable, restless, moving back and forth, never following a straight line. The zigzag has its uses in nature, hares zigzag as a means of escape, to evade an enemy who can only follow a straight line. Zickzack is also here a writing technique, allowing the text to move unexpectedly, to avoid the monotony of one thing following another. The borders between languages, landscapes, chance meetings, conversations, architecture, books, films, histories and parahistories, gastronomy, are treated with mild disdain. Be like the hare, keep leaping! This technique has its risks, the leaps may be too bold, too exhausting. Borders keep things safe not just in countries but also in writing. But the gains are the unexpected connections between what otherwise remains distanced. So the texts in this book zig and zag from one location to another, and sometimes also from one idea to another, without worrying too much about what lies in between.

SWEDEN
DENMARK
LITHUANIA
RUSSIA
* KK
* S
* W
* L
HOLLAND
* HI
GERMANY
POLAND
BELGIUM
** GZ
CZECHIA
FRANCE
* SSS
SLOVAKIA
AUSTRIA
SWITZERLAND
HUNGARY
* SAA
SLOVENIA
ITALY

Until the Bretchellmann Speaks

Strasbourg–Straßburg–Strosburi

They move silently and contentedly into the light. The old man wearing a pointed hat, on the two-wheeled cart pulled by the prancing piebald pony. The two elephants on their tricycles, their trunks held aloft, one supporting a brightly coloured spinning top. The man in the red coat in his wheeled boat, waving quietly, as though acknowledging some unseen spectators. The cowboy on his bucking stallion, the dog wearing a coat and pushing a cart, the mother duck pulling a basket with her ducklings, the woman in the white dress chasing a rat with a broom. How many more—people, animals, vehicles? The motor scooters, the submarines, the tanks, the biplanes, the gunship with a white puff of smoke emerging from its funnel, the wonderful and very beautiful steamship, the two Chinese men with a sedan chair, the ostrich pulling a jaunty white cart. The procession goes on and on, without any beginning or end, a collection of mechanical toys, miniature versions of objects in our larger world, in an upstairs room, in the grand but rather stuffy Palais de Rohan beside the cathedral in Strasbourg. The collection was made by the writer and illustrator of numerous books for children, Tomi Ungerer, a native of the city. Who are these diminutive people and these human-like animals, moving unexpectedly out of the realm of childhood and into the adult world? Do they communicate with each other, and in what language?

Strasbourg lies on the left bank of the Rhine and is the capital of Alsace, in German Elsass, a province of France. Long disputed between France and Germany, the province changed hands four times between 1870 and 1945, its status depending on whoever had won the latest in a series of wars between the two countries. In 2015 Strasbourg was made capital of a larger French province, Grand Est, and the identity of Alsace has been rather subsumed within this artificial conglomeration.

Strasbourg and Alsace, together with parts of Lorraine, are to some extent lost territories, lands which were once considered German and are now French. But Alsace had only been sporadically German, and in no way equalled the size or importance of the vast lands to the East, such as Prussia, Pomerania or Silesia, which had long been part of the German state, and which are now also definitively lost. The return of Alsace to France in 1945 was not accompanied by the kind of mass emigration, often forced, that occurred in the lands to the East, but was seen for the most part as a return to normality after the terrible crimes of the Nazis. Today large numbers of German tourists cross the Rhine to wander in the medieval town centre, reminiscent of an illustration to a Brothers Grimm fairytale, to visit the Munster, the finest German-built cathedral after the one in Cologne, to find traces of a now faded Germanic culture now combined with French style, including the delights of Alsatian cooking and Alsatian wine.

February. Light snow. Avenue de la Marseillaise. Le Michel. Traditional brasserie, four rooms, walls and ceilings coloured red, wooden tables, benches with leather. Most tables occupied. Waiters in white coats carrying plates. Saumon grillé et spätzle. Assiette Michel. Endive au jambon. Bibleskaes. Steak frîtes. Tarte au rhubarb. Torche aux marrons. Streusel. Sablé à la confiture. A conversation with Mme Itzler, born in Strasbourg and an old acquaintance.

—Well, it hasn't changed much in here, for several decades.

—No, it stays much the same. And always the same people, sitting at the same tables, having the same conversations. *Cuisine de maman*, mother's cooking.

—Mme Izler, I need some advice. Strasbourg has been for me, for many years, a kind of escape from Germany. A city which was German but is now definitely French. And now I am writing about Strasbourg, and in particular about the author Tomi Ungerer. But everything I write becomes isolated pieces—the city and the writer, his collection of toys, but also buildings, folktales, erotica, animals, more animals, clocks, European bureaucrats, football, languages and dialects, Russians, Muslims, Jews, Barbara Honigmann, even Goethe and Herder, rap singers, terrorists, and then more toys, food, rivers, streets, buildings like cats, buildings like bums. All interesting, even fascinating. But it doesn't really fit together, it leaps and bounds.

—Surely no city which you examine with care ever really fits together. That's a tedious and lazy idea. Strasbourg might at first seem pretty and pleasant, but really it makes no more sense than anywhere else. Perhaps it even makes less sense, as it's made of bits and pieces, built for different purposes. Writers just pretend to set out everything in a nice line, a montage, with a beginning and an end, because it's easier to read. So—enjoy the variety of the bits, the hopping from one to another.

—Aha ...

Mme Itzler considers for a moment and then addresses the waiter.

—Yes, two pommes streusel. No cream. And two large glasses of pear brandy, the nice one not the cheap stuff for tourists. And quickly please. My friend needs something for his confused soul, and must get on with his writing.

We walk out into the fine streets, slightly snowy, night already falling, Avenue de la Marseillaise, across Pont Royal, turning to admire the fine view back into town, quai de Maire Dietrich, where the river Ill splits into the Aar and the Ill, rue Goethe, past the grey dome of the observatory, now shrouded in mist, down rue de l'Observatoire, to a cluster of tall 1960s housing blocks, a brutal relief from the city's charm, where, almost beside the former ramparts and the boundary of the old fortified city, different parts of the world meet up, rue d'Oslo, rue de Leicester, cour d'Oxford, rue de Milan, rue de Nicosie, rue de Boston, quai des Alpes, a fine and surprising walk.... the whole world in one city. We stand on a footbridge across the Dusuzeau Bassin, looking out over the médiathèque and university buildings that have replaced the old warehouses. Madame Izler pauses and gives a final suggestion.

—Anyway, my only advice is to keep going until the Bretchellman speaks, and when he speaks then it's over, *vorbei, terminé.*

—The Bretchellmann?

—A Strasbourg legend that even good Strasbourgers don't know much about.

—Aha ...

wésse welle mer
wésse welle mer was mer sen gsen
wésse welle mer wer mer sen
eerscht nô kenne mer bstémme
was mer well ware

we wish to know
we wish to know who we have been
we wish to know who we are
only then we can decide
who we wish to become

Lines from André Weckmann's *Petite anthologie de la poésie alsacienne.* Weckmann (1924–2012) was born in Steinbourg, north of Strasbourg. His parents ran the village inn, the *Dorfwirtschaft*, where as a child he would listen to the various dialects of the visitors from the surrounding countryside. Weckmann was called up by the German army, wounded on the Eastern Front, returned and fought for the French resistance. He then became a supporter of Alsatian autonomy and an early environmentalist, opposing the construction of the nuclear power station on the Rhine. No nostalgic antiquarian of dialect, Weckmann wrote in a contemporary way in French, German and Elsässisch. For him, his childhood language was the only linguistic form in which he could express his feelings for his life and his homeland. But though one can get the general sense, the lines are almost untranslatable, everything lies in those curious spoken sounds.

The Strasbourg mechanical toy collection was originally assembled by Tomi Ungerer (1931–2019), children's book author, provocateur, graphic artist, producer of erotic images, collector of toys. Tomi (originally Jean-Thomas) Ungerer was the son of Théodore Ungerer, a distinguished clockmaker. His family was Protestant and francophone, French being the principal language of the Strasbourg bourgeoisie. When his father died in 1936, his mother moved with her children to Logelbach, near Colmar. Ungerer thus spent only his first six years in Strasbourg, but these six years were of great importance—Strasbourg was the lost city of his childhood. In Logelbach Ungerer was at first unable to communicate with the local children, who only spoke Elsässisch. After the German invasion of 1940, French was banned. Ungerer learned to speak German with the other children when he went to a school that used only German. 'I spoke Nazi at school, Elsässisch to my small friends, and French at home', he writes in *Propaganda*, the catalogue of his collection of Nazi books and images. Each language had its own use and location—school, friends, family. His feelings about the Germans, as described in his book on his childhood, *A Childhood under the Nazis*, were mixed. The Germans were an organised army, with parades, marching songs and weapons, all thrilling for a young boy, but also invaders from across the Rhine, the traditional enemy. With the return of the French after the war, and the banishment of both German languages, Ungerer was once again linguistically cut adrift. He became an illustrator, then went on extensive wanderings in Algeria, Norway, Russia, briefly joined the French Foreign

Legion, before moving to the US to become a successful writer of English-language children's books. English became his professional language, the one he used for his books and interviews and films. For many years he had little connection to Alsace. From the late 1970s Ungerer lived in Cork, Ireland, on the furthest western edge of Europe. The Council of Europe made him Ambassador for Childhood and Education in 2003, in recognition of his work in the reconciliation of Germany and France. Strasbourg created a museum in his honour in 2007, the only state museum in France dedicated to a living artist. He described his childhood as both the most disturbing and the happiest time of his life.

Kaoutar Harchi was born in 1987 in Strasbourg to a family of Moroccan immigrants. In *Comme nous existons* she describes the area of Elsau, just southwest of the centre, with its mix of rivers and canals, allotments, gelatine glue and bleach factories, tanneries and massive 1970s housing projects. Her close-knit family, speaking Arabic to one another, lived in one of these *grands ensembles*, her parents always concerned about their children entering French society. Harchi describes how at the age of ten she took her first bus ride, with a Moroccan friend, to a Catholic school in the centre, and her uneasy encounter with some French girls:

> I raised my eyes and saw the girls, these four, five girls, radiant with beauty and proud, who advanced together towards Khadija and myself ... When one of them, the leader of the group, the tallest, the one with the lightest eyes, I recall a pure transparency, approached us and asked if it was our hair that smelled *comme ça*... Then all together they bent towards us and began to touch our hair, to play with it, to wind it round their fingers, to examine the texture of the strands, to sniff it. I remember the faces of these girls. Grimacing, with the features altered, as ugly as I could believe that faces could suddenly become, ugly through the disgust inspired by the appearance of Khadija and myself. As dolls, crumpled by these dirty hands, we did not know what to say or do. So we did nothing, said nothing.

But inevitably, as she grows older, Harchi adopts the manners of French society, and begins to distance herself from the family she loves.

> I was a young girl, a girl born of parents who had themselves left their native land, I was a girl bound to her parents by a tacit pact never to live in any form of separation, and for a long time, I bore within me the fear that this second departure, my own, would resonate for Hania and Mohamed as a misfortune. A misfortune that followed their own departure.

The artist Jean/Hans Arp was born in Straßburg in 1886—French mother, German father—and spent his childhood in the city. Arp was later linked to the Dada nonsense-based art movement. La Salle d'Aubette in place Kléber, with its brightly coloured modernist decoration, was designed by the three modernist artists: Theo van Doesburg, Sophie Tauber-Arp and Jean/Hans Arp. In Arp's poem, *ich bin in straßburg geboren*, the city of his birth drifts among multiple holes. It begins:

> i was born in nature. i was born in straßburg. i was born in a cloud. i was born in a pump. i was born in a dress. i have four natures. i have two things. i have five senses. senses are a non-thing. nature is non-sense. space there for the nature there. nature is a white eagle. dada space for dada nature. i am creating a book with five buttons. art is a black foolishness. straßburg lies in a cloud. five brooms lie. four brooms sit. two brooms stand. you know nature is a black hole. you know art is a black hole. i am creating a hole in a hole and in this hole two holes, and in these two holes four holes and in these four holes five holes ... i was born in straßburg ...

The original language of the inhabitants of Alsace, Elsässisch (sometimes also called Elsässerdisch, ie, Alsace German), is mainly a spoken language, without much of a literary tradition—its written form is usually standard German. Part of the Alemannic

German linguistic group dating back well over a thousand years, it is similar to the language spoken on the east bank of the Rhine, in Baden and Swabia, and also in the northwestern areas of Switzerland. Elsässisch is barely comprehensible to many native speakers of German, and is virtually a separate language. The formal division between language and dialect, much disputed by linguists, is really a matter of degree, often resolved by a decision made by a nation-state as to what will be its official language and what will be considered merely a dialect. Insiders may feel they are speaking their own language, outsiders tend to downplay this into a dialect. Within France there are various languages relating to different areas of the country that were previously independent—Breton, Catalan, Occitan, for example—but Elsässisch is the only regional language in France relating to German. Elsässisch has its own words and its own way of speaking, the spelling varies:

Kend *(German:* Kind*), child*
Stung *(German:* Stunde*), hour*
Höönd *(German:* Hund*), dog*
Waschbel *(German:* Wespe*), wasp*
Ard *(German:* Erde*), earth*

The language includes variants on words from French:

Lalune *(French:* la lune*), moon*
Shambung *(French:* jambon*), ham*
Barabli *(French:* parapluie*), umbrella*

It has also its own insider mockery of those two rival overlords, reduced to creatures:

Kiëj *(German:* Kuh*), cow, slang for French*
Vaijele *(German:* Vöglein*), little bird, slang for German*

Like Swiss German languages, Elsässisch implies not just a different vocabulary but a different way of speaking and thinking. Whereas north German is precise, southern German languages permit a certain vagueness. For instance, speakers are reluctant to say *nein*, no, preferring a non-committal *ja ja*, yes yes, followed by *andererseits*, ... or on the other hand ... which can create some confusion. Pronunciation varies considerably across the province of Alsace, with many mutually incomprehensible variations, drifting into Swiss German to the south and Franconian to the north. Elsässisch is officially recognised by the government of France, the second most-widely spoken regional language in the country after Occitan, but like most regional languages in France—and throughout Europe—it is in decline. Its artificial preservation, supported by the European Union, is controversial in Alsace—a language needs to live and be used in everyday speech, not be conserved and be part of a museum culture. Today only about 26 per cent of the population of Alsace, mainly in the countryside, speak Elsässisch as their first language, compared to 70 per cent in 1970 and 95 per cent in 1945. This decline reflects the relentless efforts to assert French as the sole national language—the only language used in schools and government administration—as part of a re-establishment of the French state after the disasters of the war. A language provides an identity, all those who speak a language belong together, but this can also be an awkward identity, branding those who speak it as outsiders.

Why should anyone much care about languages like this, the losers in a kind of linguistic survival of the fittest? According to the UNESCO Atlas of the World's Languages in Danger, some 250 languages became extinct between 1950 and 2010. A third of the world's languages have less than 1,000 speakers. Compared to the loss of a species, the disappearance of a language is difficult to observe. On the surface little changes, it is just one step closer to the uniformity of national and global speech. The efforts of Weckmann and others to encourage Elsässisch were perhaps always going against the flow—but with the language goes a culture and a way of thinking and of being which offers something individual, distinctive.

For some French, Elsässisch is merely a nuisance, almost an insult to national pride. Surely the language of France is French? In a recent film, *Ne croyez surtout pas que je hurle* (2019), the director Frank Beauvais, born in the Moselle and living in a small village outside Strasbourg, complains anxiously about both language and culture: 'The Alsatian language is omnipresent. I rarely hear French, and even then dreadfully polluted by Germanisms ... the

Protestant, almost always right-wing stiffness of the inhabitants ... when you come from the next village you are already a foreigner ... there are a few dances dominated by polkas and German light music, at times you might think that you had been transported back 50 or 75 years.' One begins to understand why the French felt they needed to eradicate this language, still lurking like an infectious virus in the native soil.

Against this, there are certain signs that Elsässisch has become unexpectedly chic, with words and phrases appearing in the conversation of French speakers in Strasbourg—rather in the same way that polar bears and other animals in danger of extinction suddenly enter the wider consciousness. The heavy metal band Les Bredelers, curiously dressed in kilts, sing songs in Elsässisch. Street signs in Alsace are now bilingual, in French and Elsässisch (not German)—for instance rue du Savona has returned to being Sajfegässel—a token generosity by a dominant language, and a piece of folklore for tourists, a defeated language simultaneously eliminated and mythologised. But also, faced with the increasing intrusion of English words and phrases into French speech—its pollution by another global language—the reaction in Strasbourg is to resort to the remains of a language supressed by the triumph of French. So minor languages find their own way back into everyday speech, as a revenant idiom.

The theme of Alsace lying between Germany and France, and then gradually being absorbed into the European Union, would resurface episodically in Ungerer's drawings, becoming the motive for a large exhibition of his drawings, held in 2000 in Hamburg and Berlin—but not in France. Sarcastic, mocking, subversive, often mixed in with a vibrant eroticism, the sequence begins with the drawings Ungerer made as a child of German soldiers, giving the Hitler salute, beating drums, arresting his neighbours. Ungerer returned to the theme afresh in the 1970s with self-satisfied Germans devouring puddings made of ruins, watching a Jew in a cage. Then in 1989, the bicentenary of the French Revolution, Marianne appears as an ancient crone in her liberty cap, juggling with decapitated heads, screwed from behind by a uniformed Napoleon. Marianne and

Germania, always feminine, become a matching pair, dressed in sado-masochistic gear, prancing over a black hole representing Alsace. A woman in Alsatian costume cheerfully feeds sausages and wine to two babies in national dress. The mockery is merciless, both sides are equally vile, mirror images of each other. The appearance of the European Union in the early 1990s only extends the satire, as naked figures with eurostars for heads engage in orgies, a eurocrat devours his lunch while a starving refugee hides under the table, bureaucrats with their heads in boxes march off the cliff. A drawing entitled *Wohin*? Where now? shows a figure part chicken, part penis, part breast, standing alone.

'I am not pessimist', Ungerer writes, 'only a realist in a consumer society. I can only observe and what I see is a jungle of question marks.' But it is difficult to link some of these images to the man who wrote strange but optimistic tales for children, and who was sometimes presented as a symbol of Franco-German reconciliation and of the beneficial aspects of the European Union. The more one looks at the work of Ungerer, the more complex and contradictory it becomes—and the more interesting.

After centuries as an autonomous city in the Holy Roman Empire, Strasbourg came under French rule in 1681, when Alsace was conquered by the armies of Louis XIV. In a map from 1725, the city resembles some strange insect, its body reaching east–west, its sides lined by spiny scales, the new fortifications created by the military engineer Vauban. To the east, facing onto the river Ill, lies the Citadelle, now the Parc de la Citadelle. Between the Citadelle and the medieval city is an area of open land that would be filled with housing blocks in the 1960s and 1970s. Most of the original fortifications have been taken down, but the strange Barrage Vauban still survives, just to the east of the city centre, a covered bridge in the form of a long horizontal slab lying across the river, the interior space filled with the original statues from the facade of the cathedral. Occasional traces of later fortifications can still be found in the contemporary city, such as the line of the grandiose buildings built by the Germans at the end of the nineteenth century. The aquatic insect barely survives, enveloped within some other, almost formless creature.

What is striking is that the Rhine at the time was not a single stream of water, but was broken up by many islands, and the land all around the city was threaded with ponds and smaller rivers and streams, such as the Ill and the Aar, a fragmented aquatic landscape. Only much later, in the mid-nineteenth century, was the Rhine straightened and turned into the single channel of today.

Rue d'Ankara: a flat on the ninth floor of a tatty 1960s housing block. Down below, children climb the brick walls of the former military bastion of the Parc de la Citadelle. From somewhere, the dull thud of rap music. Here, a metal table, a pot of tea with jam, fresh doughnuts—proper Eastern Europe. A conversation with Mme Wissac, who moved to Strasbourg from Poland many years ago.

> —What a magnificent view, Mme Wissac! The fort, the basins for the ships, the barges moving up the river. Even forests and ponds, and right over there the hills.
>
> —People might think it's dangerous to live here. For sure it's not pretty. The blocks were built here on the cheap because the land was empty, it was an old military training ground, beside the old Citadelle. But really, it's quite harmless. This is Strasbourg, not the *cités* of Paris or Marseille. We like it here, we hardly go into the old city.
>
> —Why did you come from Poland?
>
> —When the borders opened up, many people left to find work. Our families lived in a village far to the east, near Ukraine; they'd been moved there by the Soviets after the war. We went first to Germany and then after a while arrived here, just over the border in France, and found work with the materials shop. So we stayed and now will probably never return. Our kids speak French, they go to French schools, one already lives in Paris, maybe they're now really French. We are all kind of French.

Tomi Ungerer started acquiring the toys in the 1960s, when he was living in the US. He bought from flea markets, second-hand shops, antique dealers. His collection grew to over 8,000 items, some of which are displayed either in the Palais de Rohan (significantly, on a first-floor balcony above his father's collection of astronomical devices) or in the Musée Tomi Ungerer on avenue de la Marseillaise, but the majority are now in storage. Most of the metal toys were manufactured in the US, Germany and France in the last years of the nineteenth century and the first half of the twentieth, although the collection contains toys from the 1970s and 1980s, from China and Japan. In addition to mechanical toys, he assembled a large number of paper toys, erotica, old children's books, battalions of miniature soldiers and optical instruments, propaganda. They form a heterogeneous mixture of objects that sit uncertainly with one another, just as Ungerer's own work, from children's books to radical political graphics to adult erotica, crosses the line of what is generally considered acceptable.

Ungerer's toys are usually well used, the paint flaking away, the machinery broken. They are often absurd, mocking the grown-up world, carnivalesque. The most beautiful are extraordinary objects, in particular the large metal steam-powered battleship, named Oregon, over a metre long, made with remarkable skill by the German firm Märklin, and manned by nine diminutive sailors. Each part is meticulously formed out of metal, far too fine to be simply a toy for children, with miniature guns that can be filled with gunpowder to fire pellets of bread. It hardly appears material but shimmers restlessly within its vitrine.

Some of the mechanical toys have clearly been rebuilt or reassembled by Ungerer, parts of one joined to another. The key object in the collection is a battered monkey-clown who can be wound up to draw, according to different mechanical settings, the faces of Napoleon, Queen Victoria and Louis-Philippe. This is an object that was partly created by Ungerer, using as a base a late-nineteenth-century figure of a clown, sitting in a chair and drawing on an easel, but replacing the original head with that of a monkey. The mechanical monkey, who used to be a clown, moves his pencil over the paper, as if representing the fate of the illustrator, mocking the revered figures of the actual world but unaware of the inner machinery which gives the illusion of free will.

The Strasbourg procession of beasts and humans began long ago. On his long wandering journey through Europe in 1789, the Russian writer Nikolai Karamzin arrived in the city to find it had been taken over by a revolutionary committee, and the streets were filled with drunken soldiery. His *Letters of a Russian Traveller* describe another dimly lit collection of creatures, encountered on a visit to the cathedral shortly before it was deconsecrated and turned into a Temple du Raison: 'When you enter this enormous temple, in which no clear light shines, it is impossible not feel awe; but anyone who wishes to cultivate this sacred feeling should avoid looking at the bas-reliefs on the cornices, with their bizarre and amusing allegorical figures. For instance, asses, monkeys and other beasts are depicted in monastic dress, some advance pompously in a procession, others jump and so on. One bas-relief shows a monk and nun in a most indecorous procession.' A little later he adds, 'As for the local German language, it is badly corrupted, in the best circles people always speak French.'

Jean Variot, in his book *Légendes et traditions orales d'Alsace* (1919), recounts the terrifying stories of 'Russian doctors' that proliferated around the time of the occupation of Strasbourg by Coalition forces in 1815. With long grey beards and wrapped up in grey coats, these 'doctors' wandered the streets at night, pounced on anyone they found out late and carried them off to a hidden place or cellar where they dissected their heart. Variot adds in a note that after wars people often imagine they see revenants, for instance ghosts called *Trampelthiere*, stamping animals.

Rue de Général Conrad: a small quiet canal, large trees, just beside the industrial zone of Port du Rhin, with its cranes and silos. A sky-blue spire, traditionally the blue of the Virgin Mary, criss-crossed by thin golden lines, surmounted by a golden onion dome and an Orthodox cross, and raised up by waves of sky-blue baroque arches. The new Russian Orthodox church is elegant, lightly kitsch, more like an illustration to a Slavic fairytale than anything that might actually exist in Russia. The richer Russians mostly live on the other side of the Rhine, in Baden-Baden, where there are excellent casinos to dispose of excess amounts of roubles. But Strasbourg, being almost the capital of Europe, needed a Russian Orthodox church to complement its great cathedral, the various synagogues, the new mosque, and the Buddhist temples that are springing up, in an unlikely way, in outlying villages of Alsace. Designed by the architect Dmitriy Pschenichnikov, the church was consecrated in 2019 by the Patriarch Kirill of Moscow. The interior is a pure white, the interior of the baroque arches forming an abstract modernist pattern above the large images of Russian saints below. The congregation consists of men in heat-tech jackets, older women with heads covered by shawls, and some younger women with stylish jewellery.

The medieval German centre of Strasbourg is one of the few to have survived the wars of the last century and it now seems to have suddenly grown old. Its narrow meandering streets, lined with houses of various periods, often irregular, bits of arcades, gables, all have a slightly artificial feel, a not quite believable set for the film of a fairytale.

The inner city is diminutive in scale, an urban toy over which two oversize children squabbled for many decades. Each time the switch in overlord was more violent and the cultural and linguistic change more rigorously imposed. The Germans modernised the city during their first period of re-occupation, 1870–1918, erecting a set of neoclassical buildings such as the railway station, city theatre, and various other institutions—all built in a style resembling the Berlin buildings of the period, small-scale Prussia in Alsace—and constructing the new industrial area and the basins for the port on the Rhine. The population they left for the most part untouched. On their return in 1940, during the Second World War, the Germans were more ruthless, deporting the large Jewish population to the camps, demolishing the synagogue, enforcing a strict policy of Germanisation. When French rule was restored, the authorities kept the German architecture but strictly re-Gallicised the city and the province. In the 1970s and 1980s large areas of housing blocks were constructed to the south of the centre, Strasbourg as a late-twentieth-century mass city. And then of course there is the development of the area devoted to European institutions, to the north of the centre. None of this really fits comfortably together, but the disjunctions are a relief, they stop the city becoming a touristic bauble.

Rue Ostende: beside the silos and warehouses of Port du Rhin. A white wall, LEGION ETRANGER painted in large letters. And on a smaller sign, INFORMATION RECRUITMENT. The French foreign legion. Desert forts, camels, men in dark blue coats and red trousers and those fine Kepi caps. Memories of childhood books and films, with foreign legionnaires out in the desert, *Beau Geste*, *Beau Sabreur*. A man in a rather casual uniform stands outside. A conversation follows.

—Is this really the foreign legion?

—That's what the sign says.

—And people come here to join?

—Monsieur, are you thinking of joining? Men from any country can join. But you really look too old to me. And you're wearing a hearing aid and glasses. Think hard, my friend.

A little further down the rue du Port du Rhin is the river itself. Large cranes, barges, a new container port by the Bassin du Commerce, the largest on the Rhine except for Duisburg and of course Rotterdam. The Rhine has a splendid size, with its vast slow barges, which one sees upriver, in Cologne and Dusseldorf. To the south the river reaches up into the Alps, to the north it flows into the North Sea. Here Strasbourg has a grand scale.

Strasbourg as the centre of Europe. Strasbourg as a ghost capital. Strasbourg as a miniature not-quite-metropole. The tower of the European Parliament stands to the north of the city centre, in the Quartier Wacken-Europe, at the point where the river Ill, flowing out of the city, meets the Marne-Rhine Canal. This area of flatlands is crisscrossed by canals and rivers, with locks to control the levels, an appropriate enough semi-aquatic location for the arrivals and departures of the Euro deputies and their teams of assistants.

This tower is circular, 13 storeys high, supported by a ring of flat concrete columns. Both exterior and interior are glazed to indicate nothing will be concealed, there will be no hidden deals or questionable negotiations. Occupants ascend, descend, wander around the circular corridors, discuss, perform their tasks. While the tower contains offices for the deputies, and is a visible sign of the presence of the parliament in the city, at its base is a large flat building containing the plenary rooms where the actual debates and voting are carried out. The tower, like the organisation it represents, is forever a work in progress, since parts of the upper storeys are left as a void—an eternally unfinished tower of Babel, containing multiple languages, or a Rapunzel tower, with the girl somewhere on the top floor, anxiously awaiting the handsome prince who never quite arrives.

Votes of the European Parliament must take place in Strasbourg. The parliamentarians arrive in Strasbourg for two full days and two half days every month, abandoning Brussels for the delights of Alsace, briefly filling the hotels and restaurants and boosting the city's economy. On the other days, the tower and its subsidiary buildings are pretty much empty. Most of the paperwork remains in Brussels, where the real business is carried out, for the tower is primarily a show of French-German unity, in a smallish city long disputed between the two powers.

Strasbourg claims to be the capital of European Union, with Brussels only a subsidiary administrative centre, a pleasant fantasy which has attracted any number of subsidiary European agencies. Various other administrative buildings surround the tower, including the Palais d'Europe, square in plan, vast, fortress-like, with vertical slits for windows. The diverse selection of organisations linked to, but not part of, the European Parliament include the European Court of Human Rights, the European Science Foundation, Euroscience, the Assembly of European Regions, the Human Frontier Science Programme, the Euro-Info centre, Media Antenna, Arte TV, among many others. The European Union recognises 24 languages, a number that increases as the member states grow in number. Most discussions and documents need to be translated simultaneously into all these languages, a vast and unceasing task. French and German are of course two of these languages, as is English despite the departure of the United Kingdom, but languages such as Elsässisch do not feature.

Part of what is now Quartier Wacken-Europe was formerly a garden suburb. A vestige of this rural idyll remains, creating a curious mix of relaxed local activities and European apparatus. Just to the north of the tower is the Piscine du Wacken, where the swimmers notch up their lengths. As the pools are heated even in winter, the swimmers perform in the frost and snow. Slightly to the west of the tower is Ungemach garden city, built in the 1920s by a socially minded industrialist to house the workers in his canning factory. One hundred and forty almost identical two-storey pitched-roof houses stand at regular intervals along the botanically named streets, rue des Iris, rue des Lilas, rue des Anémones, rue du Jasmin, rue des Fraises. The aims of the garden city are set out on a large stone plaque, in a slightly threatening, even possibly eugenicist tone, stating that it was designed for 'young households in good health, desiring to have children and to bring them up in good conditions of hygiene and morality'. Would-be residents were originally tested for physical health and moral character. The housing is now owned by the city as a public trust, but still the arguments over character go on, with some articles in the press arguing that the aims of the garden city are compromised by its proximity to the vast wealth of the European Union and the Eurocrats who would like to move in. Just to the north, along boulevard de Dresden, is a new development, named L'Archipel, also forever under construction, consisting of large blocks of flats, hotels and offices to house the Euro workers, if only for a few days. This bewildering zone, reminiscent of a diminutive version of Potsdamerplatz or Eurolille, reflects many of the contrasting aspects of the city, which is both small and big, toy and machine, local and continental, ideal and banal, water and land—the original Eden of the rivers and meadows, the slightly dubious garden city, the tourist boats passing by, the barely inhabited Eurostructures. During 2020, due to the complications of the covid virus, deputies were not allowed to travel and the Strasbourg parliament buildings remained empty, a sign perhaps of things to come. There is always talk of the EU abandoning Strasbourg as an unnecessary complication, especially now the centre of the union has moved further east, but for the time being it continues, a symbol of the grand idea of Europe in all its happily unresolvable contradictions.

Tomi Ungerer's children's books feature a sequence of ingenious animals—Emil the octopus, who works as a lifesaver and saves children from drowning, Rufus the bat, Crictor the snake, Orlando the vulture. These creatures are often more human than the humans themselves, brighter, more caring, more adult, capable of spontaneous action. Like animals in traditional folktales, they often come to the aid of humans who are lost or in peril—Emil the octopus rescues a deep-sea diver, becomes a lifeguard on the beach, is hailed as a hero, but longs only to return to the sea.

Such anthropomorphised creatures have a long history, appearing in ancient tales from Egypt, Greece and India, and of course in the folktales of the Brothers Grimm, where foxes, wolves, frogs, crows and other creatures cross easily from the animal to the human world, and are often humans in disguise.

In *The Beast of Monsieur Racine* an unspecified creature steals the pears of Monsieur Racine, an elderly gent. The beast 'looked like a heap of empty blankets. Long silk-like ears were flopping on either side of a seemingly eyeless head. A shaggy mangled mane topped a drooping snout. Its feet were like stumps, and it had baggy knees. It made no sound.' Monsieur Racine and the creature become best friends and cosy up on the divan. In the end the creature turns out to be two children in costume. Animals become truly human. The long soft nose of this creature, topped by hair and ominously dripping an undefined fluid, is distinctly phallic, the usually hidden sexual side of children's tales just about emerging into view. This beast is a comic version of a creature from Grimm fairytales, nice and nasty, innocent and suspicious.

Many of these animals stand in for some kind of human character. In Flix, a pug dog is mysteriously born to a cat family and brought up by cats. 'It's a genetic mishap, and a very happy one for us,' proclaims the feline father. Flix speaks cattish with a dog accent and doggish with a slight cat accent. 'In those days dogs spoke dog and cats spoke cat. They could understand each other's language but not speak it.' A reflection, surely, of the linguistic status of an inhabitant of Alsace and the difficulty of being born between two languages. Ungerer describes the diverse inhabitants of the two parts of town, for dogs Pekinese, Chows, Afghans and Shar Peis, for cats Siamese, Burmese, Persians and Tonkinese. Both dogs and cats contain therefore many varieties, neither is exclusive. In the end the pug Flix marries a poodle, their child is a little girl—a kitten.

Strasbourg's Christmas market, the Christkindelsmärik, takes place every December and attracts over two million visitors, mostly from France and Germany. The market produces a commercialised version of an Alsatian Christmas, with the narrow streets and squares filled with stalls selling goods, sweets, food, spiced wine.

In 2000 German and French police foiled an Al-Qaeda plot to explode a series of bombs at the base of the cathedral. In 2016 another attack, involving terrorists from Strasbourg and Marseille, was also prevented. In 2018 a lone terrorist, armed with a revolver and knife, killed five people and wounded eleven others near the crowded Christmas market. The assailant escaped by taxi but two days later was shot dead in the Neudorf neighbourhood of the city. The police described the man as a gangster-jihadist, a lone wolf who had been radicalised in prison. Increasingly unlikely conspiracy theories as to the 'real' motives for the attack flooded the internet after the shooting.

Small groups of armed soldiers are still to be seen in the city centre, dressed in camouflage and patrolling among the luxury shops and restaurants in the medieval half-timbered houses, carefully photographed as part of the local fauna by groups of tourists.

A large square form is marked out with eight pointed fins like botanical growths, and surmounted by a large copper dome. It stands just to the south of the city centre, below the motorway, surrounded by a large parking area. After 20 years of political wrangling, and fears of excessive Islamic influence in a Christian city dominated by its cathedral, Strasbourg now has its Grande Mosquée, the second largest in France, able to accommodate 1,200 worshipers. The design was by the Italian architect Paolo Portoghesi, who also designed the mosque in Rome. The internal central space is square, covered with a roof of exposed steel beams, the walls tiled with an abstract pattern of stones from Morocco and Alsace. The feeling is quiet, meditative, uncluttered. Men occupy the ground level, women a balcony running around three sides of the space. Most of the worshippers are immigrants from North Africa. Preaching is conducted according to various Islamic faiths, using both Arabic and French. The mosque was originally designed with minarets, prayer and study rooms, since in Islamic tradition a mosque is also a place of study, but these fell by the wayside as negotiations dragged on. Portoghesi stated his sympathy for Islamic immigrants in a Christian society and his aims in the design of the mosque:

> There is a community that has largely been present for three generations. In France, where there is a similar rootedness, there is a formidable literary and philosophical production, there is this European Islam that evolves according to its desires and not on the basis of an idea of integration of society that wants to eliminate differences. From this point of view, architecture is very important, because it allows immigrants to maintain a link, not so much physical as cultural, with their homeland. It's a very delicate thing... . Rather than experimenting with completely new paths, architecture should, in my opinion, cultivate this operation, as I have tried to do—that is, [I have tried] to confirm certain aspects of this identity but at the same time acknowledge there is obviously another place from which these people have arrived and which in turn is home to the community that is present there.

Now there are 20 mosques of various sizes in Strasbourg. A second large mosque, under construction in Meinau, a suburb to the south, will accommodate 1,700 worshippers. Largely funded by Turkish Muslims, it is designed by the Turkish architect Muharrem Hilmi Senalp in a more traditional Ottoman style, with two large minarets, missile-like in appearance. It is also planned to have the necessary study and community rooms, but curiously these are designed in an 'Alsatian' style, housed in a square, pink-coloured building with an overhanging first floor. The unlikely integration of Ottoman and Alsatian tradition appears to be still in development. Meanwhile, as of 2021, the construction of the mosque has been halted for the last two years, for financial reasons, but also because of differences of approach among the various Islamic backers. It remains a large concrete shell, with an uncertain future.

'I have realised,' Ungerer writes in *Jouets*, the original catalogue to his toy collection, 'that collecting is a mania which becomes an obsession. One finishes by living in a mass of clutter. A collection grows like a cancer. It inspires envy, the excessive taste for possession. You believe you possess it, in fact it possesses you.' He adds: 'The Alsatians are manic collectors, and this comes from a feeling of uncertainty.'

Collecting can be a remedy for doubt, loss, a way of building, or rebuilding, one's own private world. Why the need for possession? Here, the collection of clockwork toys seems a response to the family clock-making business, to the security—and fear—created by machines that measure the passing of time.

In a scene in the film *Fascinating Fascism*, directed by Celia Löwenstein, which examines the attraction of wartime fascism to young people in Alsace, Ungerer gazes at his large collection of model Nazi soldiers. All the figures are dressed in brown or black uniforms, they stretch out in a vast parade, with several diminutive Hitlers and Goerings to lead the troops. Ungerer comments on the disturbing attraction of the marching songs, the uniforms, the graphic propaganda of the Thousand-Year Reich. The toy parade inspires in him a mix of thrill, fear and disgust. Ungerer loves to provoke and shock, to deliberately adopt a stance that appears unacceptable. The collection of Nazi relics has provoked criticism that Ungerer is a *boche*, the French name for Germans during the world wars. These model soldiers, still politically beyond the pale, are not currently on display in either of the Ungerer collections in Strasbourg museums.

An upstairs room in the Jean Sturm Gymnasium, in the centre of Strasbourg. On the walls, images of microbiology. Children are building models of atoms and molecules from small balls and sticks. Some of the models hang from the ceiling on strings. A conversation with Madame Lessive, form teacher.

—The children are so well behaved.

—We are very strict. Strasbourg was for a long time a Protestant town, and associated with the Lutherans and Calvinists. This school was named after Jean Sturm, one of the leaders of the reformed church in the sixteenth century. Jean Sturm believed in balance, that education should consist of morality and religion as well as intellect and innovation. The children had to read Latin and French, to understand the knowledge of the classical world. Only those people who understood Latin or Greek could gain real knowledge. He encouraged the cultivation of individual memory and devised special exercises for children to improve their memory, so that they could remember other languages. At that time Strasbourg was a part of the old German Empire.

The children cry out that they are bored and demand lunch.

—Jean Sturm originally came from Germany, from Westphalia, but he was educated in France, so he crossed over between the nations, he is symbol of the twin ancestry of this city. Some of the oldest churches in the city are Protestant, like Saint-Pierre-le-Jeune, even the cathedral here was for a while Protestant, until the city was taken over by the French. The Protestant religion is more sober than the Catholic, here the spirit of Protestantism extends out into the Catholic countryside. Work to save your soul. But towards the end of his life Jean Sturm began to seem old-fashioned, people no longer believed that the classical world was the only source of knowledge—science and an understanding of the natural world were becoming more important.

—And Ungerer?

—Tomi Ungerer? Yes, of course he came from an old Strasbourg Protestant family. Ungerer was a complicated man, with many different, sometimes contradictory aspects to his personality. This makes him one of Strasbourg's most famous children, we have built the museum dedicated to

> him—but he is also still someone never quite accepted into this upright and correct, bourgeois view of the world, the Strasbourg behind all the medieval facades.

We are now alone. The models of the molecules spin around in the sunlight. The children have slipped out of the room for lunch.

In 1770 two German writers met for the first time in Strasbourg: Johann Herder and Johann Goethe. Johann Herder, originally from near Mohrungen, Prussia, was for a while a student of Immanuel Kant in Königsberg, then a resident of Riga, giving him a background in German, Russian, Latvian and French. At the time of his meeting with Goethe, he was writing his *Thesis on the Origin of Language*, a complex and sometimes self-contradictory work. Human language was not God-given, Herder said, but had emerged from sounds of animals, evolving gradually. He proposed that all thought is conditioned by language, so different languages produce different kinds of thought: translation between languages thus required attention not only to meaning but also to the rhythm and sounds of the original. Herder later collected folksongs from Germany and Eastern Europe, which came to influence the collections of the Brothers Grimm as well as contemporary folktales. It was the Brothers Grimm who produced the first German dictionary, applying the same organising spirit to the language as they did to their folktales. Herder believed there could be no grand theory—that things don't always need to add up, the world doesn't always fit together—a very useful proposition. On the notion of a mother language, highly relevant to a writer speaking a Prussian version of German but then living in Alsace, he wrote of language and childhood:

> Usually, we only think in the language in which we were brought up, in which we first received the deepest feelings, in which we loved, in which we dream and daydream. It is our favourite language, the language of our soul and mind. But it is no obstacle to later learning ten more languages, living and dead; to love their beauty and to collect fruits of the mind from them.

In Strasbourg Herder became friends with the youthful Johann Goethe, who had come to study law, without much success. Herder inspired in Goethe an interest in German art and culture, and the notion that the culture of Germany in the Middle Ages had rivalled that of ancient Greece. Some of the evidence for this was to be found in Strasbourg itself, as the product of a Germanic culture, even though the city belonged to the French at the time of their meeting.

Goethe frequently walked through the narrow streets to the small square in front of the cathedral. He observed the building at dawn, in moonshine, under the light of the stars. He stood amazed by the west elevation of the cathedral and described his feeling in the prose-poem *Von Deutscher Baukunst* (On German Architecture). He praised the architect of the facade, Erwin von Steinbach, as a man who worked from inspiration rather than tradition, who believed in the power of his own invention, who was able to relate the vast construction of the cathedral to the principles of form derived from nature—and who was German rather than French or Italian, with their feeble and derivative architectural constructions. Rapturously, he described how:

> An impression of grandeur and unity filled my soul, which, because it consisted of a thousand harmonious details, I could taste and enjoy, but by no means understand and explain.

Goethe emphasised that the cathedral was almost a work of nature:

> ... until the birds of morning, which dwelt in its thousand openings, greeted the sun joyously and waked me out of my slumber. How freshly it shone in the morning rays, how joyfully I stretched my arms towards it, surveying its vast harmonious masses, animated by countless delicate details of structure! As in the works of eternal Nature, every form, down to the smallest fibril, alive, and everything contributing to the purpose of whole! How lightly the monstrous, solidly grounded building soared into the air! How free and delicate everything about it, and yet solid for eternity.

Goethe's ecstatic description is wrong about many aspects of the cathedral—it is not an original creation or completely German, but an ingenious mix of French and German architecture, and von Steinbach was by no means the only architect of the facade. It doesn't matter, it is Goethe's feelings and imagination that count; out of a medieval facade emerged a more modern sensibility. Goethe's observations on the facade of the cathedral, together with his long conversations with Herder, inspired him towards an involvement with the proto-Romantic literary movement known as *Sturm und Drang*, which projected the artist as an individual creator inspired not by tradition but by his own feelings, and the work of art as part of nature, emotion, boldness, soul. Both Herder and Goethe would soon move on from Strasbourg, but their meeting there was for each the beginning of an involvement which would develop into much greater achievements.

Forty years after his stay in Strasbourg, Goethe described in his autobiography, *Dichtung und Wahrheit*, how he would ascend the right-hand tower of the cathedral, the one which has no spire but a viewing platform. At this great height—the cathedral at this time was the highest building in the world—he would have fits of vertigo which also produced a kind of delirium, a combination of fear and delight. Even in this exalted state he was able to describe with precision the landscape of the flat plain stretching between the Vosges mountains to the west and the mountains of the Black Forest to the east, with the Rhine flowing between the two:

> I saw from the platform the beautiful area around me, in which I had been able to live for a while: the impressive city, the surrounding landscape filled with magnificent flourishing trees, and the floodplains, the striking vegetation, which followed the course of the Rhine, and marked out the banks, islands, mudbanks ... a flat land laid out for humans like a new paradise, surrounded, both nearer and further away, by partly cultivated partly wooded mountains.

For Goethe the cathedral and the landscape of Alsace were a twin delight, a vast medieval form located within the streams and meadows of the Rhine valley, all relating back to the ideas inspired by Herder, and of a German cultural origin.

Strasbourg cathedral became a constant theme in Ungerer's work, almost an obsession. He drew it as a rocket launcher, shooting its single spire up into space, as a clockwork child's toy with wheels, as a mosque in an Islamic land, a beer mug filled with good Alsatian beer, a gastronomic delicacy to be carved up, a musical instrument, a tank, a medical drip, a nasty spike to be fired by a demon from a catapult, a rhinoceros horn, a scientific model, a molecule, or even as a bloody tooth to be extracted. A heap of traditional Strasbourg houses piled up to resemble an old person sits mournfully in a wheelchair constructed from the cathedral. In an unused drawing from *Flix*, the cat–dog, the alter ego of the author, flies off the cathedral in a small plane. The cathedral can morph away from its spiritual and religious functions into almost anything. As a child Ungerer had lived near the cathedral, his father worked there on the great clock, he often said he could draw it from memory. These drawings were particularly common during the long interval when he was no longer writing children's books and was living in Ireland. For Ungerer Strasbourg had been reduced to its symbol, the great cathedral, in turn miniaturised into an ever-changing set of toys for children and for the child-like adults who populate his drawings. The cathedral, like the toy collection in the old palace nearby, had become an obsession, a series that could run on forever.

In springtime, with Mme Itzler in the forêt de la Robertsau, just to the north of the city. The land is flat, sometimes marshy, with many small streams and pools, part of the floodplain of the Rhine. Birches, oaks, poplars, chestnuts. Cyclists, joggers and walkers pass by. Mme Izler speaks to me of the vanished stories of the city.

> —Of course Strasbourg has had some strange moments that have almost been forgotten now. For instance, at the end of the First World War, the city was not simply handed back to the French. The returning German sailors and soldiers

briefly set up an Alsace soviet, on the lines of the Russian soviets, inspired by the events in St Petersburg, the Rhine linked for a moment to the eastern Baltic. They proposed an independent socialist state, neither French nor German. A red flag flew from the top of the cathedral. There is a picture of these fine men in the art museum, in their brown coats and hats, holding their guns. However, they were soon chased out by the French army, who restored the comfortable bourgeois life of the city. That was the end of the Alsace soviet, quickly forgotten for an easier version of history.

In the wood are some stables, horses peer out of the stable doors. Children ride small ponies around a field. Mme Izler continues.

—And Ungerer was a writer of fantasies, sometimes dark fantasies. So not everything he said was always meant to be believed. If necessary, he made things up, rather than try to fit everything together. He is the city's most celebrated son, but he only lived here for a few years as a young child. Yes of course I love his fine children's books, the cats, dogs, octopuses and other creatures, with their human traits. They are mostly rebels, they don't quite belong to the society around them.

Mme Itzler, a person one could grow fond of, in spite of her rather superior and knowing ways, had brought a small insulated flask containing a strong Negroni aperitif, ice-cool, together with two small glasses. We sat beside a stream, in the spring sunshine, and toasted the theme of childhood in Strasbourg.

—And any sign of the Bretchellmann?

—Madame, not yet, not quite yet.

Elly Heus-Knapp, born in Straßburg 1881, near the cathedral, to a Protestant Alsatian father and Georgian mother, later anti-Nazi activist, recorded in *Eine Jugend* that her Protestant family never visited the cathedral because it was considered Catholic:

> The streets by the river are German-medieval, unaltered today, reminiscent of Nuremberg, Ulm or Würzburg. But the Sandplätzchen this side of the Ill, which consisted only of a half-dozen houses, had a completely French character and

could easily have stood in Paris. This mixture (*Ineinander*) is exactly Straßburg, the wonderful city ... From earliest childhood I knew it was different to live in Straßburg than in Darmstadt or Braunschweig or Basel. I first understood this in the games in the Schloßterrasse. The street children who played there, loud and free, hardly spoke German but another language, the Alsatian dialect. Sadly I only learned it later. So at first I was concealed in the city—how much I would have loved the Straßburg street children, the *Kneckes* as they were known ... Alsatian folk remained, in a particular way, within the cultural development of the seventeenth century. Two hundred years of French dominance had altered the upper classes, but the people remained as they always had been. Schiller said: The foreign conquerors come and go. We belong, we stay.

Oh Non Non Non Non, Oh Oh Oh Oh Oh Oh Oh
Le Noir allume les lumières de la nuit
Le Blanc éteint le sombre de nos tristes nuits
Que te dire dire sinon faut qu'on soit Amis
Noir et Blanc c'est la même je te l'ai déjà dit
(from *Noir et Blanc*)

Another wild Strasbourg childhood. Abd Al Malik (born Régis Fayette-Mikano) is of Congolese descent, born in Paris but brought up by his mother, with his three brothers, in the Neuhof district, *la cité la plus chaude de Strasbourg*. As a teenager he was a scholar at the Catholic school Notre-Dame-des Mineurs and then a philosophy student at L'Université Marc Bloch as well as a gang member involved in petty thievery, drug dealing and clashes with the police. With a small band of friends he would spend his weekends in the traditional activity of stealing from the tourists around the area of the cathedral, spending the money on flash clothes, drugs, champagne, *filles*. He writes in his autobiography *Qu'Allah bénisse la France* (2004):

The life of the expatriates of Congo and Zaire oscillated between vice and virtue, between hope and resignation. For

> the most part France was a theatre, a fixed stage set where they were hardly actors. They were little more than the remains of an Africa emptied of spirit and cast adrift. It is in the zone of the *cité*, nourishing myself in this alienated culture, that I grew up.

Many of his friends became drug addicts, several died. Abd Al Malik founded with several members of his family and friends from Neuhof the band New African Poets or NAP, which had considerable success with the album *La racaille sort un disque* (1996). He converted to Islam, changed his name, became a street preacher in the Strasbourg *cités*, went solo and produced the albums *Gibraltar* (2006) and *Scarifications* (2015), mixing rap, slamdance and jazz. Abd Al Malik became dissatisfied with conventional Islam, which he found too confining. Forever on the search for a spiritual identity he visited the Sufi masters Faouzi Skali and Sidi Hamza in eastern Morocco. *J'ai l'impression de voir*, he writes, *après avoir été aveugle*. The oscillation between different cultures continued. In 2013 he began rapping to and reciting texts from Albert Camus, backed by a classical orchestra. In Abd Al Malik's music there is a spirituality and delicacy, a lightness, different from the typical rap productions of Paris. An effect of growing up in a Strasbourg cité, in a town with surprising contrasts and an unexpectedly diverse population?

> *J'ai tout appris à l'école de la rue, mes profs des ennuis*
> *J'ai compris qu'il fallait que je change toute ma vie*
> *Il ne suffit pas d'avoir la bonne porte, il faut la bonne clef*
> *Se remettre en question, se dire maintenant je dois changer*
> (from *Au revoir à jamais*)

A major effect of the European Union, and of the Schengen Agreement, is that now there is no border, people can travel freely between France and Germany. Centuries of argument as to who owns what have, at least for now, been put to one side. Since 2017 the Strasbourg tramway has gone out to Kehl, directly across the Rhine, taking the citizens of Strasbourg across the river to do their shopping, much cheaper than on the French side of the border—Rewe, Lidl, Edeka, Kaufland, Baumarkt and so on. And casinos, cheap cigarettes, petrol. Kehl, though pleasant and quiet, typical South-German bourgeois, is the shadowland of Strasbourg. Conversation with cool young man in smart blue overalls and sunglasses:

> —Yes, of course Kehl could not survive without the money from Strasbourg. But all these French come here and can't even speak any German, as though they were still in France.
>
> —But that's what they say in Strasbourg, about all the Germans who go there and can't speak French, and think they are in Germany.
>
> —You know I'm really a student. I work here in the car park, helping the French park properly, telling them where to go, clearing their trollies. But I'm studying finance and I soon I'm going to the USA.
>
> —To become rich?
>
> —Exactly, monsieur. And to find a new life.

In Ungerer's *Moon Man* the Man in the Moon arrives on Earth, is arrested as an alien and put in jail. However, after two weeks the Moon Man has slimmed down to being a half moon, allowing him to slip between the bars of his cell and escape. He goes to a party, where people think he's in fancy dress, is chased by armed police, and finally returns to the Moon. The story is populated with absurd soldiers and police, terrified of this errant astronomical being.

Tomi Ungerer's father was the Strasbourg clockmaker, Théodore Ungerer, son of another clockmaker, Alfred Ungerer, son in turn of Auguste Théodore Ungerer, one of the two brothers who founded the Ungerer Horlogerie. The creation and repair of delicate mechanical instruments ran for generations in the family, becoming almost a calling, from which Tomi Ungerer made his escape. One of Théodore Ungerer's duties was the maintenance of the astronomical clock in Strasbourg cathedral, a task that remained in the Ungerer family from 1858 to 1989, the hereditary assignment being passed from father to son. The clock is an extraordinary piece of machinery, almost architectural in size, and repeatedly reconstructed from medieval times. It has numerous dials, scenes with mechanical figures appearing in sequence, and various devices showing the actual time in Strasbourg and elsewhere, but also the position of the Sun and Moon and the planets from Mercury to Saturn. A complex ecclesiastical computer works out the dates of feast days such as Easter. Amongst the figures are a 450cm-high sequence of Christ and his apostles, who emerge in procession at half past midday. At each quarter-hour appear in turn a child, a young man, an adult, and an old man, each passing in turn before the figure of Death. Classical gods pass by on chariots pulled by a variety of creatures representing the days of the week. A golden Gallic cockerel, mounted at the top of the clock, crows out three times, at midday, as the figure of Christ passes by. This remarkable clock, a mechanical theatre of time, offers another collection of figures and devices, located specifically in Strasbourg but devoted to the more distant spaces of the globe and the solar system. One might imagine the effect on the young Tomi Ungerer, both in terms of the sequence of wonderful machines for illustrating the passing of time, and the dedicated task of keeping them all in working order, which he escaped to find his own way in the world.

Ungerer's books for children often have violent and disturbing elements. These qualities follow on from European folktales—such as those collected or written by the Brothers Grimm or Charles Perrault, whom he admired. The world in such tales is both magical and nasty, filled with dubious and dangerous characters, the ending can be abrupt, with no moral redemption. The English writer Angela Carter, who produced new, often highly sexualised versions of such tales in the 1970s, noted how: 'the fairytale does not log everyday experience as the short story does, it interprets everyday experience through a system of imagery derived from subterranean areas behind experience.' Carter was writing for adults, but using a format traditionally assumed to be for children. Folktales, with their token characters— kings, princesses, peasants and animals—and events that unfold against a rural backdrop of fields and woods, can either be read simply for themselves, that is, as a tale to amuse, or as something deeper.

Ungerer did not offer psychological musings and his books for children are not exactly fairy or folktales. Their sexuality is never on the surface, but suggested, and in the background—a contemporary children's book could not be otherwise. But they often use the atmosphere and format of such tales, which narrate without explanation, which love grim details, which offer unexpected twists and turns and which often end suddenly. In the dark and rather scary *Three Robbers* (1961), which derives from an illustrated Munich tale from the 1890s, three armed bandits dressed in spooky black clothes and pointed hats rob stagecoaches by spraying pepper in the horses' eyes, smashing the carriage wheels and threatening the passengers with a blunderbuss—only to come across an orphan girl who reforms them and persuades them to use their ill-gotten gains to set up an orphanage where all the little orphans get to dress in red with matching caps. There is something not entirely positive about the tale, the bad becomes good, but remains much the same in appearance. In *Zeralda's Ogre* (1967) the ogre (who looks remarkably like Ungerer) devours children, and is shown with a large bloody knife and a cage in which can be seen a captured child.

> A sniff! A snuff! How hungry I feel!
> Five or six children would make a nice meal!
> A sniff, a snuff, a snip, a snup!
> When I find some children I will gobble them up!

Again the ogre is reformed by a small girl who cooks him large meals without using children—the new dishes include Roast Turkey à la Cinderella, her little feet still wearing pink high-heeled shoes, Pompano Sarah Bernhardt, and Chocolate Sauce à la Rasputin, all lavishly illustrated. Ungerer later commented:

> there is definitely an obsession with food, I was born in Alsace and the Alsatians just love to eat ... but the link to food goes back further than this. During wartime there is always an obsession with having enough food. When I was a child during the war, I would draw cellars and attics full of food, with strings of sausages hanging, and barrels of food ... even though, of course, we never had anything like this as we were very poor.

The story has a happy ending, the ogre marries the (fortunately now grown up) girl and they have many children. But certain traits are inherited, in the final image the boy holds behind his back a knife and fork as he considers devouring his baby sister.

While these stories can be read aloud to children in a straightforward way they emerge from something darker, whether specifically Ungerer's own childhood experiences or a more general world of evil and fear, which cannot be presented openly in children's books but which is hinted at, often in the corner or background of Ungerer's illustrations. Any hint of sexuality is pretty much forbidden in contemporary children's books but there is certainly something strange about these small girls that seduce bandits and ogres. Ungerer was banned from some US public libraries because of adult erotica, but already in his children's literature there are intriguing signs that all might not be quite what it seems.

Ungerer's illustration for the cover of *No Kiss for Mother* (1973) shows a thoroughly angry kitten, his arms folded, sitting at the table but furiously declining to consume his milk and bowl of soup. The disgruntled kitten refuses to kiss his doting mother and behaves in a violent way, throwing his alarm clock out the window, spoiling family meals, punching and kicking at school. Finally his mother thumps him, and in a sort of happy ending he sells his weaponry and buys her some flowers—on condition she gives him no thank-you kiss. The pictures throughout the book have a wonderful creepy feel—mice are dropped into hand mincers, spiders scare teachers, a waiter carries a large cooked bird on a silver platter, rats are pulped on a jam factory production line, the kitten sits on the toilet pretending to brush his teeth while reading a Ratman comic, a bottle of schnapps adorns the breakfast table. The drawings are in black and white crayon, careful and refined compared to the directness of the action. Ungerer wrote that this book was his most autobiographical, and of his mother: I never tolerated that she kissed me or touched me, I never liked that.' The atmosphere is that of the 1940s, very French, there's even a Gestapo officer in the scene where the mother hits the child. This a wild anarchic childhood world, disturbing, slipping back into the violence of those days of the German Occupation, but combined with a sharp wit. *No Kiss for Mother* was written as a deliberate reaction to the many soppy children's books which paint an idealised version of childhood and family life—and which now largely dominate the children's book market. It was widely criticised by parents who saw it as an attack on traditional American family values. By this time Ungerer was already in trouble with the FBI, for his links with civil rights and anti-war movements, and shortly after publication he departed for Canada. Unsurprisingly, it was to be almost his last children's book until 1998, a break of almost two and a half decades.

And cats as buildings? In the village of Wolfartsweier, near Karlsruhe, on the right bank of the Rhine, Tomi Ungerer and the architect d'Ayla-Suzan Yöndel designed a kindergarten in the shape of a large cat. The cat sprawls in an amiable kittenish way, somewhere between a geometrical block and an animal form. Its eyes are formed by two circular windows, either side of a triangular bewhiskered nose, the entrance is of course through the mouth. The paws stretch out on either side. At the rear a slide resembling a tail allows for speedy exit. The flat roof is clad in a greenish material resembling fur. The effect is playful and absurd. Rather than a miniaturised version of an existing object, as in the toy museum, there is an enlarged creature which somehow also accommodates the function of a school for children.

Such animal buildings are not unusual. Various locations boast dog buildings, sheep buildings, tortoise buildings, dinosaur buildings, all enjoying a childlike enjoyment of being both big and small. The Wolfartsweier kindergarten is cleverer than just being a giant cat, as it manages to be both playful feline and architectural, with its orthogonal form, large windows and light, pragmatic interior. It was constructed as part of the Europe without Borders' initiative, as a Franco-German cooperation.

And so from cats to bums. In 2009 Ungerer was asked by the municipal council of the small Swabian town Plochingen to make a proposal for a new public toilet. Ungerer's design, which he termed *arschitektur*, was for a small square building surmounted by a large pink arse in place of the more customary dome. Above the entrance would be written in gothic script *Übung macht den Meister*, practice makes perfect. A photo from the period shows Ungerer proudly presenting his proposal in the rather dreary city hall. Whereas the kindergarten in the form of a cat had met with general approval, the arse-like toilet crossed the line of what was deemed acceptable and managed to upset the inhabitants of the small town, who were expecting something more dignified. The politicians of Plochingen lacked the courage to construct this piece of Ungerer humour, claiming that Muslims might be offended—South German pietism disguised as an unlikely sympathy for Islam. A more moderate design was constructed. Karlsruhe has its cat, Plochingen still awaits its bum.

Alsace has traditionally had a very uniform population—the Alsatians with their lects, supplemented by the arrival of the French, mostly in the cities, and, according to who owned the province, the Germans. In addition, there have been the Jews, who have settled uneasily, being subject to outbreaks of vile mass persecution in the Middle Ages. However, Yiddish (sometimes referred to as Judeo-German) is very close to the Alsatian language, both deriving from what is called, in the impossibly complex terminology of linguists, Middle High German.

The poet Claude Vigée (born Bischwiller 1921 as Claude Strauss) was descended from a family of Judeo-Alsatian cloth merchants and fled at the time of the German invasion of 1940 first to the South of France, then the US, then Israel. Vigée kept the faith with his use of dialect, writing in *La lune d'hiver*: 'I am an Alsatian Jew, so doubly Jewish and doubly Alsatian'. His poetry is sometimes in French sometimes in German, and still also sometimes in Elsässisch.

> My maternal grandfather, Leopold, who came from the countryside, continued to speak Judeo-Alsatian until his death in 1937. Rather than master classic German, or French, he used this dialect all his life, within the family, in his native village of Seebach ... From him, at five or six years old, I learned through osmosis the Judeo-Alsatian dialect, living and complete, which my paternal grandparents had not spoken for 50 years, and my parents never.

In 1939 there were 20,000 Jews in Alsace. By 1945, after six years of Nazi rule, effectively none. But today there are estimated to be

50,000 Jews in Alsace, partly returnees, partly Sephardic Jews arriving from Africa in the 1960s. Very few still speak Judeo-Alsatian.

One member of this thriving community is Barbara Honigmann, who came from a Austro-Hungarian-Jewish family, of some complexity. Her parents had close and rather dubious links to the Soviet espionage agencies and her mother was originally married to the English spy Kim Philby. Honigmann grew up in East Berlin under the communist regime but emigrated with her husband to Strasbourg in 1984. She still lives in Rue Edel, south of the city centre, which she describes in her book, *Chronik meiner Straße* (2015), as one of the ugliest streets in the city, where immigrants arrive and move on as soon as possible. She writes that the area has become a kind of Jewish zone, as large numbers of immigrants moved in from Eastern Europe after the collapse of the Soviet Union. But there are also:

> many Arabs, Turks and Kurds, Africans of every kind, who often pass by in long coloured clothing and high headgear, and sometimes one sees an African priest in a long white outfit with a golden cross ... also Pakistanis, Indians, Sikhs with turbans and women in saris, Asians who are perhaps Chinese or Japanese or Korean ... Portuguese, Russians and other East Europeans, Albanians, Romanians, Bosnians ... but they don't behave as in Paris, they walk slower and in smaller numbers, we are in the provinces here.

This rather exotic multiracial community—a familiar sight in big cities but not expected in smaller towns like Strasbourg—includes of course the 'Innerfrench' and the Alsatians, who remain distinct. Some of the Jews come from families that returned to Alsace after the German Occupation, having survived deportation to the extermination camps. Honigmann remarks of one pair who live in her building that 'they speak with each other in the Judeo-Alsatian dialect, since they originate from small Alsatian villages, she from Merzwiller and he from Ingwiller; this dialect is now not much heard and will soon be lost, since most Jews, or at least their children, moved to the city and have become assimilated into the French language.'

Annie Ernaux, in *Les Années*, writes of her childhood in Normandy (yes, the other side of France, but the experience is comparable) and the difference between her local way of speaking and standard French:

> We recited the grammatical rules of proper French. As soon as we returned home we found without thinking our original language, which did not make us think about words, only about things to say, which belonged to our bodies, to slaps, the smell of Javier water, apples cooked throughout winter, the sound of piss in the bucket and the snores of our parents.

Local languages and toys are both part of a limited, small-scale childhood world. Language is learnt as a child, in the family, normally spoken and not written; other, more official languages are acquired later. Toys are of course usually childhood objects, miniature versions of the adult world. The language one speaks affects the way one observes and defines the world. Local languages are a particular form of expression and understanding, spontaneous, instinctive, reflexive, compared to languages learned as an adult, which are more considered. A local language creates a semi-private world, accessible only to those who understand its cultural atmosphere. A toy is also personal, belonging to the child, a fantasy object for creating a private world. As a child grows up, and needs to learn other languages to communicate, so his/her understanding of the world must also change. Similarly, toys are at some stage put away, the child moves on to adult objects. The comfort of the original language of childhood still remains, to be resorted to when required. And toys also can make a curious return, as in the Ungerer collection, not just as nostalgic objects but viewed differently, from outside, from an adult point of view.

The upper floors of the Strasbourg Tomi Ungerer Museum are devoted to displays of his work as children's illustrator. But visitors who venture without much prior thought down to the basement find another side to Ungerer—erotica and pornographic images. For alongside his work as a writer and illustrator of children's books, and as a graphic artist, Ungerer produced provocative sexual drawings. *Fornicon* (1969), for instance, consists of a series of erotic images showing women and sexual machines, sexual toys, witty, cruel, brutal. Ungerer produced a book on Hamburg dominatrixes. Such images, exhibited without problem in Paris, were seen in the US as entirely unacceptable from a children's author. How do we judge such this worrying combination of supposed childhood innocence and adult sexuality today? What is merely edgy, what is clearly oppressive to women? Ungerer followed many paths at the same time, dark and light, joyful and painful. Perhaps he was a more disturbed and confused personality than is usually allowed of a writer of children's books. The traces of these various paths were always there, they might already be found in that room with the toys, in the illustrations of a certain jovial cruelty often found in children's books. The mechanical sexual devices, usually phallocentric, are perhaps a depraved version of that mechanical clock in Strasbourg cathedral, the movements of the planets reduced to male erotic desires. Ungerer himself wrote towards the end of his life:

> Looking back at this mind-boggling diversity I have to face all the different identities (not split but united) that constitute myself. All haunted by death and sex which drive *la condition humaine*.

The long-term manager of Arsenal football club, Arsène Wenger, was born in Strasbourg in 1949, but the family soon moved to Duttlenheim, some 20km away. Wenger's father managed a bistro, Le Croix d'Or, and a shop for spare car parts. He was also manager of the local football club. Wenger was brought up speaking Elsässisch. In his autobiography, *My Life in Red and Blue*, he recalls his childhood in the village: 'The area I grew up in was steeped in religion. In those days you had to receive permission form the priests to play football because that meant missing vespers.' Regarding the position of Alsatians he comments: 'Neither here nor there, that was our misfortune. But to possess a little from here and a little from there, that is also our wealth.' In Wenger's case this meant being able to use the strengths of various kinds of football.

He began as a fan of German football, with its concentration on strong aggressive play, and as a teenager supported Borussia Mönchengladbach, but he was also a fan of the fluid Total Football approach at Ajax. He became manager in turn of the local team Mutzig, then Nancy, Monaco—and Arsenal.

More from Jean Vigée. The poet writes of the moment in his childhood when he realised that objects have different names in different languages, and how this undermined his understanding of his familiar surroundings:

> Our teacher, Mlle Zimmermann, announced to us, in dialect, that we would now begin to learn French. We opened the illustrated book, where a fine rabbit was running, and she said, 'E lapin ésch e Hààs'. It was thus that I officially learned my first word in French, along with 30 amazed fellow pupils.... So they taught us that the real name of a Hààs was a lapin. All this did not seem clear to me. What was this real name? Since forever we'd known the name of this animal that we saw running in the fields. But now it had two names—of which neither was true, and as a consequence a doubt rose up about all the names of people and things.
>
> (Jean Vigée, 'E lapin ésch e Hààs' in *Le parfum et le cendre*, 1982)

In *Tortoni Tremolo*, one of Ungerer's later books, a musician is cursed by a witch. His name changes continually—Temelo Notrito, Metrolo Rottoni, Lotremo Initrot—and the notes of the music he plays become small pellets which pour out of his instruments and cause chaos. He finds these pellets have different tastes according to the type of music—'lullabies had a soothing effect, marches got you going, and the mariachis were soothing'—and sets up a mass-production of musical foods. Names changing unexpectedly has a familiar tinge, but musical sounds taking on physical, gastronomic form suggests a folktale world where such metamorphosis is natural, music feeding not only the ears but also the stomach.

One cold January morning, a meeting with Mme Willer, director of the Tomi Ungerer Museum and author of several books on the artist. The conversation is in French, with an occasional sprinkling of German, the quiet around us periodically interrupted by groups of schoolchildren.

—It's much better that you speak, Mme Willer, and I just listen.

—Very well. Ungerer came from a very conservative Strasbourg family. His relationship to the Alsatian language, Elsässisch, was distant. He spoke it in school, during the time of the German Occupation, but it was not an integral part of his family life.

—The Ungerer family home had many children's books in both German and French, such as Wilhelm Busch's *Max und Moritz* and Hansi's *L'histoire d'Alsace contée pour les enfants*. Also folktales, *contes*. These books are often satirical, they propose a strange world for children, parallel to the adult world, in which terrible but humorous things might happen. Children's books can say things which cannot be said, in adult books, or at least not in the same way.

—His mother used to play French and German songs on the piano. Later Ungerer produced his own *Liederbuch* of German children's songs.

—He wasn't at all a bitter man, but he knew how to mock, how to take what others see positively, for example, the great gastronomic tradition, and to send it up as greed and gluttony. He did sometimes feel ignored by Alsace, that his achievements and books were not really recognised. But in the mid-1970s he began to give parts of his collection to the city museums, starting with the toy collection.

—Ungerer had a word for Alsace, *l'escargotisme*, snailness, referring to the tendency to do nothing, to sit inside a shell and complain. But he also showed the snail coming out of its shell, entering another with the stars of the European Union. He drew Marianne, the female symbol of France, pulling the tongue of a small boy—the prohibition and destruction of the native language.

A fine sunny spring day. Standing with Mme Itzler at the centre of the pedestrian Pont des Deux Rives, which spans the Rhine. The French bank to the west, the German bank to the east. The city lies slightly downstream. The port beside the river, with its basins, warehouses and cranes is visible. In the distance the single spire of the cathedral.

—So did it all work out? All those different pieces you were worried wouldn't fit together?

The wide slow-moving river stretches out to the south to the Alps and to the north to the North Sea.

—Oh ... yes, Madame. Really I just left them to find their own way, seeing how they might sit next to another, not too close and not too far.

A large barge, towing another barge of similar size, approaches slowly on its way downstream.

—It sounds almost like a method. So long as you have the right pieces the spark will flow between them. Strasbourg isn't the city that people often think. And it is so fine to be out here near the river, away from the city, with no one around.

A man on the barge shouts out something to us in a language we don't understand, and waves his arms, perhaps in greeting, perhaps slightly obscene.

—And did the Bretchellmann speak?

Birds follow the barges, flying up into the sky and down almost onto the water.

—Hmm, not so that I have heard.

The barges pass under the bridge.

—Ah well, maybe soon ...

An earlier subversive figure still remains in Strasbourg, but is now silent. In the cathedral, very hard to make out, just below the great organ overlooking the nave, are three late medieval automatons—a trumpeter, Samson prising open the jaws of a lion, and a bearded figure known as the Bretchellmann (named after the bretzell, a traditional salted bread in the form of a knot). The figures were formerly set in motion by levers linked to pedals on the organ. The Bretchellmann moves his arm, as through eating a bretzell. Jean Variot, again in his book on the legends of Alsace, records that a man would hide behind this figure and

> during the divine service, vespers or night-prayer, would burst out laughing, roar and cry out, even sing bawdy songs, mocking the faithful in the nave, deriding mercilessly their naivety, above all that of the country folk, not even sparing the canons and the clerics piously singing in the choir. Of course the voice was really that of a man, concealed in the lower reaches of the organ. The clergy repeatedly tried to silence the Bretchellmann, but he was popular and survived. Then there began a rivalry between the Bretchellmann and the mechanical cock placed on top of the astrological clock, who to the joy and astonishment of the crowd would beat his wings and sing out like a real cock, echoing around the church ... the two adversaries insulted each other with an unprecedented violence, asking the crowd to judge their quarrel, they cried out so loudly that they made inaudible the sound of the organ and of the clergy ... but up until our time the dispute between the Bretchellmann and the cock remains unresolved, nobody has been found with enough intelligence, science and courage to dare to determine the question of delicate and hidden rights which lies behind the issue.

The hidden voice of the mechanical man and the cries of the clockwork bird, later renovated by Tomi Ungerer's father—the struggle seems to imply some absurd rivalry between mechanical religious toys. The bearded Bretchellmann was provocative and outspoken, possibly dangerous, calling out against authority. O Bretchellmann, automaton with a human voice, why are you so silent today? Lay aside that bretzell, speak out man, speak out!

If the visitor returns to the collection of toys, these diverse themes surface and reflect on one another. What appears at first to be missing may be only slightly hidden. In the Ungerer toy collection there are no mechanical poets, nor Russian travellers. But there are several men of mildly artistic appearance, wearing long coats and hats waiting outside a diminutive railway station. No dominatrix, but there is something curious about the diver with a propeller in place of a penis. No obvious Eurocrats or Eurojudges, but an eminent lawyer in a black suit, making a speech. No cat kindergarten but a cat beating time on a drum circles around, accompanied by a dog with a trombone. No fascist soldiers, or even legionnaires—they remain in storage, patiently awaiting the call for the next mass rally—but there are numerous armoured vehicles, ready for action. Any more Russian figures? Soldiers perhaps, with red flags? Very soon it will be time for them to make their appearance, but many hundreds of kilometres to the east. In fairytale tradition, these clockwork figures are merely in disguise, barely hidden signs of other personalities. For what are these wonderful trumpeter elephants, writer monkeys, musician swans and trotting ponies but ourselves in another form, emerging from the past or from the future, into an uncertain present.

Now You Understand
Königsberg–Kaliningrad

In the arrivals area of Khrabrovo airport hangs a wall-size black-and-white photograph of a large town featuring nineteenth-century buildings, church towers, a castle, bridges and parks. This appears to be the city one is about to visit, but it's actually Königsberg, the capital of East Prussia until it was almost completely destroyed 70 years ago and largely replaced on the same site by the Soviet city of Kaliningrad. Which is the material city and which is the immaterial? The answer is not so obvious, because after many years of absence the city shown in the photograph is now very tentatively returning to life, prompting an uneasy relationship with the lively if battered and often self-contradictory socialist city that superseded it. Complicating things further, each of these two Baltic cities is itself multiple, consisting of parts of other cities, some submerged, some only partly visible, some solidly present, some envisaged but never constructed, vying with one another for a place in the same location.

Königsberg's most celebrated inhabitant, the philosopher Immanuel Kant, attempted to specify the limits to understanding in his *Critique of Pure Reason* (1781). Here Kant proposed that the world is divided into 'phenomena'—which we experience through our senses and through reason—and what he termed 'noumena'—which exist beyond what is knowable and which therefore can never be understood. Noumena are the very essence of things. That which we experience with our senses is a manifestation of this essence. Kant's proposal stems from a long and evolving tradition of envisaging the world as divided into knowable and unknowable, understandable and not understandable. Philosophers have endlessly debated what Kant actually meant by this distinction, without ever quite arriving at any definitive conclusion. Kant himself even rewrote his theory various times, forever slightly altering the argument and changing the defining terms. But the essential idea of Kant's twin terms, phenomenon and noumenon—the appearance and the reality—remains. This way of understanding the world around us might now be adapted to examine his native city in its twenty-first-century incarnation, as the synthetic Königsberg–Kaliningrad. The twin city is indeed part material and understandable to the visitor, part immaterial and always slightly beyond what can be comprehended. Boldly challenging Kant's assertion that we know nothing of noumena, the conjoined city might even offer some inkling as to its elusive nature.

Adding a refinement to his theory, Kant went on to compare that part of the world which can be understood to 'an island, enclosed by nature, itself with unchangeable borders, the land of truth—enchanting name—surrounded by a large stormy ocean, the sea of illusion'. For Kant, Königsberg was itself like an island. He rarely travelled beyond the boundaries of the city, and then only to a small house in the countryside. 'Such a city', he wrote, 'can be a perfect place for acquiring both knowledge of people and knowledge of the world, where these can be gained without the need to travel'.

Ulitsa Portovaya: a large wharf building, brick walls and metal roof, beside the river Pregel. Long rows of expensive cars, mainly

Mercedes and BMW, Toyota and Lexus SUVs, alongside some Italian sports cars. A few potential buyers. Two smartly dressed women carrying folders of papers approach:

—All these vehicles are for sale.

—Really? I'm only visiting the city. Where do they come from?

—There are assembly lines for BMW, Chevrolet and Hyundai near here, in the dockyard.

—And the others?

—From across the border. All our vehicles are imported legally, and with all the proper customs and registration documentation. Our prices are very competitive. We are not isolated here in Kaliningrad, but we have links to everybody, we can obtain any vehicle you wish. And yes, we can take credit cards or cash—euros or dollars, even roubles, even pounds sterling.

An enclave is a portion of a territory, a kind of island different in character from the other nations that surround it. The Kaliningrad oblast is such an enclave. Covering an area of 15,000km^2, it belongs to Russia even if it lies well beyond its borders, over 1,000km from Moscow, bounded instead by the Baltic Sea to the west, Poland to the south and Lithuania to the north and east, a flat landscape, projecting out into the Baltic, on either side the curious Vistula and Kurisch Lagoons, protected by their long narrow sandbanks. For the Soviet Union Kaliningrad was a strategic possession, the Baltic here is ice-free even in winter, giving an ideal location for the Soviet Baltic fleet—further east in the Gulf of Finland the fleet was icebound in a severe winter.

The city's local football team, FC Baltic Kaliningrad, plays in the second tier of the Russian football league. One recent match was against FC Luch-Energiya Vladivostok—and so a team from the westernmost point of Russia met its equivalent from the east. The two cities sit more than 10,000km apart, across an eight-hour time difference, and for the away team, FC Luch-Energiya Vladivostok, this meant a 14-hour flight with one stopover. The match ended 0–0.

Kaliningrad was part of the USSR from 1945, when Stalin took it as a personal prize from defeated Germany—its former self, Königsberg, having been for the most part reduced to ruins by RAF bombing raids and then by street fighting as the Red Army wrested control. The German population, already reduced from 370,000 before the war to just 70,000 in 1945, were all expelled over the following two years. The Jewish population, about 3,500 before 1933, declined to almost nil, but has since risen to about 2,000 through immigration from Russia. The new population, which arrived after 1945, at first consisted mostly of Soviet military personnel, who were then followed by large numbers of Russians, White Russians, Ukrainians and many others from the more distant Soviet republics, all hoping for a new life. In the city archives there are even unlikely photographs of new inhabitants arriving by camel, possibly from the southern republics of the USSR. And yet it was from out of this very diverse group of people, with no experience of living in the Baltic, that the current, actually rather homogeneous, population emerged.

The Kaliningrad oblast remained a restricted area until 1990, off-limits to foreigners and as a military base hard to access even for native Russians. But with the collapse of the Soviet Union the borders were opened. Initial reports in the Western media described it as an urban disaster zone, the 'Black Hole of Europe', associated with car smuggling, drugs, prostitution and other forms of criminality. In the nearby port of Baltiisk, home to the Soviet Baltic fleet, the warships and submarines quietly rotted away, their nuclear armaments reportedly dumped into the sea—one more toxic agent added to the polluted mix of industrial effluent and untreated sewage. Over the years, however, these negative associations began to flicker with other, more positive affiliations. And so at one moment Kaliningrad was presented as the 'Calcutta of the North', at another as the 'Russian Hong Kong', a crossroads between the capitalist west and the new business zones of the east. There were even tentative proposals, firmly rejected by both the Russians and other neighbouring countries, for the oblast to be integrated into a reunified Germany, or to become a fourth Baltic state along with Estonia, Latvia and Lithuania, in a new confederation united by peace, trade and interchange. Indeed, for some years Kaliningrad enjoyed the status of a Special Economic Zone. Factories were set up to manufacture automobile parts and digital technologies, with Western companies such as BMW and Cadillac providing considerable investment. However, since 2004, when Poland and the three Baltic states joined the EU and the visa-free Schengen Zone, the oblast has been cut off from both the surrounding countries and the main Russian territory, with only a corridor linking it across Lithuania to Belarus and the Russian border. More recently, amid a general heightening of international tension, Russia has threatened to rebuild its Baltic fleet and to install missile launch pads in the city.

In the confused political geography of the southern Baltic there have always been mixtures of ethnic populations within nation states that are often isolated from their governing countries and then unexpectedly reconnected, which in turn isolates others, like some complicated game of Go. In the case of Kaliningrad, its status was inherited from Königsberg, since from 1920 to 1940 East Prussia was itself a German enclave, surrounded by Poland and the USSR, cut off from the main body of Germany. The status of an enclave is usually uneasy, uncertainly linked to the homeland, surrounded by potential enemies, but determined to assert its own identity. As a result, it tends to induce an individually minded populace, often proud of their special status and unwilling to be merely part of a larger block. Even at the time of being a supposedly closed city, Kaliningrad's citizens were known for being distinct. In 1969, *Der Stern*'s Moscow correspondent, Dieter Steiner, visited the city and reported that the youth were more relaxed than elsewhere in Russia—young men sported Beatles haircuts and mischievously sang 'You don't know how lucky you are, boy, back in the USSR'. Photographs from the late 1970s also show lines of bridal couples in suits and miniskirts wandering with guitars on the Baltic beaches, hardly the typical image of the Brezhnev years. Königsberg even had its own distant reply to this appropriation of 1960s culture. The long-legged model Veruschka, sounding Russian but actually German, was born in Königsberg in 1939 as Countess Vera Gottliebe Anna Gräfin von Lehndorff-Steinort. Her aristocratic Prussian father, a key member of the German Resistance, was later executed for allegedly attempting to assassinate

Adolf Hitler in the 20 July Plot. As a result Veruschka spent some years as a child in a German labour camp. After being 'discovered' aged 20 by the photographer Ugo Mulas, she became one of the it-girls of the swinging sixties, was featured in fashion magazines and appeared memorably in Michelangelo Antonioni's film *Blow Up* (1966), in which David Hemmings makes love to her with his camera. If history had been a little different she might have been strolling along that Soviet Baltic beach.

Ulitsa Frunze: a series of dilapidated 1980s housing blocks, ten storeys high, constructed of prefabricated concrete panels, located beside an urban highway. In front of the nearby Palace of Weddings stands a relief sculpture in concrete proclaiming the ideal socialist love match. A Soviet couple—he in a suit with slightly flared trousers, she in a loose-fitting dress—are shown standing lovingly together. Doves flutter around them and an olive tree sprouts unexpectedly at their feet. Just beyond the sculpture there's a restaurant frequented by fashionably dressed women sporting considerable quantities of jewellery. Man in smart suit and tie, black boots stands outside.

—Is the Palace of Weddings still open?

—Of course, people always need to get married. Are you thinking of getting married?

—No. Not quite now.

—True love thrives in Kaliningrad.

A small group emerge, led by a bride in a short white gown and veil, and a groom in a tight suit. They stand for a moment to the side of the relief while a photographer records the scene. A large black American car pulls up, the driver gets out and waits.

Kaliningrad still contains urban elements from many different periods, often so altered that the original is hardly discernible. For example, the island of Kneiphof, surrounded by the arms of the river Pregel, was once the heart of the German city, a densely populated mass of small houses alongside the cathedral and town hall. Renamed Pregel Island, it is now a quiet park, scattered with sculptures of miscellaneous Soviet worthies, including a noble Yuri Gagarin, and oversize proletarian workers. Beside the ruined castle, on a large pedestal originally occupied by Bismarck, is a bust of Alexander Suvorov, Russian field marshal and national hero at the time of the Napoleonic wars. Few of these people ever came to Kaliningrad, but they are here to provide a kind of moral support, to suggest a Kaliningrad that was always in its heart of hearts Russian.

Slicing across Pregel Island, from north to south, is Leninsky Prospekt, originally conceived as the grand avenue of the city, in imitation of streets such as the Nevsky Prospekt in St Petersburg, but in reality a multi-lane highway lined with housing blocks. Going north, this avenue passes both the site of the city's former castle and the now vacant House of Soviets, a late-1980s building nicknamed The Monster—two failed seats of government. It then turns northwest to Ploshchad Pobedy, the new centre originally created by the Soviets as a place for military parades. Leninsky Prospekt is crossed at right angles by another multi-lane inner-city highway, Moskovsky Prospekt, which is also lined over much of its length with typical 8- to 12-storey blocks of Soviet housing.

Amongst the trees of the park by the river are numerous statues of Russian and Soviet literary figures. Feral cats prowl around, paying no great attention to the worthies. A group of schoolchildren eagerly ask questions of their teacher, who replies with a certain lack of confidence.

> —Is that really Alexander Sergeyevich Pushkin?
>
> —Yes that must be Pushkin.
>
> —Or maybe Lev Nikolayevich Tolstoy.
>
> —No, Tolstoy had a large beard.
>
> —If only there were signs to say who they are.
>
> —I wonder if Anna Akmatova is here. She is my favourite poet. May a prison dove call in the distance, and ships sail quietly by on the Neva ...
>
> —Or Marina Ivanovna Tsvetaeva. I love her. Where is Tsvetaeva? I have looked long enough into human eyes, now emblaze me, make ash of me, black-sun night ...
>
> —Where is Elena Andreyevna Shvarts? She must be over there beside the river, perhaps smoking a cigarette and

drinking vodka. The sun once sang of safety, as it rose above, but then the sun knew of nothing, of dark destroying love ...

—Children you have learned well. Surely they are all here. Everyone comes to Kaliningrad. But Russian writers need no signs. We all know who they are. The golden age, the silver age ...

—And what age are we in now.

—Hmmm. Maybe the plastic age, the digital age ... no, children, it is now your age, yours to decide.

Elsewhere to the east and south the inner city is made up of an assemblage of housing blocks of various sizes and from various periods, sometimes fitting into the German street pattern, at other times forming their own grid. A ring road based on the layout of the old city walls encloses the inner city, passing various old brick forts, but even this is incomplete, with bits missing entirely and lacking bridges over the Pregel. The city has also now spread out uncertainly beyond the inner ring, with microrayons such as Leningradsky, Tsentralny, Moskovny—always similar names in every Soviet city—and networks of quiet streets without any apparent order, with suburban villas, huts, factories, parks and allotment gardens reaching out to a second, also incomplete, ring road 12km in diameter. Already in this description one can see that nothing is very clear in Kaliningrad—small scale and large scale, urban monsters and diminutive elements, natural and artificial, almost disappearing and not quite appearing, all without ever seeming to quite overlap.

The disappearance of Königsberg and the appearance of Kaliningrad in its place was a vital part of the Soviet image of the city, providing the foundation myth from which its urban plan emerged. Large areas of Gdanzk/Danzig or Warsaw could be reconstructed after the war because there was an assumption of continuity, that the Poles had always been there. Even Wrocław/Breslau, the home of German modernism, had been once in the original Kingdom of Poland, so could be rebuilt as it was. Königsberg had been founded on territory once inhabited by Slavs, but many centuries ago, claims boosted by the new Soviet owners, but the city was essentially German. Königsberg had to be seen to vanish so that Kaliningrad could be born. But just how much of the city was actually destroyed in the last years of the war is a matter of varying opinion. In the Soviet film *Meeting on the Elbe* (1949)—one of many shot in the city—Kaliningrad plays another town, Torgau on the Elbe, where US and Soviet troops met at the end of the war. In the opening sequences Soviet tanks surge past the remains of the old city gate and other nineteenth-century fortifications, as though displaying, through their effortless progress, the difference between modern and ancient warfare, Soviet power and German decadence. The old city centre is shown as a mass of ruins, variously inhabited by noble Soviet military, degenerate American capitalists concerned only with looting artworks, German spies and traitors. Confusingly, in this blending of different cities, part of the film was shot in Riga, further north along the coast in Latvia, and so there are interiors here that cannot belong to Königsberg at all.

Photographs taken from the ruined tower of the castle in the early 1950s illustrate the same central area as the film, but now the ruins have been replaced by a flat, vacant landscape stretching away into the far distance. The raw material of the city centre has vanished, Pregel Island looks like a field in the countryside surrounded by a river. Other images show the new city infrastructure—a wide straight road, the remains of what was once Langgasse, but which will become Leninsky Prospekt, its only vehicles being two trams moving in opposite directions. In the foreground are some empty plinths, previously supporting statues, and a small group of people, the only humans in this open landscape, wondering whether to cross the road.

In contrast there is another film, directed by Grigory Levkoyev in 1949 and simply titled *The Kaliningrad Oblast*, which shows people going about their daily lives. Cars pass down Mira Prospekt, crowds saunter in Ploshchad Pobedy, workers populate busy factories. There are happy farmers and fishermen, orators making noble speeches, animals in the zoo, children going to school, a football match in a stadium, a thriving Soviet city which had always existed, with few signs of the ruins. Documentary or mere propaganda? The film undoubtedly puts a rather positive gloss on life in the city, but Levkoyev was an interesting director with a background in making dramas with emotive scenes from Soviet history, now adapted with considerable visual flair to the latest territorial acquisition. The Kaliningrad of the period, usually characterised as a tabula rasa, must actually have been those very different cities at the same time—a disaster zone and a new beginning, simultaneously erased and reborn.

The vanishing of the material city also leaves space for the immaterial, not least in the way the Germans who had been expelled from Königsberg continued to imagine its survival in its prewar state—the nineteenth-century city of traditional streets and squares, with its castle and cathedral, a lost paradise, forever unchanging since there was at that time no knowledge of any subsequent developments. German publications such as *Merian* went so far as to continue to produce guidebooks to the city's sights long after they had all been demolished. As a result this city of the imagination always remains in a perfectly preserved state. Even after the opening of the border in the 1990s, and the arrival of large numbers of German tourists intent on rediscovering their former homeland, the old image somehow remained stronger than the new reality. Many of these visitors tended to ignore all aspects of the Soviet city and the achievements of its inhabitants, and instead searched for any sign of what had long vanished, only to leave in frustration, complaining that there was now nothing to see. The journalist Karl Schlögel, writing in 1993, shortly after the border opened, describes former inhabitants returning to find the city they had left in 1945:

> They follow paths that no one can follow. Their eyes move in constant search, as though there might not be any stopping place in the endless collection of blocks and towers. They fix on one building as though might compare it to what they have in their head. They lower their eyes and in resignation move on when they memory finds nowhere to latch onto ...

> They remain rooted before the battered letterboxes with German lettering. Their hands, pointing at something on the horizon, search for a fixed point from which the surrounding space can be ordered, connected. They halt at a street curve, exactly where 'the tram always squealed when it went around the curve'. They point with a finger in the air where there is nothing to be seen.

For the Soviets, in contrast, Königsberg was the symbol of fascist military power, a German outpost in what they maintained had really always been the territory of the Slavs. A 1945 *Pravda* on Königsberg seems to have been lifted from the pages of a gothic novel:

> Taciturn and gloomy are the palaces, in their silent rooms are the archives and libraries of war, behind their thick walls, in schools and lecture rooms for war, decade after decade wars and robberies have been planned. Around the city stand the massive buildings of the defensive ring. In the centre of the capital stands a fortress of solid stone, of enormous size, within which corridors, casemates and galleries are inserted, cut through and excavated. These reach deep under the earth.

Renaming this city and province—after Mikhail Kalinin, one of the original Bolsheviks and Stalin's very dodgy henchman—changing its population, rewriting its history, destroying its fabric and creating a completely new identity on the same site were all interlinked strategies for asserting the claim that it had always been Slavic territory. Use of the name Königsberg, or indeed any use of the German language, was strictly prohibited. All streets and buildings were renamed, all written city records and documents were either destroyed or moved to Moscow. The same system applied throughout the oblast, where all towns were renamed, usually in a random way—Tilsit became Sovetsk, Wehlau became Znamensk, Pillau became Baltiisk, the new port for the Baltic fleet. Whereas in Alsace or Südtirol the original German names for the towns exist alongside French or Italian translations, here in the Kaliningrad oblast a completely new set of names replaced the old ones. Since the German-speaking population had gone, and the German language had thus been eradicated, the oblast could assume a completely different nomenclature. And since the Russian language had been standardised by the Bolsheviks, and was taught in a standard way in schools, the citizens of the oblast quickly lost their original lects and languages. The Kaliningrad oblast is a zone both littered with memories of other peoples, but also, at least in theory, free of the past, a new beginning.

The prewar Königsberg population had always been an ethnic mix, of Germans but also Poles, Lithuanians, Latvians and Jews, each with their own name for the city. The old Polish name was celebrated by the essayist Andrzej Mencwel in his love letter to the city, *Kaliningrad, moja miłość* (Kaliningrad Mon Amour): 'That I stubbornly use the name Królewiec is not a sign of revisionist refusal. Królewiec, the equivalent of the German Königsberg, has an extensive centuries-long use, and is as familiar as Rzym, Lipsk or Gdańsk. I just use the name which offers itself and has a historical background.' Today, these older names are beginning to return to the oblast, having lost, as Mencwel says, some of their nationalist associations. Even Russian maps now show a variety of names, often transposed into Cyrillic script.

For Russians Königsberg used to be the first city encountered when travelling to the west, and the last on returning to Russia. The city was seen as a sign of a different culture, complimenting St Petersburg, as a great Baltic city modelled on Western European ideas. The distinguished Russian traveller Nikolai Karamzin passed through in 1789 and commented on all the usual tourist sites, the palace, the great cathedral, where he fell into a deep reverie, a secret passage that supposedly led outside the city, the gardens, the coffeehouses—and the shape of the soldiers' hats. He met and talked to Immanuel Kant, of which more later. Anton Chekhov, Vladimir Mayakovsky, and Sergei Esenin accompanied by the American dancer Isadora Duncan, all passed through at various times.

The destruction of the German town and its partial replacement by a Russian city hardly registered in Russia, since the Kaliningrad oblast was a military zone and difficult to access. The

Lithuanian writer Tomas Venclova described going to Kaliningrad in the 1960s to try to locate the former house of the writer E T A Hoffmann and finding only the remains of a road without houses ending up in an abandoned duckpond. Vencolva's friend, the dissident Russian poet Joseph Brodsky, briefly visited Kaliningrad twice, in 1963 and 1968, and produced three interesting poems on the city. The first visit was enabled, rather absurdly, to report on the swimming team in Baltiisk, a military port outside the city. From this trip came the poem *Otrivok* (Fragment), where he sits mournfully in a hotel by the harbour, drinking brandy and gazing at the warships. The second much longer and more complex poem has the German title, *Einem Alten Architekten in Rom* (To an old architect in Rome), and begins with a mysterious carriage clattering through the squares of Königsberg, the occupant unspecified but possibly the philosopher Immanuel Kant. Again the atmosphere is melancholic.

> Rain nips at the stones, the leaves, the edge of the waves.
> Teasing language, the river mutters vaguely,
> Its fish permanently surprised
> look down from the rails of the bridge, as though
> Left there by an exploding wave
> (even if the rising tide has left no mark).
> The carp shines in its steel armour.
> The trees murmur something in German.

The carriage travels through the city which seems suspended between various times, encounters a modern Kaliningrad tram, the bust of Field Marshal Suvorov, a gothic church, playgrounds. All that murmuring in German defines the mood, the old inhabitants are gone but the trees still speak their language. At the end of the poem the carriage, already disintegrating, wanders off towards the coast and the sea.

Finally, there is the one poem derived from Brodsky's second visit in 1968, a sonnet, *Otkritka iz goroda K* (Postcard from the city of K). Once again the subject matter is the ruins and the past, but it suggests the two different cities still occupy the same place, in defiance of the laws of physics.

Water
Shakes in its dull mirror the ruins
of the Kurfürst's palace; and maybe now
listens better to the river's prophecy
than in those presumptuous-days
When the Kurfürst built it.
Someone
roams amongst the rubble, stirring up
last year's leaves ...

Joseph Brodsky was one of the very few Russian writers of the period to show much interest in the city, stirring up those old leaves that were meant to be forgotten. But Brodsky was a dissident from Leningrad, formerly St Petersburg, another Baltic port and the Russian city deliberately constructed as Slavic version of a Western European city. Königsberg was both a reminder of St Petersburg, which had also been badly damaged in the long siege during World War 2, and also a suggestion of Rome and its classical ruins. Brodsky looked back out of the Soviet present to a European past that now hardly existed in Kaliningrad, or was carefully concealed.

Other Russian writers would, quite a bit later, follow on from Brodsky's lead. Yuri Buida, from Znamensk—formerly Wehlau—and of mixed Russian, Ukrainian, Belorussian and Polish origin, gives us his own version of the city in the short story cycle *The Prussian Bride* (2012). The Russian characters are haunted by the deported former occupants of the city. The mood is distinctly spooky. When a Prussian coffin is opened Buida writes:

Before us, her arms folded on her chest, lay a young girl ... she was wearing a white dress, seemingly of gossamer or the stuff from which butterflies wings are cut, and white shoes with gold heels. A tiny heart-shaped watch ticked at her wrist ... the girl sighed, and at that same instant her airy dress and the smooth skin were turned into a cloud of dust, which settled slowly along her knotted spine. We gazed entranced at the yellow skeleton, at the white shoes sticking out absurdly with their gold heels, at the heart-shaped watch, still ticking, at the thick hair in which the dark-yellow egg of her skull was nesting.

More recently Valery Galzov, a professor at the local university, reported in a 2015 article, 'The War and East Prussia in the Memory of the Inhabitants of Kaliningrad', that the children of Kaliningrad now consider the vanished German population as part of folklore, 'as inhabitants of the underworld, gnomes, dwarves, ghosts, the secret people of Königsberg'. Fuelling these characterisations is the long-imagined view that there were caches of hidden German treasure, either buried in haste before their departure or lying under the ruins of their houses, all waiting to be unearthed.

These extensive treasure hunts are described by Yuri Ivanov in *From Kaliningrad to Königsberg*, which tells wild tales of the (mostly fruitless) excavation of graveyards and the gardens of Prussians mansions and cellars. Ivanov, who arrived in Kaliningrad in 1945 as a child member of a military band, witnessed goods trains in the city being laden with the last material traces of the German populace—sofas, carpets, pictures and cases packed with porcelain. But the centrepiece of these legends was not any single domestic trove, but the fate of the almost mythical eighteenth-century *Bernsteinzimmer* (Amber Room), whose panels were said to have been made from more than six tonnes of amber harvested in globules from the Baltic Sea. Designed by the baroque sculptor Andreas Schlüter for the Prussian King Fredrick William I, it first went on display in the Berlin City Palace in 1707, but when a visiting Peter the Great took a shine to it, the room was packaged up and gifted to him. Reinstalled in his palace, Tsarskoye Selo, just south of St Petersburg, it remained there until 1941 when German troops looted the place and brought the Amber Room back to Königsberg. Ivanov claims that part of the room was secretly erected in the city castle, and that the only person allowed to enter, the Königsberg museum director Alfred Rohde, would sit for many hours in solitary contemplation of the Baltic sunlight glimmering through the translucent panels, the last person to experience the extraordinary atmosphere of this architectural highpoint of a particular German culture, at the very moment when the light was becoming shadow. As the Russians advanced on the city, the panels were placed in packing cases in the cellar of the castle—and then they disappeared without trace. These cases may still be underground in Kaliningrad, or at the bottom of the Baltic with the transport ship *Wilhelm Gustloff*, sunk by a Soviet submarine in 1945, or in a mine or, most likely, long since destroyed. Yet in Kaliningrad the myth of the Amber Room lives on. In the meantime a perfect replica, which took 14 years to create, has recently been unveiled back in the Russian palace of Tsarskoye Selo.

Ah—enough old Germans. Ah—enough rain and melancholy and looking to the past and wandering in ruins. Kaliningrad is a Russian town, with Russian inhabitants, and has been for 75 years. It does not always have to look back into the past. It has its own thriving Russian culture. It's a fine sunny day. The streets in the centre are thronged with people. The traffic is dense and hardly moves. Cars, some rather luxurious, are parked along the streets. People are fashionably dressed, they move energetically. Cross the Ploshchad Pobedy, move through the large shopping mall with its electronic screen, expensive electronic goods, clothing and jewellery, stroll up along Ulitsa Prof Baranova and enter the crowded market hall. Here in a market hall that almost exceeds in vivacity the Boqueria Mercado in Barcelona, are goods from all over Russia and its former Soviet republics. The different types of food are each in carefully separated zones. Here are great piles of apples, pears and melons, here the freshwater fish and here the saltwater fish, here dozens of varieties of sweets wrapped in brightly coloured paper, here through the glass doors the milk poured out from metal casks, and just a bit away the various kinds of yogurts, here the nuts and varieties of raisins from the now independent southern republics, here diverse golden honeys, also from the south, in large glass jars, and here the animal fats—bear fat (Russian bears?) badger fat, pig fat, hare fat (no more hopping), dog fat (dog fat?), here the rye breads and wheat breads and oat breads, brightly coloured cakes and buns. People hang around in the market, watching carefully what is going on, often on their mobile phones, you can never be quite sure who these people are, guards maybe, or members of some gang. At the back of the market is the zone for cheap clothing, decorated dresses for little girls, jeans, leather boots, and a great variety of Putin T-shirts.

A 1980s building on Ulitsa Komsomolskaya is the location of the city archive (GAKO): the one room, accessible to the public, features several ancient computers and is deserted apart from an archivist sitting at a desk. The woman speaks a small amount of German.

> —No, we do not have any of the watercolours of Navalichin, or any of the other socialist architects. We do not know what happened to them. But many records, particularly the more valuable works, vanished in the 1990s. Perhaps they were sold or stolen. You can look on our computers and see all the records of photographs taken in the socialist time. Then if you have a USB stick, we can give you copies, for a small fee.

On the computer screen appear a sequence of images of schoolchildren, teenagers on a beach, small-scale military parades, workers in paper mills, farm labourers, wide streets without cars, shots of a city under construction—people and locations it is difficult to link to anything which exists today.

Kaliningrad was planned as an ideal Soviet city, free from the past, a completely new city for a completely new era. Dmitri Navalichin—artist, visionary architect and conservationist—arrived in Kaliningrad shortly after it was taken over by the Soviets. He was head architect for the city from 1948 to 1955 and for the oblast as a whole until 1957, aided by a second Leningrad architect Arseny Maximov. Both men had been educated in the architecture school in Leningrad, which then had a reputation for being heavily influenced by Scandinavian design, and both had also trained as watercolourists and so arrived with a visual, almost scenic attitude to town planning, typical of a period when great emphasis was placed on architecture as urban theatre.

In the late 1940s Maximov produced numerous watercolours picturesquely imagining how a new city might grow out from among the ruins of Kaliningrad. But since the Soviets did not know how long they would control the city, and feared its imminent return to the Germans, the ruins were rapidly pulled down and the bricks—the material fabric of Königsberg—were taken by barge along the Baltic coast to Leningrad, where they were recycled as part of the reconstruction of that Russian city on the Neva. Archival photographs of the empty city centre are thus explained. Somewhere in St Petersburg today there must still be buildings made from the bricks of Königsberg houses.

Both Navalichin and Maximov originally favoured maintaining at least some aspect of the Königsberg street pattern and rebuilding many of its more celebrated German landmarks, such as the castle. These visions, however, would immediately fall foul of the Moscow central state institute for urban planning, GIPROGOR, which demanded the elimination of all traces of the German city. Navalichin therefore changed tack and became a proponent of wholesale redevelopment, producing a succession of increasingly grandiose schemes for a radically new Soviet city. His boldest project envisaged the construction of a massive building in full Stalinist style just north of Pregel Island, as the centrepiece for a radial plan with wide avenues reaching out towards two sets of concentric ring roads. At the points where the radial roads met the ring road, large vertical buildings were to be constructed, and there was to be a fine new bridge over the Pregel. Much of this plan was imitative of Moscow's own radial design, with its geometrical system of wide avenues and seven Stalinist high-rises (or 'Seven Sisters') at the intersections with the ring road. Navalichin's scheme was illustrated in a set of splendid watercolours—highly formal yet also rather fantastical—in which almost nothing of the original city survives. The luminosity of the paintings contrasts with the brutal nature of what was actually being proposed.

The Navalichin schemes were also highly impractical, produced at a time when the city's population was very small and the German workforce had all been expelled, leaving few labourers or skilled workers available for construction. There were, moreover, no architects to speak of other than Maximov and himself, no factories to produce the cut stone, or bricks or materials to build the new city. It is not surprising, then, that very little of his plans became a reality. Instead, over most of the 1950s, the city stumbled along with the most basic resources, its population living in the remnants of the built fabric. The piecemeal construction that did take place tended to be sited outside the city centre, where it was relatively easy to build small-scale housing blocks and gardens, unimpeded by any existing street pattern. In the inner city, the German plan, which formed the basis for the underground system of pipes and cables, was gradually taken over and adapted to service large, collective housing blocks rather than the nineteenth-century terraces.

As a result, the city grew very slowly and with moderation. The only significant element of Navalichin's plan that was realised was the new 'grand' avenue running north–south. Leninsky Prospekt is today a six-lane urban highway lined with banal Soviet blocks, rather than the elegant neoclassical buildings favoured by Navalichin. Construction moved so slowly that the avenue's street lighting was not installed until the late 1960s. The envisaged bridge over the Pregel was also only built in the 1970s, again in a style rather more mundane than magnificent, and the great sports stadium that Navalichin had proposed for the east of the centre was only constructed for the 2018 World Cup, held in cities in Ukraine and Russia. Time moves slowly in Kaliningrad.

However, the clearest visible signs of the urban scenery imagined by Navalichin are actually not along that central avenue but in an area northwest of the centre, beside Prospekt Mira, or Stalingradsky Prospekt, as it was at that time. In this more peripheral part of the city, less affected by wartime bombing, a number of large villas survived in the Amalienau and Mittelhufen neighbourhoods. The Soviet officer class and officialdom moved in, adopting much the same lifestyle as their German forebears (still evident today, in the form of high fences and large SUVs parked in the drives). But the modernist appearance of some of these buildings ran counter to the Stalinist model then in favour in Moscow. And so, in a time of extreme poverty and with a large part of the town in ruins, the Soviets devoted considerable energy to a programme of converting the facades into a more acceptable style. Along Prospekt Mira and Ulitsa Karl Marx just to the north various houses were given a new neoclassical dressing, with formal doorways, pediments, pilasters, screens of classical columns and Egyptian pylons added at roof level. The result is a strange Stalinist street theatre, the additions almost arbitrarily attached, random parts of a hastily assembled classical construction set. Elsewhere, the city opera house was also given a new facade, but like much of the civic building this took so long to complete that by the time it opened in the 1960s neoclassicism had fallen out of fashion and Khrushchev's more utilitarian architecture was the preferred national style.

In the late 1950s, and with his vision for Kaliningrad looking increasingly outmoded, Navalichin took up a post in Moscow as an architectural restorer. However, he would move back to Kaliningrad in 1989, at the time of *perestroika*, just a few years before his death, to list and record the few remaining German buildings, an unlikely return reflecting his first concerns for the preservation of the main elements of Königsberg. His colleague Maximov remained in Kaliningrad and died in 2003. His watercolours, shown in exhibitions in Germany in 1992 and 2005, would become part of the new, softer Russian approach to the architecture of the German city.

A group of about hundred sailors, all in uniform, walk down Marshal Bagramya Promenade. They stop and throw their hats in the air. A small group of passers-by cheer.

—What are they celebrating?

—A victory. A fine victory. Maybe football.

Nearby, moored beside a wharf on the Pregel, are a line of ships from various periods, part of a display of Ocean Museum. The very fine Irbenskiy lighthouse, bright orange, with high beacon-masts, which used to be moored off the Gulf of Riga. The diesel-electric submarine B-413, part of the Soviet Union's pre-atomic fleet, and which used to be part of the Baltic fleet based in the Baltiisk port just outside Kaliningrad. And, finest of all, the 100m research ship *Vityaz*, which has wonderful cabins filled with the possessions of the crew, dining rooms laid out for formal meals, chess sets with figures in navy uniforms and sea creatures, charts, maps, instruments. A young woman in a chic blue trouser suit explains.

—*Vityaz* was originally a German ship called *Mars*, a luxury cruise ship with 38 crew and 12 passengers. There were individual cabins for the crew, decorated in medieval style. It was considered one of the most elegant ships of its time. And so it is still. In 1945 it was one of the last ships to sail from Königsberg, with inhabitants fleeing the city. It was handed over to the Soviets.

—And what did the crew research?

—The crew discovered and mapped underwater mountains. *Vityaz* became the most famous research ship of the Soviet Union. It had libraries, laboratories, special storage for specimens. It had the quality of a ship out of Jules Verne, scientific but with great style. The crew dined on the finest seafood, freshly pulled from the oceans. *Vityaz* sailed almost one and a half million kilometres across the world's oceans, was visited by the famous French aquanaut, Jacques Cousteau, measured the depths of the Marina trench, the deepest point in the oceans, discovered innumerable deep-sea creatures.

—And why is the ship here in Kaliningrad?

—The ship finished its life here in 1979 and was going to be scrapped. How could anyone scrap such a wonderful ship? Instead it was saved and carefully restored. Perhaps it is the finest object in Kaliningrad.

We walk along the corridors, down the metal stairways, along the deck. We stand in the bows and look out, as though imagining ourselves to be far out to sea, with the great depth of the oceans below us.

Far easier and cheaper to produce than buildings are monuments, and Kaliningrad, like any Soviet city, has a significant number of them, largely dedicated to military victory. Among the most striking is the Monument to the 1,200 Guardsmen, located at one of the entrances to Victory Park, and featuring two sets of charging soldiers, waving flags and weapons, mounted on two massive plinths. The first postwar construction of any kind in the city, it celebrated the dawning of a new era, and was for many years a popular spot for wedding photographs. Nearby, on Ulitsa Rokossovskogo, a dark green T-34/85 tank, dedicated to the Red Army, is mounted on its own concrete plinth; along Sovietsky Prospekt stands the Memorial to the Pilots of the Baltic Fleet, featuring two concrete aircraft pointed, like paper airplanes, towards the sky; while on Moskovsky Prospekt a torpedo boat sets off at a jaunty angle from a concrete wave to commemorate the Baltic Seamen. Beside a lake next to the former castle there is a statue to the submarine commander Alexander Marinesko, who in 1945 sank the transport ship *Wilhelm Gustloff*, resulting in the death of over 9,000 people, the greatest maritime loss of life in history. The story is related by Günter Grass in *Crabwalk*, a book still considered controversial in Russia for its criticism of the memorials to Marinesko, much loved by Soviet veterans. In this particular memorial Marinesko stands within a cutaway section through the submarine's hull, peering through his periscope at what is now a smart new housing block. The combined effect of all these military monuments, which are uniformly kept in perfect condition and often surrounded by bunches of flowers, is a strange mix of nostalgia for a heroic but vanished past, and an almost pop art sensibility, with brightly coloured boats, guns, planes and tanks parked in the middle of the city. At the same time, as Kaliningrad's USSR generation gradually die out, and other purely Russian nationalist forces make their voices heard, these monuments have gradually become detached from their point of origin, relocating to a contemporary world where the Russian ownership of the city has acquired a rather different meaning.

Through their own materiality, which preserves something now past and therefore immaterial, the monuments suggest the quality of Kant's elusive twin terms, phenomenon–noumenon. For the victorious soldiers of the Red Army in 1945, however, the distinction no longer held. 'Now you understand, it's a material world', they wrote on the Kant memorial beside the cathedral. Designed by Friedrich Lahrs in 1924, the bicentenary of Kant's birth, the *Kenotaphion* has a flat roof supported by a row of square Bauhaus-style columns of pinkish volcanic stone. In 1993 it acquired a tablet quoting Kant's famous declaration: 'Two things fill the mind with ever new and increasing admiration and awe, the more often and steadily they are considered: the starry heavens above me and the moral law within me.' The memorial, next to the cathedral on Pregel Island, is a popular spot, and has even overtaken the Monument to the 1,200 Guardsmen as the preferred backdrop for wedding photographs. Bridegrooms in cream-coloured suits and brides in layers of white imitation brocade and chiffon queue up to lay flowers at the tomb, usually accompanied by large quantities of sweet Russian champagne.

On Prospekt Mira, set back a little from the road in a small square usually occupied by a few relaxed idlers, is yet another memorial, the Monument to the Conquerors of the Near Universe. A large vertical circle, curling out of a metal base, accommodates a cosmonaut looking up with one hand raised to the sky. The cosmonauts to whom the monument is dedicated are the three Kaliningrad citizens Alexey Leonov (the first man to make a space-walk, in 1965, and one-time Soviet candidate for the first man on the moon), Roman Romanenko (one of the first cosmonauts on the *Mir* space station) and Aleksandr Viktorenko (also a *Mir* cosmonaut). The monument acts as a kind of framing device, for through the great circle one can observe not only the changing atmosphere of the night sky but also the movement of the moon and the luminous planets.

Immanuel Kant, though clearly Prussian—even if he claimed, rather bizarrely, that his grandfather was a Scot—was never going to be eliminated from this socialist city, and over time has become an honorary Russian. In contrast to the west, where he has been valued for his philosophy of freedom and his almost mystical transcendental idealism, in the Soviet Union Kant was remembered primarily for his social thinking, and in particular for his emphasis on moral duty. More fundamentally, his idealistic philosophical system had prompted in turn the dialectics of Johann Herder and the historical materialism of Karl Marx and Friedrich Engels, leading thus to the revolutionary socialism of Lenin. In spite of his interest in both the material and the immaterial, Kant was therefore a point of origin for the whole socialist system. And so while almost all forms of German presence were erased, the Kant memorial on the side of the cathedral was one of the very few monuments guaranteed to be preserved.

Within Kaliningrad, Kant has steadily gained in materiality. A famous scene where the philosopher dines with colleagues appears in kiosks across the town on stamps, postcards, cups, plates and other souvenirs. In the 1990s, as Leningrad was reverting to being St Petersburg and Stalingrad to Volgograd, it was questioned why Kaliningrad continued to be named after a long discredited Soviet functionary and member of Stalin's inner circle. Since the city could not go back to a name derived from its German past, some suggested it should become Kantgrad or Immanuilisk, in honour of Kant. The matter remains unresolved, but Kaliningrad University has been renamed Immanuel Kant Baltic University, and a statue—a 1992 copy of the one that used to stand near the site of his house—now graces an overgrown park near the entrance to the university. The original was lost after it was buried after the war in the grounds of an estate outside the city.

Consistent with the logic of dualism there is naturally also an anti-Kant. A few yards from this statute is the entrance to the underground bunker belonging to Otto Lasch, the German commander who led the disastrous last stand against the Red Army. Inside is a terrifying and claustrophobic Cold War waxworks in which an elegantly periwigged Lasch, looking more like a late-eighteenth-century aristocrat or philosopher than a Nazi general, stands by his actual phone waiting for the last orders from the Führer, while a waxwork SS lieutenant nearby holds the leash of an authentically barking mastiff. In the background, various tableaux, created with loving care, show the town going up in flames as Red Army troops rush in. Underground, in this bunker, is the last carefully preserved nightmare of Nazi East Prussia, while in the garden up above stands the gentle figure of a philosopher, apostle of perpetual peace.

Kant was well known for his daily walks through the city, always following the same path and the same schedule. He would cross two of the bridges, the now vanished Krämerbrücke and Grünbrücke, into the lower city, and reputedly composed elements of his *Critique of Pure Reason* whilst walking along a small street leading out into the countryside. In the nineteenth century this street was renamed in his honour as Philosophendamm, by which time it ran through railyards rather than fields. Since renamed Ulitsa Elblongskaya, it is now lined with typical housing blocks and workshops and warehouses. A few chestnut trees and lakes still thrive, surrounded by the dockland sheds and cranes.

The Russian interest in Kant is longstanding and pre-dates any linkage to later social philosophers and thus to socialism. Nikolai Karamzin, as mentioned above, visited the philosopher in 1789. The encounter was casual, he passed by Kant's house and was received by 'a slight thin old man, immaculately white and gentle'. They talked for three hours, mainly about metaphysics, a conversation Karamzin had trouble following since 'Kant speaks rapidly and not clearly; as a result I had to mobilise all my auditory nerves to listen.' Kant spoke of the impossibility of ever obtaining what we desire, the moral law which binds all men, the sense of good and evil, the ignorance of the future of even the wisest man. His final words were of the future where 'Even here reason extinguishes its lamp and we remain in darkness, only phantasy can travel in this darkness and create phantoms.' 'His house', notes Karamzin, 'is small and inside there are few furnishings. Everything is simple, except ... his metaphysics'.

Moskovsky Prospekt: a small flat in a housing block. Access from the exterior is via a narrow entrance and stairs; the lift is broken. Inside, the spaces are all immaculately clean, and there are just two rooms, one decorated with op-art wallpaper, offering views south over other blocks and fields. The kitchen has an old-fashioned electric stove but the bathroom is more contemporary. On a table sit two glasses of tea. The occupant is a middle-aged lady, Larissa Shalamanov. In another room a young girl sits by a large computer screen, playing a game involving Wild West cowboys. Her mother pours out the tea, and adds small portions of jam.

> —So, you have come to Kaliningrad to do some research. You want to know what is happening today. Kaliningrad is individual, we are Russian but not like the rest of Russia. We are a kind of Baltic state, but not like the others. Moscow is

really only interested in us because of the naval base, the city is here to serve the base. Here the Baltic never freezes, the submarines can go out all year round. And now, of course, we have the missiles, pointed at you, at the west. You must know we have some democracy, we vote for our duma and we have some independence. But in the end we are just a province.

—And new architecture?

—There are always plans, great plans. Look down over the fields, there are plans to build houses and factories there. But no money. Many people here have so little money. The city has never really been rebuilt so we still have wonderful fields right here in the centre. With fruit trees. In summer we go down and pick plums, apples, pears, berries.

—Your daughter has a fine computer.

—Here in Kaliningrad we are also linked to the Western world. You can buy everything in Kaliningrad if you have some foreign currency.

The *microrayons*, those massive Soviet housing zones that characterised so many Eastern Bloc cities, were usually located just outside the traditional city centre. But in Kaliningrad, where there is no traditional inner city, what is usually peripheral becomes central. Microrayon 16, the most spectacular in Kaliningrad, lies along the east part of Moskovsky Prospekt, where a wall of mid-1970s blocks, ten storeys high and each at least 100m long, runs parallel to the six-lane highway. Their facades are lined with the vertical strips of the lift shafts and with panels pierced with bold circular openings. Whatever the dubious state of the buildings, one has to feel something for the boldness of urban construction on this scale, accommodating the population of a small city.

Somehow the grand scale also tolerates various levels of subversion, even gentrification. Besides the usual kiosks selling vegetables, meat, bread, flowers, there is a liberal peppering of private enterprise—pet salons, travel agencies, banks, garages as well as various operations with no obvious function. An optimist in this Baltic climate has even set up a business selling fibreglass swimming pools of considerable size, their bright blue interiors holding out the promise of a different lifestyle. In the blocks themselves the standardised panels have been adapted by the inhabitants, balconies filled in, window systems changed. And then there are also large-scale revisions, with the entire facade being pulled away over all 12 storeys and a new corporate-style office building inserted vertically into the elevation, with a brand new facade of burnished bronze panels, clearly a large financial investment. These architectural additions are a reminder of those classical elements attached in the 1950s to German buildings in Prospekt Mira, but now it's Soviet megablocks that are being adapted to the tastes of a Westernised contemporary capitalism. Just beyond this line of buildings a modern Scandinavian-style housing block is under construction, with elegant windows and timber balconies. What is one to think of this strange mix of dilapidation and revival, where one would expect to encounter a bleak Soviet slum but instead finds unexpected signs of new life, poverty and wealth closely intermingled? Should one share the optimism of the swimming pool salesman?

The housing blocks along Moskovsky Prospekt are generic, and identical to any other block in any other Soviet city. But in Kaliningrad there are also more individual buildings revealing a local version of 1970s Soviet architecture, modest, uncertain, but with a certain pop sensibility. In visiting these buildings, which often appear unexpectedly in otherwise bland neighbourhoods, one can almost discern another Kaliningrad about to emerge. Among them is the main bus station beside the vast expanse of Kalinin square, a long, low box with a facade of silvery panels, almost op-art in its dazzling reflection of the light. A few hundred metres away, on the lower half of Leninsky Prospekt, is the Ol'štn (Allstein) cafe by the then city architect Eugene Popov. A concrete building set between two stair shafts, with a roof distinguished by large vertical slots vaguely resembling historical dormer windows, it is adorned with period graphics of an elk and other creatures—socialist realism shifting into folklore. The nearby Oktober cinema is another long, horizontal form with elaborate glazing panels and a rooftop lined with a horizontal sign in elaborate script announcing the revolutionary month. Elsewhere, opposite the House of the Soviets, the House of the Allies—actually the telephone office—is a cube with a facade of panels with pyramidical reliefs, again reflecting the light in different directions, the whole again surmounted by a decorative Soviet-style frieze. And in the city zoo, one of the oldest and largest in Russia, there is a self-contained children's town, constructed in 1982 and composed of concrete reliefs and mosaics again with Slavic motifs by the local artist Nikolai Batakov and architect Pavel Gorbach.

Kaliningrad Zoo, Prospekt Mira: entry via gates surmounted by black stone statues of a penguin, a walrus and a bear. Inside, trees, cages, pits, animals and considerable numbers of visitors. Hippopotamus House. Dim interior with fetid atmosphere. Large pool with the backs of two hippopotamuses just visible above the surface of the water. A group of schoolchildren are being addressed by a zoo keeper wearing a smart uniform:

> —The hippopotamus is the symbol of our zoo, and also perhaps of the city. The original Kaliningrad hippo was called Hans. He was one of only four animals to survive the storming of the city by the Red Army, along with a deer, a badger and a donkey. Actually, before the war he had been named Rosa, maybe confusing to have a female name, but he received a new, yes, very German name, Hans. During the attack on the city poor Hans was unfortunately shot seven times, and he lay for several days in a ditch, with nothing to eat or drink. He was nursed back to health with doses of vodka, and he survived for 15 years, into the period of Nikita Khrushchev.

Silence, as everyone gazes at the backs of the animals, which remain motionless.

One building above all is particular to Kaliningrad, and usually seen as a symbol of the failure of the socialist city. Dom Sovjetov, the House of Soviets, is referred to locally as the 'Monster'. But perhaps, like many monsters, it is simply misunderstood. The building stands beside the site of the former German castle, which was finally demolished in the late 1960s on the direct orders of the USSR secretary general Leonid Brezhnev. Many proposals had been made for the site since the time of Navalichin, but nothing had been constructed, the void at the centre of the city a sign of the inability of successive Soviet authorities to decide on any consistent identity for Kaliningrad. But eventually a decision was made to replace the castle with a single tall building surrounded by open plazas—feudal militarism giving way to socialist open space. Much criticised today with the cliché 'bleak and windswept', open plazas were seen at the time as innovative propositions to create spaces matching the communal ambitions of the state, not so different from the open city spaces in Warsaw, Dresden or East Berlin, as well as in many cities in the west. With these criteria in place, a series of competitions were held for the site in the early 1970s, the chosen winner being the Moscow architecture cooperative Meczenev-Institute, led by Julian Schwarzbreim.

Schwarzbreim, an architect of Jewish descent originally from Kiev, was by no means a typical 1970s apparatchik. He had designed an elegant circus building in Sochi, and would go on to produce another in Yekaterinburg, a square form with curious murals and an innovative open lattice-dome structure (such formal circus buildings were an important part of Soviet urban culture, and their absence in Kaliningrad is yet another sign of its separation). In 1973 his cooperative produced a daring plan for the centre of Kaliningrad, shrinking Pregel Island to a small area surrounding the cathedral, finally sinking the Atlantis of Königsberg, and turning this part of the Pregel into a lake, accessed by a series of new bridges. The whole was a kind of Brasilia on the Baltic, with the House of Soviets, towers and stadiums combining to offer a bold urban vision—ultimately too bold for the government of the period. Schwarzbreim was also an enthusiast of the 1920s constructivism of Ivan Leonidov, and his lively mix of blocks, technical inventions, lightness and daring revealed his awareness of international developments of the period, in particular Kenzo Tange and the metabolist movement in Japan. Even in those plodding Brezhnev years, why shouldn't Kaliningrad have been able to leap out of its indecision and mediocrity and find a place on the international architectural stage?

The House of Soviets was to house two government bodies, one for the city and one for the oblast. Neither body was known for any kind of architectural innovation. The Schwarzbreim proposal was for two 19-storey vertical blocks, each broken up into an upper and lower element by large U-shaped horizontal beams. At the base were two other large box-like elements, one above the other, each facing different directions, surrounded by an open plaza. The design was a composition of different rectangular forms, all with a certain dynamism, and inspired by Oscar Niemeyer's double blocks at Brasilia and Tange's 1960s Dentsu project in Tokyo.

Almost immediately, however, cost-saving measures fundamentally altered the nature of the structure. Only the cheapest materials were available and the Kaliningrad workforce was not capable of building a sophisticated piece of metabolism. Rather than being clad in glass, as intended, the two blocks were faced in concrete panels, so they appear just as heavy as the supporting structure. The ground level then became cluttered with supporting walls and a confusion of columns: instead of floating, the structure remained resolutely earthbound. Construction started in 1970, but without skilled workers progress was slow. In 1975 all construction projects in the USSR were called to a halt to concentrate the state's limited resources on buildings for the 1980 Moscow Olympics. Money remained tight in the years immediately afterwards and by the 1990s there were no funds left of any kind for Kaliningrad. By then the building's structure was mostly complete, but there was still no exterior cladding and no interior fitting out. And so it gradually became a vast ruin, visible from all over town, an all too prominent sign of the inability of Kaliningrad to complete such an ambitious project. For the 2004–05 celebrations of the anniversary of Königsberg-Kaliningrad, glass was inserted in the voids of the windows, and the building was painted a mix of light blue and white, as though camouflaged to fade into the Baltic sky. The glass was so badly fixed that a number of panes fell out and the building was soon walled off for safety. The great House of Soviets remains forever incomplete, a forlorn face with two eyes formed by the ends of the U-beams, a large forehead and a horizontal mouth of low-level boxes. At some predetermined signal, will this humanoid figure, half-buried in the soil, suddenly come to life and tramp off across the flat lands of the oblast like some B-movie sci-fi robot? Probably not. The robot face remains impassive, stolidly waiting.

As the House of Soviets wastes away, some have called for the old German palace to be rebuilt, a ghost returning in place of the very building which succeeded it. The building is permanently threatened with demolition, but still in place. More than that, Schwarzbreim's Monster has even experienced a return to fashion, or at least acceptability. Within a general re-examination of Soviet culture two decades after the collapse of the USSR, the brutalist architecture of the 1970s and 1980s has attracted increased attention. French photographer Frédéric Chaubin's 2011 book *Cosmic Communist Constructions* shows images of Kaliningrad's House of Soviets alongside other examples of late Soviet architecture, such as the 1985 Druzba Sanatorium in Yalta and the 1976 Tashkent Circus. The building resurfaces in another compendium of Eastern Bloc brutalism, Nicolas Grospierre's *Modern Forms: A Subjective Atlas of Twentieth-Century Architecture*. Grospierre also finds space for the facade of the Kaliningrad bus station and the children's town zoo. Some of this interest is merely a half-mocking appreciation of the wackiness of Soviet brutalism, but there is a deeper and more sympathetic aspect too. In the republics detached from the control of the centre, such as those beside the Black and the Baltic seas, architecture did develop its own very particular path, usually heavy-handed, but also individual, maybe even witty. For the moment, though, the House of Soviets still stands as a sign of yet another Kaliningrad which became material, but was never quite filled with the breath of life.

In Kaliningrad's public archive there is a photograph that shows a man, woman and young girl sitting on a barge moored on the river Pregel, looking out across the water at a series of housing blocks under construction. The smallness of the family on the barge contrasts with the scale of the building on the shore, but there is also a certain optimism to the scene, a city is being reconstructed around housing and homes for families like this. The scene could almost be from Jean Vigo's *L'Atalante*, or from any number of Italian neo-realist films of the early 1960s. It looks like Kaliningrad, but is not easy to place. Something is missing. An enquiry to Markus Podehl, German architectural historian, reveals that the photograph is of Navalichin's grand avenue, but before the wide road bridge over the Pregel was constructed. Today several lanes of traffic stream across it. Looking again at the photograph, the objects and people in the scene appear solid, unambiguous, understandable. But at the same time one gets a sense of a quietness, of a pause, a lull before something unexpected occurs.

Leninsky Prospekt: the basement of a Kaliningrad department store, one of the few bookshops in the city. On the shelves there are many books on Soviet war heroes, as well as on football teams, cookery and car maintenance.

—Do you have any books on Soviet Kaliningrad?

—No, why would people read them, that period is over.

—But you have books on Königsberg, which is also over.

—Yes, people are interested in the past if it far enough away. People like beauty.

—And postcards?

—The only postcards we have for sale are those here, also of the Königsberg bridges, all seven bridges.

—Euler?

At this late stage another figure emerges alongside the philosopher Immanuel Kant, affording a further method for considering the city: the Swiss mathematician Leonhard Euler, deviser of numerous innovative mathematic and algebraic formulas. In later life he became blind, thus living in a world of gradually vanishing phenomena, increasingly inclined to mathematical explanations. It was in his youth, however, as a resident at the court of the empress Anna Ivanovna in St Petersburg in the 1730s, that Euler famously formulated the classic Königsberg seven bridges problem. At the time the city had seven bridges: *Krämer* (chandler), *Schmied* (blacksmith), *Holz* (wood), *Grün* (green), *Köttel* (a place name), *Höhe* (high) and *Honig* (honey). All of them spanned the river Pregel, with four of them linking the central island of Kneiphof (now Pregel) to the north and south banks, one connecting Kneiphof to the area to the east known as Lomse, and two forming part of a route that ran across Lomse from the old city in the north to the cattle market in the south.

The question that Euler asked—and which he first considered so simple as to be barely worth a mathematician's time—was whether it was possible to walk across each bridge in turn, but only once, so that all bridges were crossed. There were two caveats: the islands could not be reached by any other route, and all the bridges had to be crossed completely, so no going halfway and coming back. By reformulating the question in algebraic terms and eliminating all other information other than nodes and connections, Euler eventually proved that it was *not* possible to cross all the bridges in this way. But at the same time as he ruled out a material path across the bridges, Euler's methodology prompted the emergence of an immaterial path, in the form of graph theory. A trail in a graph that visits every edge exactly once is now known as an Eulerian path.

Euler's surprisingly difficult brainteaser was made more complicated when two of the city's bridges were destroyed by Allied bombing in 1944, and two others were removed a decade later to make way for a new highway over Pregel Island. But the highway bridge is itself ambiguous, not least because it structurally attempts to jump right over the island, since the Soviet strategy was to ignore anything relating to the German city, and so the island as a whole was no longer considered part of the urban fabric. Of course, the Euler theorem cannot cope with ambiguity: either there is a link, or there isn't. But today, counting the multi-lane highway as two bridges gives us a total of five bridges, making a Eulerian path possible, so long as one begins and finishes on one or other of the islands.

The seven bridges problem doesn't only relate to Königsberg, but can be applied to any system with a similar amount of nodes and connections. The science of topology, which emerges from Euler's problem, is the study of the spatial relations between figures and objects. Objects which appear very different can be considered similar, merely deformed through twisting, flattening or stretching. For instance, a plate is only a flat form of bowl; a doughnut is like a cup with a handle because both are a mass pierced by a hole; a triangle, square and circle are all simply the same form arranged in a slightly different way, creating an inside and an outside. But topology becomes much more sophisticated than these simple examples in the way it measures degrees of connection and distortion. Beginning with a problem which appears architectural—of a set of bridges—topology reaches out into mathematics, algebra and other sciences. And so while in Kant's phenomena and noumena we are shown a world irretrievably divided into the knowable and unknowable, in Euler's seven bridges problem we gain a methodology for linking the world we experience with the most complex abstract ideas.

No one—apart from a topological mathematician—could ever follow an Eulerian path around the bridges of Kaliningrad, and so what relevance does this abstract problem have to the city of today? Euler took an actual material city and transformed it into an immaterial problem whose solution could be applied to similar questions at any scale. Reducing the city to lines and nodes removes most of what makes the city interesting—the material world of that bizarre list of bridge names, mixing proper names, colours, trades and foodstuffs—but it also allows one to relate the island and its bridges to other systems of points and connections.

The questions in Euler's puzzle are also specific to Kaliningrad as an enclave, both separate from and connected to the exterior. Which point connects to which? What happens to the whole complex if one adds or removes links? Can one go backwards as well as forwards? And could one even move through the whole system, along the Eulerian path, without repeating previous errors, without being stuck in a historical dead end, unable to move either forwards or back?

Euler's connections and nodes can be used to consider other urban locations. For example, a public square can be compared to an island, as an identifiable space linked in various ways to its surroundings. In Kaliningrad this unusual mix of different elements from various cultures is particularly clear in the area around Ploshchad Pobedy—Victory Square—named Steindamm in the nineteenth century, then Hansaplatz, and for a brief period Adolf-Hitler-Platz. In the immediate postwar period the Soviet authorities decided to make an enlarged version of this square the new centre for the city. The intention was to create a grand open space for military parades, featuring tanks, troops, banners and the party officials up on a dais. What fills this urban space today is a jumble of traffic lanes thronged with assorted cars, trucks and buses, cars parked almost at random, advertising signs, half-hearted attempts at pedestrianisation. At the centre of this lively square is yet another monument to the war, a 20m-high column. Beside the column there was once a large statue of Lenin, standing on a plinth made of recycled German gravestones, but in 2004 he was quietly relocated, no longer an appropriate figure to be placed in front of an Orthodox cathedral in the new capitalist Russia. He now stands in a more discreet location to the south, near the main railway station, not far from his dodgy Bolshevik comrade, Mikhail Kalinin. Four buildings around Ploshchad Pobedy could be seen to exemplify the changing architecture of the city, some elements being rather different from how they appear, materiality thinly concealing an undefined immateriality.

Firstly, on the southern side of the square is a large box-like structure with vertical pilasters on the facade, a flat grey roof, functional, undistinguished, seemingly a product of the early 1960s. In fact this building was once the elegant Handelshof, a trade hall designed by Hanns Hopp in 1923 in north German expressionist *Hansa* mode. The first building in the city with a reinforced concrete frame, the Handelshof featured a grand interior courtyard with a glass roof, an arcade of shallow pointed arches running along the base, a division of the clinker brick facade into horizontal bands and a remarkable entrance flanked by sculptures of Fortune and Mercury by Hermann Brachert. Under the Soviets the Handelshof was used as a municipal hall and today it continues to house part of the city administration. Already badly damaged during the war, in the Khrushchev years it was trimmed of its remaining architectural details. To rescue the building from despised German modernism, the clinker brickwork was covered with a coat of plaster, and a horizontal canopy added to the facade.

But Hopp, originally from Lübeck, was responsible for the design of other Königsberg buildings which brought into the essentially nineteenth-century city the spirit of 1920s *moderne*, including the minimalist facades of the Park Hotel (1929) and the long, glazed Bauhaus forms of the city's school for girls (1930), both of which still survive largely in their original state and offer a fresh approach to the architecture of the city, ultimately one of its many untaken paths. A declared member of the left wing, alongside other Königsberg architects such as Robert Liebenthal and Kurt Frick, Hopp ran into problems with the Nazi regime in the early 1930s and was lucky not to be eliminated. The war over and Königsberg in ruins, he moved to Dresden, then in East Germany, and was responsible for part of Stalinallee in Berlin, amongst other buildings. A genuine idealist, he continued to work for a succession of dubious regimes, and in the late 1950s even produced a project that turned the centre of Berlin into a lake, with a large central building, all slightly reminiscent of Navalichin in Kaliningrad.

Secondly, opposite the former Handelshof is another German building with an impressive elevation, the North Railway Station from 1930, neoclassical in appearance and seen as a forerunner of fascist state buildings, but harmless enough. Navalichin had proposed adding a Russian-style tower to the station facade, which he found excessively Germanic. There is even a vignette of him in Levkoyev's 1949 film on the city, *The Kaliningrad Oblast*, explaining his proposal to passers-by with one of his signature watercolours. However, during the early 1950s this variety of German architecture, built just before the fascist period, was close enough to the approved Stalinist style of stripped down neoclassicism to be acceptable to the Kaliningrad authorities. And so the building survived unaltered. Later converted into the Seaman's Hotel, today it is occupied by various corporations, its once modernist facade now covered with advertising signs. The only evidence of the actual train station, from where one departs for the small towns that line the oblast's Baltic coast, is a small ticket office behind the main building.

Then, slightly set back from the right-hand side of the former station, is a surprising intruder from another place and time, offering yet another path. A reproduction of Moscow's Cathedral of Christ the Saviour, constructed at a slightly reduced scale but still appearing oversized in relation to its surroundings, was manufactured at great cost in 2006. The original nineteenth-century cathedral in Moscow, a pastiche of medieval Russian architecture, was demolished in 1931 to make way for the new Palace of Soviets. A replica was then rebuilt in 1995–2000. The Kaliningrad model is thus a copy of a copy of a building. Its five golden onion domes and rather two-dimensional facade give it a surreal appearance, as though it had been created for a film set, because medieval Russian buildings such as these, genuine or fake, are entirely untypical for the Baltic. The new cathedral can hold a gathering of over 2,000 believers. The purpose is naturally to confirm, via a grandiose architectural structure, firstly the presence of the Orthodox church in the centre of Kaliningrad—a city created by the atheist USSR—and secondly the continuing power of the Russian mainland at a time when the nature of the enclave is coming under question.

The fourth and last of this quartet of buildings, just beside the cathedral, is a large and glitzy Western-style shopping mall, its exterior covered in illuminated advertising placards and its interior filled with shops selling mobile phones, jewellery, lingerie, sports cars, cappuccinos and other items appealing to the more affluent citizens of the city. These consumer goods look right at first glance but on closer inspection some seem slightly strange—the familiar mobile phones are just a little different, the various cafes imitate Western chains but the products are just a little exaggerated, the cakes a curious shade of purple, the fizzy drinks a little too bright. Alongside the real, genuine consumer items, much of what is sold here is in fact fake, imitation packets holding imitation contents—a fake consumerism that matches the ersatz religion of the cathedral next door.

In Ploshchad Pobedy an urban game has been played out over successive decades by competing interests, yet somehow the result is an intriguing urban mix. Today these various interests—political, economic and social, some visible, others less so—continue to unfold over the centre of Kaliningrad without any obvious resolution. Among them are paths to an outdated future, with a succession of architectural proposals—for mini versions of downtown Frankfurt, with its clusters of towers, for postmodern tallboys and for deconstructivist shards. Competition winners have been proclaimed, and then quickly forgotten as neither political will nor external finance has been forthcoming.

There are also paths back into the past. In 2000 a German publisher produced a detailed proposal for rebuilding all the houses of Pregel Island, restoring it completely to its pre-1945 state in the tradition of Gdansk and Wroclaw, but this time as a vast island hotel, presumably mainly for visiting German tourists, afloat on a reconstruction of their sunken city. In the same spirit, a set of houses called the Fishers' Village has been erected to the east of Pregel Island in a contemporary version of the Hansa style, vaguely medieval, vaguely German, deeply fake.

And then there are paths running simultaneously backwards and forwards. In 2014 the city's planning office held an urban design competition for the city centre that was won by the St Petersburg collective Studio 44. The project proposed the renovation of the House of Soviets, the restoration of the castle, the addition of a number of large cultural buildings, the re-landscaping of Pregel Island to evoke the old street layout and, as an additional selling point, the reconstruction of Köttelbrücke and Schmiedbrücke, reviving the principal bridges of the Euler mathematical problem. Predictably this project was also shelved as developers linked to Moscow put forward other proposals. No doubt more projects will follow, until finance and political power reach some form of agreement.

There are even signs of a path back into the times of Soviet control. For the USSR, Kaliningrad was of vital strategic importance because it offered an ice-free naval base on the Baltic. But after 20 years of military decline, the recent revival of Russia's nationalist expansionism under Putin has seen new frigates assigned to the Baltic fleet in Kaliningrad, each armed with nuclear-capable Kalibr cruise missiles. Elsewhere in the oblast, Iskander-M short-range ballistic missiles have also been deployed. This gives a new, rather terrifying relevance to all those Soviet monuments of slightly cartoonish tanks and torpedo boats scattered through the city, which not so long ago had seemed like historical relics.

The bar of a large 1970s hotel in Leninsky Prospekt. Men in smart suits. Women fashionably dressed, with surprising amounts of jewellery. Two old men, with large beards, sitting in armchairs, smoking cigars. Mobile phones, laptops, tablets, briefcases. Some young women, heavily made up and in short skirts. Intense conversations. Groups of tourists, mostly in jeans and T-shirts, slightly tatty. Bar staff in tuxedos. Woman in jeans and smart fur coat speaks with self-confidence:

—*Sind Sie deutsch?*

—No, I am from Scotland.

—Ah, Scotland. I love Scotland. Whisky. Bravehearts. Sean Connery. The Scots our friends. So cool. And fine cows with long hair, which wander in the mountains and stand beside the lakes. You know where I am from?

—Maybe Russia.

—Yes, but from Kamchatka. So far away, to the east. I am an economics student. Here in Kaliningrad. And you know my aim is to make money. So much money. But always with soul, with heart, just money no good. And maybe live in a big house, in Scotland, with a fine Scotsman, and some fine cows. *Kakoy prekrasny son*, what a dream, always to have dreams.

From the small station behind Ploshchad Pobedy a train runs north, past villas, housing blocks, factories and sheds. The carriage is almost deserted, the conductor plays *Grand Theft Auto* on his smartphone. The countryside starts as soon as the last buildings recede into the background, with clusters of oak, birch and conifer, ponds and lakes, meadows, open fields. There are few houses or inhabitants out here. This was all once cultivated, but the land, long untended, has gradually reverted to its pre-agricultural state, as it was before even the Prussians arrived. It is here that you realise that the city itself is an island, surrounded by this quiet, delicate, almost prelapsarian landscape, which extends almost without interruption to the Baltic coast. You also understand how Kaliningrad is another of those Baltic cities build on flat lands, little different in level from the sea. This is an aquatic landscape of meadows, pools, streams, marshes, where a change of sea level may in the future produce a very different relationship between land and sea.

Yes, now you understand, it's a material world? Euler and Kant, part of the vanished German world, remain twin guides to the contemporary Russian city? Euler transformed the bridges of Pregel Island into an abstract mathematical problem on the nature of connections, in the process giving rise to new topological forms. Kant proposed a world of noumena beyond our understanding alongside the material phenomena we can experience. Euler's abstract paths and patterns of connections link to Kant's theory—the world we experience through our senses as a reflection of a shadowy abstract realm. Wait long enough in Königsberg–Kaliningrad and an unexpected Eulerian path, one that looks suspiciously like an old path but which is in fact new, usually appears. Time anyway now to leap away from the river Pregel back to a more comfortable landscape beside the Rhine. Ah, Kaliningrad, mon amour, you have your own beauty, at first hard to discern, a difficult maligned city, but it is through your individuality that I have learned to understand, or at least moved a little way towards understanding.

Paradise on Erft
Hombroich Insel

Beside the river Erft, to the east of Düsseldorf, 11 brick pavilions by the sculptor Erwin Heerich function as a kind of fragmented gallery for one man's collection of art. Four other Heerich buildings are housed on an adjacent site, a redeveloped NATO rocket station formerly manned by Belgian soldiers and with missiles directed at the Soviet Union. Together they form the Museum Insel Hombroich, home to a small collective of artists, musicians and poets.

The initial idea for the 'museum island' with galleries in the landscape and a resident artistic community stems from the complex, contradictory personality of Karl-Heinrich Müller. Born the son of a factory worker in a suburb of Düsseldorf in 1936, Müller grew up in the flat, marshy Rhineland of the city's southern edge, a foretaste, he would later say, of the similarly amphibious landscape of the banks of the Erft. Soon after the war he set himself up as a property developer in Cologne, where by means of considerable ambition—and largely by being faster and more driven than anyone else—he built his firm up from a one-man business with a communication network that relied on the payphone on the street to one of the largest industrial property concerns in Germany, employing more than 400 at its peak.

Walther König, founder of the König art and architecture bookshop in Ehrenstraße in Cologne and a significant *capo* in the unofficial Cologne–Düsseldorf art world mafia, seemed to be an obvious source for information on Müller. Brief informal interview with the chain-smoking Herr König, in the presence of his son Franz König. Both wear dark grey suits and open white shirts. They sit at a large table on the first floor of their shop, surrounded by shelves filled with art monographs. The conversation begins with arrival of a tray with a bottle and three glasses.

—A small schnapps?

—Thank you.

—Yes, we have our collection of monographs here. Thousands of them, no one can really guess how many, and from so many different countries. And on the next floor we have even more, and then yet another floor. Here, look at this one from Russia, it's very rare, perhaps one of the very few available on the market.

—How would I find anything here?

—There is a system, but only we know the system.

—How well did you know Karl-Heinrich Müller?

—He was a business acquaintance but also friend. I would often be invited to dine at his house. On one occasion we even had a grand lunch together at the Hombroich Insel—a wonderful meal in the cafeteria. All the tourists, who are given only boiled potatoes to eat and water to drink, sat and stared at our delicious food and fine wine. We really enjoyed ourselves. I admired Müller, he was a money man, but also a mensch, open, generous. Other people liked him too, as a man, but at the same time here in Cologne he was also known as the *Heuschrecke*, the locust, because of his tendency to devour everything in his path. He was a businessman, a successful property dealer, used to wheeling and dealing.

—How did Müller become attracted to art?

—He was intrigued by artworks, first as commodities and then as high-quality objects. He soon got to know the right dealers, and he also knew many of the artists at the Kunstakademie, especially Erwin Heerich and Gotthard Graubner, with whom he was good friends. He saw art as something to collect, but also as a kind of purpose in life. He felt at home with artists.

—Müller seemed especially drawn to the work of the pre- and postwar Düsseldorf artists, but why not the big names like Joseph Beuys or the Bechers?

—He could be impatient, he couldn't be bothered to spend time on extensive negotiations, which meant he often missed out on a deal. At the same time Beuys, in particular, was considered by some people here to be an ideologue, a constructor of temporary installations, not an artist to collect. Maybe in part Müller was right, there are many museums with Beuys creations which are gradually rotting away.

—How did Müller deal with the artists?

—He was generous, perhaps even too generous. He allowed them a great deal of freedom.

—And what will happen now that he is no longer here to direct his art foundation?

—Difficult to say. The charm of Hombroich is the people who created it. Without them it is danger of becoming a museum.

—Maybe just time for another glass of schnapps?

Müller's first forays into art began in the 1970s. Initially he focused on primitive and archaeological objects but, prompted by his meetings with dealers such as Sami Tarica in Paris and Alfred Schmela in Düsseldorf, he soon started to purchase work by artists from the 1930s and 1940s—notably Hans Arp, Francis Picabia, Kurt Schwitters and Jean Fautrier—whose paintings were then relatively affordable. Müller collected art in the same way he built up his property business, by buying in bulk, by selling high and buying low and by making deals at the right moment. For instance, in the early days of his collection he swapped a fine Hockney for a large number of ancient Chinese Ban-Chiang sculptures. He had a feeling for the quality of individual pieces, but he also clearly loved quantity, and never seemed to know quite when to concentrate rather than diversify. Soon his interests expanded to take in antiquities from the Near and Far East, where he made various trips, as well as the undervalued artists of the local Düsseldorf school. With this expansion his collection became increasingly eclectic—he bought a number of Tjurungas from Australia, a series of Alexander Calder mobiles, several Cambodian stone heads, some wonderful ceramics from the Near East, a few Pacific Island sculptures and a remarkable ballet costume by Matisse. Müller seemed to have no fixed boundaries, introducing any number of other cultures into the rather narrow art world of Düsseldorf. 'I believe art belongs to nobody', he announced in an interview in 2004, 'art is a self-sufficient living entity', as if the idea of it being a floating commodity was alien to him, and as if art didn't actually belong in increasing quantities to Müller himself.

As his collection outgrew his house Müller cast around for a more suitable place to install it. In 1982 he bought the Hombroich estate, then comprising only a modest house, a number of smaller outbuildings and a rambling garden that had long run wild. Over the following years he added other pieces of adjoining land, the process of acquisition only hampered by his locust reputation—when this wealthy property magnate started buying land, people tended to wonder why, and the value of surrounding properties went up. But with his 1994 purchase of the land of the former rocket station, a few hundred metres to the northwest of his main estate, Müller finally acquired 62 acres to complete the Stiftung Insel Hombroich.

By all accounts Müller was a well-loved figure, at least among the art community, a person who would listen and was open-minded and generous—a sort of contemporary version of a Renaissance prince, whose dubious dealings in business could be separated from his public persona as a Maecenas or patron. As Walther König attests, Müller would play out this role partly by hosting lavish feasts and celebrations in the cafeteria at Hombroich, with cakes in the shape of the pavilions and with artists and musicians and other guests invited from all over the world. He was also an enabler, trusting others to do what he could not, notably encouraging Erwin Heerich, who had no architectural training, to design buildings, the artist Gotthard Graubner to show an orthodox mix of artworks, and the poet Thomas Kling to bring in other writers and playwrights. At the same time he offered his patronage to scientists and commissioned composers for island concerts. It was Müller, too, who conceived the idea of the artists' community, providing ateliers on the site for his friends. Yet he wasn't self-aggrandising. He didn't build play lord of the manor and build himself an imposing house, but lived in the upper part of the old coach house, above the ground-floor studios of his closest collaborators, Graubner and Heerich.

One might recall those typical late medieval Rhineland paintings of the crucifixion or nativity whose cast of characters includes a peripheral figure kneeling or praying, supporting the piety of the event. Such a character was in reality the artist's patron and his appearance, quietly edging into the scene, was a form of acknowledgement. A photograph of Müller in the meadow operates in a similar way, peripheral yet also clearly fundamental, a slight smile on the lips and an eyebrow raised, as though he was aware of what was going on and was playing a longer game. For Müller was also highly individual, bold and impervious to conventional criticism, treating his art collection in ways others wouldn't dare, not least in his apparent disinterest in conservation. 'For me', he says in a 1992 interview with Peter Sager, 'it is not strange that a painting grows old'.

There were three initial members of the Hombroich community, an inner circle which in the early stages directed almost everything: Müller, the essential mover for the whole enterprise; the sculptor Heerich, who designed the buildings; and the painter Graubner, who coordinated the choice and display of artworks. But as Hombroich Insel developed and as more land was purchased, others were added. The sculptor Anatol Herzfeld (usually referred to only by his first name) moved in, living and working in a barn on the island, now surrounded by his artworks—a metal piano, wagons, bits of human figures. The art critic Volker Kahmen lived in the original property on the estate, the Rosa Haus, which he also made the base for an archive specialising in German-Jewish literature. There were others who lived at least part of the time at the rocket station, located on higher ground above Hombroich: the poet Kling, assorted artists including Ute Langanky, Katsuhito Nishikawa and Oliver Kruse, composer Christoph Staude, a team of biophysicists and a large cast of miscellaneous characters who flit across the Hombroich story. What brought them together was not dogma, not a party line; Müller's aim was only to find a self-sufficient, loose-knit group of individuals, from a variety of disciplines, and give them free rein to produce their own work.

One can easily imagine the difficulties that could potentially develop among an isolated community of artists—a group of people not usually known for their ability to keep their egos in check. Müller writes in *Stiftung Hombroich Insel* that there were outbreaks of 'biting jealousy, bitter criticism and excessive vanity'. Yet somehow he managed to insist on the 'careful holding together and measured development that create natural growth'. Müller's circle seems to have been a sort of version of the Knights of the Round Table, where each has his place, with 'no hierarchy, no ranking', and the king oversees rather than commands. But in reality did rival artists vie for space or recognition from their benevolent patron? Walking around the island one can see, for instance, how the metal sculptures of Anatol begin to infringe on the space of the Heerich studio, but then how Heerich carefully uses the *Hohe Galerie* (High Gallery) just beyond Anatol's studio for a carefully thought-out display of his own rather more elegant sculptures.

How did the community relate to the private lives of the individuals in the outside world? Müller writes of how the island (*die Insel*, feminine in German) 'is a path on which one collects communal experiences and results through different experiments in various areas', adding rather surprisingly that 'the island has no place for masculinity'. Yet the community was largely male. Müller frequently refers to the community as 'a family'. But what did the actual families of Müller, Heerich and Graubner think of their husbands and fathers vanishing off for long periods into their island garden sheds? One never really discovers the answer to these questions. What is apparent, however, is that the community of talented artists living and working in Hombroich, despite its complex dynamic and periodic descents into squabbling, seems to have functioned remarkably well under Müller's generous and open-minded guidance, perhaps because on the island and rocket station there is plenty of space, with each occupant able to find their own privacy.

Approached from across a meadow, the *Hohe Galerie* first appears in the distance as a long brick wall, lined by a row of tall, wispy poplars planted almost too close to the brickwork. Only up close do you realise it is a three-dimensional volume. You enter through a high wooden door with an oversized round handle. The interior is long and high, church-like, and divided into two, the second half rather higher than the first. The walls are painted white, the floor is white marble, the glass of the roof is milky and there are no windows. The roofs of the two halves also slope in different directions, picking up either north or south light. After a while you become aware that this minimal difference produces two kinds of diffused light, one slightly bluish, the other reddish. The illumination varies according to the weather and the position of the sun, always changing. Arranged inside are several large Heerich sculptures in black stone, like tombs of some departed island inhabitants. A few leaves and twigs from outside drift in and lie across the white floor. In the adjoining half of the building there is a second door, diametrically opposite the first. Leaving the gallery, you initially feel like you've made a mistake, exiting the same way you entered, but this door opens onto a timber bridge which crosses a stream, leading onto the landscape of the island. The building in this sense is the most minimal of labyrinths, the two halves almost identical, but distinguished by slight variations in light, one half relating to the landscape of the marshes, the other to the overgrown English garden of the island as a whole.

A pause in all this art talk. Two women, mother and young daughter, Ulrike and Lisa, walk beside the river Erft. Shadows of fish flicker between the surface of the water. It all seems a bit too pleasant. The daughter speaks first.

—Nature is best when it is disturbing. It should not be so easy. It should not be so beautiful and so carefully looked after.

—It so quiet here, in nature there should surely be animals.

—They must be here, not far away. There are always animals near the river, but you cannot always see them.

The painter Gotthard Graubner advised Müller on the purchase of artworks and was also responsible for how these works were displayed, which is unique to Hombroich—and an indication of Müller's mistrust of professional art curators. In Heerich's pavilions there is no artificial lighting, no signage, no air conditioning, no security guards, no CCTV. The collection is almost all on display, and what's on show remains in position, there are no temporary installations. The art therefore speaks for itself, and also looks after itself, coping with the fact that the galleries open directly onto the exterior, whatever the weather. It is up to the viewer to reach their own conclusions about the artwork, no signs or captions are going to tell them what it is or what they should think. Because there are various galleries and not just one large building, the in-between also becomes important—the landscape of fields and woods out of which the next building emerges, and a space whose navigation affords time to consider what they have just seen.

In addition to the overall layout Graubner also challenges conventional categories of art display. Sometimes the rooms show just one kind of object. For instance, the *Tadeusz Pavillon* features only paintings by Norbert Tadeusz, brightly coloured complex compositions, slightly expressionist in feel, just as the *Hohe Galerie* is solely occupied with sculptures by Erwin Heerich. Graubner's own work consists of large canvases saturated with pale colour, indefinite but giving an impression of an uncertain depth, abstract but with the drifting atmosphere of Caspar David Friedrich or J M W Turner. For a period in the early 1970s he produced a series titled *Nebelräume*, fog spaces. Graubner has a pavilion dedicated to himself, but perhaps appropriately enough for a painter whose work is concerned with the nebulous, it is empty. This building is formed of one large circle intersected by a smaller glass circle. Light enters from the south-facing glazed facade and reflects off the curving plastered wall of the larger interior, as if the building were a kind of model of the human eye, the glass as lens, the plaster as retina. In other pavilions Graubner uses Müller's eclectic tastes and dislike of art experts as an opportunity to gently subvert traditional art categories, deliberately mixing periods, places of origin and styles. It is not that anything can go with anything, but certain objects play off and question others. So pre-Columbian artefacts are shown alongside 1920s paintings, Oceanic sculptures next to Albert Jensen's bright and fizzy electro-diagrams, ceramic and bronze figures of camels, cows and horses from early Asia and Mesopotamia—relics of intense but long-forgotten natural religions—are now confined to glazed cupboards, sharing space with Graubner's own paintings, where abstract atmospheres drift across the canvas. Do the ancient cows communicate with the modern mists, and in what language? 'I placed particular emphasis on the spatial relationships between the groups', Graubner wrote, 'every picture, every sculpture, every object must speak its own language in order to blossom. Art-historical links should be conveyed through the art and not via tracks of knowledge.' Objects speaking their own language hints at a touch of visionary mysticism, at a revelation of the natural world. But what kind of conversation takes place when each speaks his own language? The effect could have been a babble, but here the works speak not with words but with colour, form, material, texture, intention. The effect is both deliberately unsettling and revealing. Stepping from room to room you are never sure what to expect next.

The mix of objects at Hombroich, all from different times and periods, is simultaneously confronted with the strong local identity of the Rhineland, with its combination of industrial and natural landscapes—factories and river ports set within heaths, marshes and flat alluvial plains. Hombroich Insel is less than 100km from the Dutch border, in an area which until recently spoke Lower Frankish, very similar to the Dutch language. The buildings in the streets of Düsseldorf have a Dutch feel, very different from Berlin or Munich. This whole area was for a long time occupied by a scattering of smaller states, with ever-changing borders, before becoming a part of Prussia and then integrated into the nation state of Germany. In a long interview with the poet Kling in 2004, Müller spoke of the Rhineland's capacity to shape both plants and people. He went on to describe it as a 'wonderful, godly earth', as some kind of chosen land.

Düsseldorf lies on the Rhine, of which the Erft is a tributary. Much of the cultural mix Müller put in place in his island museum can be seen to have its source in the nearby city, and in particular its Kunstakademie, founded in the eighteenth century and located just north of the old town in a grand building beside the river. Running around the ground floor of the academy is a wide and high corridor punctured by doors lined in reddish marble, which open into large ateliers belonging to the individual professors. The *Meisterklasse*, a studio led by a distinguished artist, was the school's original pedagogical system and it remains largely the same today, mixing considerable respect for personal artistic authority with a certain tolerance for individual creativity. In the 1970s and 1980s the Düsseldorf Kunstakademie was seen as the best in Germany, and the city's art scene was of international importance. Beside Heerich and Graubner, graduates of the school included Joseph Beuys, Binky Palermo, Norbert Tadeusz, Gerhard Richter, Sigmar Polke, Bernd and Hilla Becher, Andreas Gursky and Thomas Demand. And as the Rhineland became the centre for any number of competing art movements, completely reinventing the German artworld—pop, neo-dada, formalist, Fluxus, performance, minimalist—the Kunstakademie became the location for rival art factions.

Heerich and Graubner were part of the same student generation as Beuys and Richter. As students of the sculptor Ewald Mataré, Heerich and Beuys were initially close friends. Mataré was famous for his sculptures based on animal and plant forms, but his work was banned by the Nazis as 'degenerate'. After the war he attracted more public commissions, including the great doors of the south portal of Cologne cathedral, where he was assisted by Heerich and Beuys (Beuys even famously inserted his own shaving mirror into the bishop's coat of arms, still visible today). The young artists then collaborated again with Mataré on the reconstruction of the limestone sculptures of mourning parents by Käthe Kollwitz beside the Cologne church of St Alban—Beuys produced the father, Heerich the mother. Both later became professors at the Kunstakademie.

In his own work Beuys took Mataré's concern for nature and spirituality, and for the ideology of Rudolf Steiner, into wilder directions, following his own self-delineated path into an art based on social, political and spiritual principles, mixing in equal parts shamanism and charlatanism, ever self-promoting, part of the much-contested public culture of postwar Germany. In contrast, Heerich remained closer to the Mataré tradition, sculptural, object-based, moving towards abstraction and non-figuration, following a quieter, more considered way, uncontroversial, almost hermetic, where ideas were expressed through the simplest materials with a precise, almost mathematical process rather than sudden inspiration.

The contrast filters through into Hombroich, where there are no examples of Beuys's work even if he remains a ghost in the machine, absent in his own artworks but present elsewhere. For example, various artists seen as preceding him, such as the collagist and poet Kurt Schwitters and the painter and performance artist Yves Klein, hang in a number of the galleries, and his shamanism is there in the form of tribal objects from Mesopotamia and Oceania. Anatol, whose work is scattered around the island, was once a student of Beuys. In an act that has now attained semi-mythical status, in 1973 he paddled his master across the Rhine in a hand-carved canoe, Beuys in the prow in a 'Sea of Galilee pose', to celebrate the restoration of Beuys's professorship at the Kunstakademie (he had been fired the previous year when he continued to accept large numbers of students into his class after they had been denied admission by the school). On Hombroich Anatol occupies the same spirit of the old shaman, but he is slightly second-hand Beuys, without the fiery aggression of the original. Norbert Tadeusz was also a former student of Beuys. Perhaps Beuys himself was too extreme, too loud, to feature directly in the quiet detachment of Hombroich, so has to slide in sideways.

The Kunstakademie influence on Hombroich goes further. Just to the north of the academy lie the remnants of the 1926 Düsseldorf Great Exhibition, dedicated in the fashion of the times to a mix of art and social hygiene, its buildings including a planetarium and a series of large exhibition halls, all built to a formal geometry, lined in clinker brick with white interiors, high doors and stone floors. In contrast, a street just south of the academy was once the location of the Ratinger Hof, a venue notorious from the 1970s on for its mix of Krautrock and punk bands, such as the offshoots of Kraftwerk, Neu and LA Düsseldorf, or Die Toten Hosen. The pub was also a meeting place for students and teachers from the academy, and attracted personalities from both popular and high culture. One well-known regular was Thomas Kling, who in his early series of poems, *Ratinger Hof zb*, celebrated the frenetic activities in the pub, boosted by cocaine and amphetamines made from aircraft fuel. Kling's performances with the drummer Frank Köllges were titled *Sprachinstallationen*, speech-installations, moving poetry away from being book-oriented to a live event in a club. So the Düsseldorf Kunstakademie was flanked by indications of what would become the twin poles of Hombroich—the geometrical brick-faced buildings of Heerich below, and the last traces of the Ratinger Hof with the presence of Kling in the rocket station above.

Of Kling, more later. For the moment an extract from Kling's long poem *Eine Hombroich-Elegie*, filled as ever with his strange, untranslatable, German compound nouns:

dies sind die geheimtinten der gegend
erlenzittern über den namen den moornamen
im trockenen überm tiefen grundwasser
spiegelt sich bebende schrift
einzeln aufsteigende blasen …
und elastik
der kopfweiden gespalten morsch
luft böden mit spliss brombeerdickicht dies
sind die einfachen tinten der gegend

these are the secrettints of the region
aldershaking over the names the moornames
in dryness over the deep groundwater
mirrors quavering writing
single rising bubbles …

and elastic
the willow divided ragged
air earths with split blackberrythicket these
are the simple tints of the region

Located almost at the centre of the Hombroich island is the largest of the pavilions, *Labyrinth*. The square-shaped building is surrounded by marshy land, very different in quality to the otherwise endemic outgrowths of the shaggy English garden. In the waters of the Erft and the man-made ponds swim rodents of surprising size, while up above the tree tops float buzzards and falcons. Approaching the pavilion, you first encounter a dense hedge concealing what appears to be a high garden wall. Between the hedge and the wall is a gravel path. As at the *Hohe Galerie*, you walk along the path and discover that the wall is actually part of a large building, with four identical sides, each perforated by an identical door on its corner, again unusually high. Entering at random through one of the doors, you find yourself in what seems to be a sequence of identical square rooms, distinguishable only by the light coming through the angles of the glass roof. How many rooms are there? Is there a route for navigating through them? Somewhere in what may be the centre is a large space, with atmospheric paintings by Graubner and Asiatic and Mesopotamian sculptures. The sense in these rooms is of light, uplifting spaces, filled with so many fine objects that you hardly have time to properly absorb them. A number of the internal walls are thick enough to contain within their depth ingenious glazed vitrines displaying ceramic objects. You begin to find your way through the placement of these art objects. Finally, you come to a door, identical to the one through which you entered. You step outside once more, onto the same gravel path between wall and hedge, uncertain as to just where you are or how you might proceed.

Erwin Heerich tended to use the phrase *begehbare Skulptur* (walk-in sculpture) rather than 'pavilions' or 'chapels' to describe his Hombroich creations, implying that he saw them as volumetric art pieces which visitors could enter rather than simply observe from a distance. But just when does a *begehbare Skulptur* become a building? Is it a matter not just of form but also of function? But function alone doesn't define a building. For the sake of simplicity, and not because the issue is resolved, in this text they are called pavilions, a term used to define small, independent structures of open use.

Heerich's favoured material for his earlier, smaller sculptural work was cardboard, which he chose as a fragile, neutral, amorphous material that could be folded to create three-dimensional sculptures, a skin rather than a mass. While there is a distinction in scale between the works he produced on paper and those he later constructed in bricks and mortar, all of Heerich's buildings are reducible to his earlier sequences of sculptural objects and drawings. The pavilions were first conceived on graph paper, Heerich drawing out the basic elements in plan, section and axonometric. These rudimentary diagrams were then sent to the office of a local architect, Hermann H Müller, who developed them into a typical set of construction drawings.

Heerich's sculptural work—which used wood, metal and stone, as well as cardboard—essentially consists of a large number of small, three-dimensional objects based on orthogonal geometrical forms, which are either added to or cut away. These moves are often explored in isometric drawings, such the sequence of studies from 1982 in which he looks at how a series of cuts are made into cube. Sometimes the first steps are very simple, such as a piece of wood cut in a certain way or with an angled section removed. Yet these somewhat elementary actions then build up to produce objects of increasing complexity. For example, he produced series of metal cubes, sometimes adding together cubes of diminishing size, at other times cutting smaller cubes out of larger ones, to create elaborate three-dimensional puzzles. Often Heerich would have such pieces photographed as a group, so one piece in the family reflects off another. Many of the individual components are comparatively small, but once aggregated they can form larger figures, like his furniture designs, or larger still, the massive stone objects found in the *Hohe Galerie*, or ultimately, of course, the pavilions themselves, freestanding sculptural containers within the landscape. Viewed in its entirety, Heerich's work constitutes a vast array of possible geometrical forms, carried out at all scales. The work appears calm and detached, but this apparent rationality barely conceals a battery of tricks and deceptions that delight in baffling the viewer or occupant.

In the handful of interviews that he gave, Heerich remained evasive about his intentions, but stressed both that his work is organic—one piece grows from the next—and that it lies largely in the realm of thought: 'For me, sculpture is the bringing out of a form, whose coming into being shows a self-referential system of organisation—like that of a fruit or mussel in the organic world.' He also emphasised that his work is not purely material: 'The existence of my work lies in the zone of what is conceived (*gedacht*) rather than made (*gemacht*).' He enjoyed the fragility of his materials, the actual objects are not what is important. The world of Heerich is thus both natural and conceptual. What we are seeing, whether sculpture or building, is really the physical manifestation of an idea, reflecting back to the theories of Kant in Königsberg, of a material world based on the immaterial. It is not clear how we would understand the idea without the existence of the objects, but the idea comes first. This almost spiritual approach to sculpture—the equivalent of the word made flesh—provides the particular and rather undefined qualities of Heerich's work, the feeling that one is experiencing more than just one aspect of the physical world. Part of its ingenuity stems from the way Heerich was able to move between families of objects, between sculptures and models, all based on some unseen idea, and then apply this approach at various scales. Many of his simple objects are already architectural in nature, without needing to be models for buildings. They lack only interiors, almost always being solid figures, intended to be seen from the exterior.

Sculptors producing architecture is hardly something new—Renaissance architects, for instance, moved with ease between the two fields. In more recent times, the question of the nature of the two professions—functional or non-functional, fine or applied art—has generally been more closely defined, but one such hybrid, originating in the US land art movement of the early 1970s, seems to have had an influence on Heerich. Among these artists, Mary Miss and Alice Aycock created large-scale structures, often based on American vernacular forms, typically sited in the landscape. Aycock's *The Beginnings of a Complex*, a temporary construction at Kassel for the 1977 Documenta, offers an interesting parallel to Heerich's own pieces. It consisted of a series of medieval-style timber walls, shafts and towers, which the visitor had to experience in person, crawling through tunnels and clambering up ladders. Aycock's work was shown in Germany in a number of large exhibitions in the early 1980s. Some of this interest in mazes, walls, towers and passages is reflected in Heerich's architectural vocabulary, but with the difference being that Aycock is concerned with extreme psychological states, while Heerich, though also playful, is quieter and more meditative. Aycock never considered her work as anything but sculpture.

Other artists lie closer still to the aesthetic coolness of Heerich. The US sculptor Donald Judd, originally a philosophy student, produced sculpture with industrial materials such plywood, steel and Perspex, and moved between the requirements of pure art and functional design. He coined the term 'specific object' for his geometrical, non-representational work, deliberately avoiding the terms 'sculpture' or 'painting', and rejecting even more explicitly the word 'minimalism', since in his opinion his work was never reductive but always offered considerable complexity. Disliking the way artwork was shown in temporary exhibitions, Judd developed instead particular locations for the display of his work, first in a house in New York, and then in a former US army base in Marfa, Texas. Judd may have crossed over between art and design, but he was careful to distinguish between the two. In his 1993 essay 'It's Hard to Find a Good Lamp', he wrote:

> The configuration and the scale of art cannot be transposed into furniture and architecture. The intent of art is different from that of the latter, which must be functional. If a chair or a building is not functional, if it appears to be only art, it is ridiculous. The art of a chair is not its resemblance to art, but is partly its reasonableness, usefulness and scale as a chair. These are proportion, which is visible reasonableness.

> The art in art is partly the assertion of someone's interest regardless of other considerations. A work of art exists as itself; a chair exists as a chair itself.

Some of Judd's concerns are reflected in Heerich's work—the production of 'specific objects', the insistence on permanent rather than temporary exhibitions, the interest in the links as well as the differences between art and design. However, Heerich was much more open to viewing three-dimensional artworks as potential architecture and was not deterred by notional requirements of function. His sculptural work and drawings already have certain architectural qualities, a concern with clear geometrical form, proportion, material. It was actually Müller, the non-artist, who first proposed to Heerich that his work might be enlarged to an architectural scale. And having taken on this proposition Heerich played with the idea of reasonableness, usefulness and scale with a boldness that might have been frowned on by Judd, and in a way which later becomes more problematic as the demands of function struggle with the perfection of the sculptural object.

A piece of architecture almost always has a site, a particular location—unless it is some kind of mobile architecture. Sculpture is usually assumed to be at first siteless, it could be in various locations, even if it is later given a site. Heerich's pavilions are particular, their form is almost abstract, but they are placed in particular locations—in a wood, beside a lake, on a hill—and belong there. They become rooted, part of the place, and it is difficult to imagine them anywhere else.

Heerich's buildings at Hombroich can be divided into three categories: those which act as pure *begehbare Skulptur*, such as his empty *Turm* (Tower); those which have the function of displaying Müller's collection, such as *Labyrinth*, *Hohe Galerie* or *Zwölf-Räume-Haus* (Twelve-Room House); and then those with more complex functions, such as *Caféteria*, or his artist's residence and archive in the rocket station. Again, at what point does one of these constructions move from being a piece of art to a piece of architecture? The distinction between the three categories is actually not as neat as it first appears, for at Hombroich form clearly does not follow function. But nor does function follow form, as conventional pragmatic function is also fairly irrelevant. For instance, the *Graubner Pavillon*, which is at present empty, once contained sculptures. The issue is neither to do with scale, for the structures vary in size; nor with habitation, for even the *Turm* allows a certain temporary habitation; nor with interior space, for all possess interiors, though these are often at odds with the exterior. If the function changes, the building remains relatively untouched. The rocket station archive, for example, was originally used by biophysicists for certain experiments, but now contains shelves of books. These could easily be stripped out and, with its unusual blank ground floor, blind courtyard, two symmetrical stairs and general air of existing to baffle as much as to accommodate any particular activity, the building could either simply be designated a *begehbare Skulptur* or, with the addition of some artworks, serve as a gallery. It is only when Heerich becomes too concerned about function, for instance in the stairs and glazing of the tall, thin *Wohnhaus* (guest house), which are clearly architectural, that his buildings become weak and drift away from being the pure manifestation of an idea.

Heerich's buildings never feel like scaled up versions of a sculptural object. They are not like Claes Oldenburg's extruded domestic objects—clothes-pegs, hammers and forks—which are simply larger versions of originals, using different materials but visually the same. With Heerich, in contrast, a material and conceptual transformation takes place alongside the artefact's rescaling. For instance, within the archive of his work on the rocket station site one can see a solid object which will become the *Hohe Galerie*, a box-like form featuring two opposing diagonal slopes, even if this object is not yet a model of the building to come—it has no scale, it can be rotated in various directions, it has no interior; rather, it is a kind of *ur*-form from which various other forms may emerge. When this becomes the *Hohe Galerie* the object is given a horizontal orientation, plaster turns into re-used clinker brick, the diagonal faces become glass and an interior emerges, with white walls and a marble floor. All of this is latent in the *ur*-form, yet still needs to be reimagined and transformed to become a building. If Heerich had simply scaled up the original model he could have made the building in concrete, which would have resembled the original, but he avoids this, and by using clinker bricks gives the exterior a texture, linking its appearance to that of other buildings of the Rhineland. In addition, by giving the object a particular site, between two rows of high trees planted close to the walls, and with a particular north–south orientation, he further transforms the original, which of course had no specific location. Does the *Hohe Galerie* necessarily belong to one side or other of the line proposed by Judd? Heerich has taken the issue further so that his *Hohe Galerie* belongs to some new category that goes beyond the old divisions.

In spite of the abstract nature of his work, Heerich was also interested in the vernacular. The photographs of Bernd and Hilla Becher had brought the industrial architecture of the Ruhr district into the art world, showing how banal structures, usually disregarded, had their own aesthetic qualities. Heerich made use of brown clinker bricks, timber doors, glazed roofs and industrial windows. The use of clinker and simple materials is widespread throughout the Rhineland. The plain forms in brick suggest also a link to the *Backstein* tradition throughout the north of Germany, to building complex objects with the simplest of materials.

Heerich produced a very large number of drawings, many of which are now in plan-chests in the archive of his work at Hombroich's rocket station. These immaculate drawings were made by hand, mostly with that traditional architectural instrument, the Pelikan Graphos ink pen, and its successor, the Rotring Rapidograph. Despite the uniformity of their paper size and line weights, the drawings are very varied, often using architectural iconography such as plan, perspective and axonometric, or showing what might be imagined as a three-dimensional object, but more often they are abstract or play with being potentially representational, as though uncertain whether to be pure abstract art, slipping off into a graphic reverie, or part of the ordinary world of three-dimensional forms. The lines appear mechanical, but seen close up their slightly shaky, hand-drawn qualities become more apparent, with the spaces between lines often uneven. Many of these drawings are based on the setting-out of a two-dimensional grid, which is then distorted to create illusionary three-dimensional forms. The lines of the grid are pushed in or pulled out, project in or out, play with moving from two to three dimensions, so that the viewer is presented with various ways of reading the drawing. The standard repetitive world of the grid, expanding to infinity in all directions but also limited by the size of the paper, becomes a surface out of which other forms are born. Often this grid is contrasted with areas of flat black, brushed on rather than drawn, not as a background but as a sort of continuous anti-space, set against the complexity of the grid. The clear lines, the areas of black, the use of standard drawing techniques, all seem to imply the creation of a definite and comprehensible world. On closer examination, however, internal contradictions are revealed; the drawings deliberately don't quite add up, the suggested spaces contradict one another so that no unified understanding is possible. This love of physically impossible spaces is later transferred into certain pavilions—the *Turm*, for instance, is spatially baffling; the exterior, at least on first inspection, does not seem to match the interior.

This mix of plodding consistency and unpredictable, leaping progress is also present in Heerich's buildings, which evolve with continuous ingenuity but are always based on the grid. These are not the pure grids, considered as an end in themselves, rather they are stepping stones from which a system of proportion for objects and buildings is derived. To an architect these drawings appear alarmingly basic. In an age of increasing sophistication in architectural graphics, due in part to digital technology, is this really how buildings are designed? By counting squares on a piece of graph paper and marking them off with a pen? The *Zwölf-Räume-Haus*, for instance, is just as its title suggests, 12 rectangular rooms, each 1 × 2, placed within an envelope of 4 × 6 squares. That's it: 24 squares measured out on graph paper. The only difference between rooms is the number of doors they feature—one, two or four. The plan resembles the layout for a board game or a geometric puzzle rather than a building—but it works, and because everything is reduced back to the idea, it makes for one of Heerich's more successful buildings. The relationship of grid to building becomes compromised when the perfection of the repetitive, abstract line has to adapt to the awkwardness of actual architectural materials, but this is invisible to a casual visitor. The ideal system gives way to everyday built reality.

The use of grids becomes more sophisticated in other buildings at Hombroich, when Heerich cuts out complex shapes from basic box-like forms. For example, the *Archiv* (archive) on the rocket station and the *Turm* on the island are each boxes with square plans from which elements are then removed, at the lower level in the former and higher up in the latter. Likewise, the design of the *Schnecke* (Snail) proceeds by cutting away parts of a square plan, here (unusually for Heerich) using a triangular cut to produce a plan folded in on itself, with a remarkable piece of brickwork tapering to an acute point. These in turn lead to other versions of design by subtraction, such as the *Fontana Pavillon* on the rocket station, whose plan, again set out on that familiar graph paper, is formed by a series of cuts of increasing size—1, 4, 9 and 16 squares—removed from a larger square. The drawing is absurdly simple, but achieves a remarkable power through the minimal manipulations of the lines of the grid.

Ulrike and Lisa have moved away from the river, up to an open area of grass. Lisa begins to kick a log in frustration.

—1, 4, 9, 16. Numbers. Grids. Squares. Shapes. I'm bored. I want to go home. I'm hungry. Now, now, now.

Lisa is pacified for the moment with a bag of brightly coloured Haribo Starmix. Her mother makes an attempt to explain.

—Yes, all these grids and these geometric shapes. This headwork, this abstract, philosophical approach. And all this purity, this search for perfection, for abstract beauty. I love it, I feel for it, but also sometimes it's really too much. I know, it's special here, it's not like anywhere else. It's not like a conventional gallery, because there is no CCTV and the doors are open, in the middle of the woods and the gardens. But something is lacking, there's something awkward, that doesn't quite fit.

Lisa looks baffled. An author from London emerges from one of the galleries, walks across the grass and sits down beside the two women. They look at him with mild surprise.

—Finally I have found you two. I was wandering through the galleries. All are wonderful and original. But I wanted to ask you. Do you think that this is all very German?

—That would be a cliché. What is German? We are German, or almost. German means lots of different things. All those clichés: rational, functional, clean, orderly. It makes me so angry. What shit. *Was für eine totale Scheiße.*

—But Mama ...

—My child ...

Together all three walk across the grass towards the woods. The English author continues.

—Is this area typical of the Rhineland area? I remember so well that film, *Kings of the Road*, by Wim Wenders, his best film. The open countryside, the size of the river, the little houses, the actor having a shit beside the road, it all felt large-scale and wild. I have a romantic idea of the Rhineland, a place to wander, to drive big trucks and motorcycles.

—Englishman, such an old film. With really not many women. And made mostly by the Elbe, along the old borderline, as well as a bit by the Rhine. But around here the Rhineland is a mix. It can't be defined. Big river, big money, big cars, big fashion, big art. But shabby as well. The best bits are where the shabby bits meet the smart bits. And here by the little river Erft, everything is hidden away in the woods and the marshlands.

—But Ulrike, do you remember that phrase in the Wenders film, 'the Yanks have colonised our subconscious'?

—Of course. But in the film they were talking about American pop music, which supplanted German popular music, and about road movies, which are also American. It's a clever throwaway phrase. Our subconscious is something deeper, it cannot just be taken over.

—And the island?

—It's also different here on Hombroich Insel. It's not American here, neither the buildings nor the artwork. These buildings derive from geometry, from shapes, lying just below the surface, not quite visible. Geometry underlies everything. Of course this can't called be a subconscious, only beings have that, not buildings. But there's a similarity, a sense of something hidden, something informing what you experience. Like the geometry that gives shape to those medieval churches, the *Backsteinkirchen*. Here on the island this geometry finds a modern form, and relates to the surrounding nature. And geometry is not always clean or pure, it can also be dirty. Dirty geometry, *was für eine Idee*!

They walk in silence through the woods. There are many people here, families enjoying the fine weather. The occasional sculpture is sited in the clearings. A woman plays on a flute. The sunlight shines unexpectedly through the trees. A large orange cat sits on a branch, yawning and contentedly ignoring the complexities of geometry. Just beyond the woods can be seen fields with cows. Lisa cries out:

—Mama I know what subconscious is. *Unterbewusstsein*. It's a German word and so it's a German idea. It's not American at all.

—Lisa, for a child you know too much and are quite irritating.

—And Ulrike, this garden?

—This beautifully organised garden is also a kind of surface. And just under the surface is something else, something older. Nature is saved from its beauty by not being very nice. Dead hares, dead birds, wasps, spiders, beetles, traces of urine, shit, mud.

—German art and nature?

—So much of German art shows a love of nature. Dürer and his hares. Extraordinarily precise. And Caspar David Friedrich with those wonderful scenes of mountains and the sea and the woods. Even the more brutal works of Anselm Kiefer. All these paintings are so beautiful that they almost make me cry. They reach deep down inside me. But we must never really trust pictures of beautiful nature. The best nature stinks. Like the actor in the beautiful film taking a shit. Nature is only real when it's revolting.

—Ukrike, this conversation is quite confused.

—That's the good thing about conversations. They can go round in circles and go nowhere in particular but still be revealing. Not like scholarly articles by clever English authors.

—Hmmm. Do you think we might go with Lisa for the boiled potatoes and mint tea in the cafeteria?

—Yes, yes, I am so tired of walking and kicking and thinking and talking. Let's go now, even if just for potatoes with yogurt sauce.

The cafeteria lies just beyond the pond. It serves indeed a rather Calvinist offering of boiled potatoes, yogurt sauce with parsley, apples, mint tea, water. The building has a square plan, with cubical blocks at each corner and a sloping glass roof between these blocks. It is functional, with a kitchen, toilets, storerooms, dining space. so tests the idea of a *begebahre Skulptur*. But somehow this doesn't really change its form. One could also imagine it empty, or also with objects. Or that even it might be replaced as cafeteria by the *Zwölf-Räume-Haus*, as 12 interesting top-lit rooms for dining.

It is difficult at first to discern just what method does determine the arrangement of the Heerich buildings. They appear to be simply scattered across the site, without any particular relationship to one another. This apparent randomness is in direct contrast to the objects themselves, which are always geometrically composed, and also to the way Heerich organised his sculptures for shows, set out as though conforming to some invisible orthogonal layout. However, on closer examination, an order is discernible, although it is not a geometric network but a more ad-hoc system that develops over time, responding to Müller's gradual acquisition of more land. In Hombroich this system divides the site into three main landscapes and three phases in time (a fourth phase in place and time is higher up at the rocket station).

The first three buildings, the *Hohe Galerie*, *Graubner Pavillon* and *Orangerie* (Orangery) (1983–84), were constructed on the sites of existing buildings within the original English garden on the island. But Müller soon realised that these would not be sufficient to house his collection and so commissioned three further buildings— the *Labyrinth*, *Turm* and *Caféteria* (1985–88), which lie as a triangulation of freestanding pavilions amongst the ponds and streams of the flatter landscape to the north. The larger pavilions are located where the land is level, so as to avoid the need for expensive foundations. The next trio, *Tadeusz Pavillon*, *Zwölf-Räume-Haus* and *Schnecke* (1991–93), experiment with various geometrical forms, and are set on the higher agricultural ground, beside fields and woodland. To these should be added the two buildings added later (1992–98), also on the higher ground, the *Kassenhaus* (entrance building) and a workshop for the artist Graubner, which are a little different in nature from the earlier work.

In considering these 11 structures as a group, built in sequence but without a masterplan, one can see how Heerich evolves his technique of placing abstract forms within an unpredictable landscape. In many ways there are parallels to a similar ambiance and scale in the gardens William Kent designed at Stowe, but whereas in an eighteenth-century English picturesque landscape one folly leads to another, and prescribed views are clearly set out, at Hombroich the buildings are often concealed, with no obvious route between them. Instead of a sequence of clear visual links, they provide points of transition between one type of landscape and another, or act as gates leading the visitor through the woods, streams, ponds, marshes and fields—and as passive eyes, filtering the light and registering the changes to external luminescence, but rarely allowing any view in or out. This is a more ambiguous vision of buildings in the landscape, a modernist version of *The Household Tales* of the Brothers Grimm, where buildings of slightly dubious identity and with questionable inhabitants are to be found in the woods, and where the way forward, or backward, is never clear.

Questioned by Christina Schroeter in a 1994 interview about the role of nature in his work, Heerich offered an unexpected and revealing answer. He didn't speak about architecture sitting benignly within the natural environment, about adapting to nature, or about any kind of aesthetic sensibility, but rather spoke about nature as a system of design, as an inspiration for sculptural forms. 'I observe the permanent, the substantial, in nature and try to allow these observations to influence my work. Morphology and metaphysics interest me. Through them archetypical sculptures come into being, which evolve organically.' For Heerich nature is not visual, but prompts ideas about form: morphology, metaphysics, archetypes, organisms. He sees his work as relating to nature because it follows an organic system, with one form evolving from another. For instance, one can see the evolution of Heerich's pavilions in terms of cells, a word relating to both biology and architecture. The *Orangerie* is one cell, the *Hohe Galerie* two, the *Zwölf-Räume-Haus* naturally 12. These cells seem to multiply as time goes by, like some slow biological animation. Then there are also complex single-cell pavilions, like the *Turm* and the *Schnecke*, where the cell morphs out of a simple form. 'The walls', says Heerich in the same interview, 'are the skins of the organism', as though describing the structure of a biological element rather than a building.

This is nature as a process, a continuous morphology. It is also very different from its depiction in more established German art-historical traditions, such as Caspar David Friedrich's romantic vision of landscape, which conveys nature as a spiritual experience, or the dark ecstatic forests of Anselm Kiefer, which comment, poetically or ironically, on the Nazi version of the sacred German land of *Blut und Boden*, or, more immediately, the shamanistic performances of Beuys, with his hares and stags, which usher a mystical understanding of the natural world back into contemporary life. But at the same time Heerich's viewpoint does relate to another very German vision of nature, deriving from the work of late-nineteenth-century scientists such as Ernst Haeckel, who categorised natural forms into continuously evolving families, and then related these systems to some grand idea of a natural religion which lies behind the material world—once again that odd mix of morphology and metaphysics. Haeckel produced wonderful illustrated books showing the families of forms. Through his sculptural systems Heerich is creating his own version of nature, his own evolutionary family tree.

When he places this family of forms in the landscape of Hombroich, whether in the overgrown garden beside the Erft or the open land of the rocket station, he is not merely producing a contemporary version of the picturesque. Hidden amongst trees or out on the plain, their brick walls are unforgiving, their geometry—which Heerich describes as 'the locating of people within space'—makes no attempt to blend in. Rather, the pavilions are a set of organisms, with their own nature, placed within the equally artificial nature provided by the museum island's landscape architecture and the anonymous and deliberately artless NATO rocket engineers.

At the time Müller bought the land around Hombroich Insel, it had long been a kind of lost landscape, a German version of Daphne du Maurier's *Rebecca* or Alain Fournier's *Le Grand Meaulnes*, a forgotten domain, overgrown and virtually deserted. This feel of the lost garden is reinforced in the work of the landscape architect Bernhard Korte, who created the apparently natural environment in which Heerich's abstract forms are located. In studying aerial photographs of the site, Korte discovered long dried up branches of the Erft, which he then excavated to provide streams feeding new ponds and marshlands. Elsewhere he played up the mix of exotic and local planting, making the English garden something like a tropical version of Devon. Korte even indulged in his own form of botanical archaeology, uncovering in the humus of the formerly dead river's arm, seeds from plants from many thousands of years ago. These plants, with their wildly idiosyncratic names—frogspoon, feverpoppy, poisonous henfoot, hedgehog-ear, cuckoo-light-carnations—provide much of the herbaceous infill between Heerich's pavilions.

Korte's mix of old and new garden forms is in this way integrated into the long history of the island. Around its perimeter, the estate's fields were originally farmed with hefty German crops—turnips, potatoes, cabbage—while in the eighteenth century the inner areas were laid out in the fashion of the time as a formal garden, with long, radiating avenues of trees reaching out into the fields. In 1813 the estate was bought by a Wuppertal industrialist, Peter de Weerth. Three years later he built the Rosa Haus as its main residence. As a prelude to Korte, in the land immediately beyond his house, Weerth introduced exotic plants such as hemlock pines, tulip trees, trombone trees, robinia and deciduous cypresses, some of which have now grown to immense proportions with trunks over five metres in diameter. At the same time he turned the formal garden into an English landscape garden, of winding paths, streams, woods and picturesque figures.

By the early twentieth century the estate had changed hands and was now owned by the youngest son of a family of industrialists from Cologne, an eccentric named Wilhelm Lensing. He hung chandeliers from the trees, plucked the wood-violets for salads, placed odd sculptures in the shrubbery, devised automated bird feeders, and lived much of his later life alone on the island as an affluent hermit. It was actually Lensing who first started to dig out the dried tributaries of the Erft, getting the water and the energy flowing again, a form of garden acupuncture, but also using the resulting network of streams to demarcate his land from the surrounding fields and create an increasingly inaccessible home for himself. He recorded much of this landscaping on a box-camera, preserving its transformation on glass-plate negatives, and as a kind of forerunner of Müller, revelled in the privacy of his own private Arcadia along the Erft.

When Lensing died in 1962 he was an almost forgotten figure, but a local woman, the widow of a journalist from Neuss, Frau Vicky Kreuels, was able to shed some light on his character. Frau Kreuels, who lives in a third-floor apartment in a small street in nearby Neuss, is something of an Anglophile, having worked in London in the early 1950s as a maid to a rich aristocrat. Cheery and conversational, she responded well to a visit by an English author, and recounted stories of encounters with Lensing in the late 1950s.

> —Yes, I have prepared some breakfast. Some eggs, cheese, bread and jam. And you drink coffee? Ah, tea, so very English.
>
> —Excellent. Thank you, no milk.
>
> —I went to England once, a long time ago. Just after the war. I remember it was so cold and foggy, but the English gentlemen were charming. Almost I might have married one, but I was homesick and came back to find my true love.
>
> —And Lensing?

—Lensing was at first sight an unprepossessing man, but he was really a *sehr sensibler mensch* (a sensitive soul), quite lonely and old-fashioned in his ways, but still very sharp—for instance, when he was teased by an assistant in the local bakery he registered her terrible teeth and politely suggested that before laughing at him she ought to see a dentist.

—What is your connection to Lensing?

—When Lensing died his house was cleared. The people doing the work had no understanding of what is valuable, they just threw things away. My husband Albert, a journalist who had connections to Lensing, salvaged some glass-plate negatives from a pile of possessions waiting to be destroyed. Without Albert all these photographs would have been lost. Later he used several of them in an article on Lensing for the local paper.

—And where are they now?

—In the attic, but the box is much too heavy to bring down. But there are some reproductions here. Yes that is a fine one with the tractor.

The photographs, retrieved from a cardboard box in Frau Kreuels's attic, have the quality of the technology of the period, slightly blurred owing to the long exposure times and rather flat due to the lack of focal depth, which gives them an inevitably melancholic air. Imitating in a painterly way the style of late impressionism, they nonetheless have just a suggestion of the photography to come, of *Neue Sachlichkeit*, even a touch of the celebrated Rhineland photographer August Sander. Their subjects include a large gathering of well-dressed figures on the lawn in front of the Rosa Haus; two youths standing on a bicycle-powered punt while two men look on from the reedbeds; cows grazing on the bank beside the willows; or Lensing himself, round-faced and tubby, accompanying two colleagues on a shoot. Lensing, ever the uncertain dilettante, practised photography for only a few years before he became bored and put his equipment and plates away. Comparing these images to the same scenes today, more than a century later, we find the well-dressed figures have been replaced by tourists, and Heerich's *Hohe Galerie* or *Orangerie* have risen up in the background.

Rosa Haus, the nineteenth-century property at the centre of the estate, formerly the home of Lensing, is inhabited by the critic Volker Kahmen, a long-time friend and colleague of Müller, and one of the few insiders remaining who is still able to recall the early days of the Hombroich project. Kahmen, besides being one of the first to write about the Düsseldorf photographers Bernd and Hilla Becher, is also the author of other more general books on photography and on abstract art. The Rosa Haus contains the literary archive that Kahmen set up, with its large collection of literary autographs, such as those of Franz Kafka and Paul Celan. Somewhere upstairs, apparently, is Kahmen's own remarkable collection of art, studded with works by friends like the Belgian painter René Magritte—although it should be said that with Kahmen, as with so many aspects of Hombroich, facts and myths tend to overlap. Kahmen himself is a very private individual and has a reputation for refusing all interviews, but a meeting is arranged through the good offices of the Hombroich archivist. In the small entrance hall of the house are a number of cabinets in which Kahmen has placed an extraordinary geological collection of minerals, fossils and prehistoric tools, interspersed with unexpected miniature artworks, each item's title and date of acquisition recorded in minute script on a paper slip. Kahmen sits at a small table by the window, and speaks expansively, even if there is something lightly ironic or slightly evasive about his responses.

—Müller was an industrial property developer. He liked things done in mass. It was the same with art. He bought in bulk. I sometimes acted as his artistic adviser, and would also be asked to comment on the quality of a particular piece. His collection is very good, but of course there were also beautiful things he didn't seem to value—most famously, a Hockney.

—Do think Müller had limits, did he know when to stop?

—Müller was a businessman, he always wanted more. He would blow things up and up, like an air-balloon, until ... well, you know the Grimm brothers fairytale of the Fisherman and his Wife, where the wife never knows when to stop asking for more, until they lose all sense of scale.

—Was it Müller's idea for Heerich to build the pavilions?

—Müller and Heerich and Graubner were friends. Heerich made such beautiful objects out of cardboard, and also in steel and stone. He made these with his own hands, and so controlled the work. Müller saw the possibility of turning these objects into buildings. In the early days everything was regulated by the authorities, and it was very difficult to secure planning permission. To get around these problems the first buildings were called 'renovations' or 'sheds' and placed on the sites of existing buildings. Then they were called 'chapels', because chapels are uninhabited, they require no complicated functions and no one can really object to a chapel. There was no artificial lighting or security guards or air-conditioning because there was not enough money. At first this was out of necessity, then later it became standard in all the buildings.

—Do you think the transition in scale was always successful?

—In his sculptures Heerich did the work himself. He was a very fine craftsman. But with the buildings he was dependent on others—on an architect and on workmen, and so he lost some of the control.

—Why did Heerich not receive more international recognition?

—Heerich was quiet, modest, with his small-scale cardboard sculptures and fine gridded drawings. He never became an international name. Other artists at the time made more noise.

—Is there something particularly German about Heerich. Is his art German?

—German art was destroyed by the event of 1933–45, by the Nazis. It has taken a long time to find its way back. But yes, Heerich has given something back, returned something that was missing, an abstraction but also a kind of wit. These buildings, they are not always to be taken so seriously. They are to be enjoyed. They are a big game.

—What did Heerich mean when he claimed that the buildings were not just physical forms, but also that they are to be considered signs of another world?

—Well that it is of course complex, and relates back to the ideas of the Königsberg philosopher Kant and beyond, phenomenon and noumenon, that there is a world that we experience without senses, but this is just a sign of another world, which we cannot experience. It's an idea that runs through parts of German culture and through Heerich's world of forms which emerge from geometry.

—In your book, *Eroticism in Contemporary Art*, you include Heerich as an artist with erotic aspects ...

—Ha ha, did I write that? No, there isn't much eroticism in Heerich. In that book I was really writing about *Sinnlichkeit* (meaning), not about erotica—my argument was that there was meaning in abstract art, which at that time was ignored—but the publishers changed the title of the book to something that would sell more copies.

On higher ground on the western edge of the museum estate, where the landscape has a different feel, almost agricultural, with open grass fields and enveloping woodland, you encounter the *Tadeusz Pavillon*. It is another clinker box, this time with a large square window cut into its facade. By this time you might feel you have seen so many of these boxes that there can't be many tricks left in store. But it still manages to surprise. You enter as usual through an oversized timber door, as though going into a space you have already experienced. Inside you see a series of very large oil paintings by Norbert Tadeusz, which appear to combine a vibrant atmosphere of human anatomies in all possible positions, with the occasional suspended Francis Bacon-like animal corpse, as though a butcher had moved into a circus. Of course, the interior space of the building has none of this carnivorous performance, but remains as ever cool and slightly baffling. The large window that dominates the outside has vanished and is nowhere to be seen, until you realise there is a second interior higher up, cutting through the first one across the centre of the building. Initially there appears to be no way of accessing this other space. But once outside again, behind the building, you find a mound and a stair which allows you to enter this second space—an empty horizontal shaft which reaches across to the window and a view over the fields. It is only back in the *Caféteria*, aided by a second helping of apple puree and mint tea, that you figure out the *Tadeusz Pavillon* is a building with two spaces that do not connect, one a gallery, the other a viewing room.

Swimming in the pond is a large grey creature. Uli and Lila stand beside the pond, with the English author.

—Lili, do you know what kind of creature that is? It looks like a big otter.

—That's easy. I know all about animals. It's a *Bieberratte*. But its Latin name is *Myocastor coypus*. They eat leaves and plants.

In 1994 Müller bought a site made available by the end of the Cold War, a decommissioned NATO rocket station located about 1km away from Hombroich Insel, and separated from it by a road and railway line. The presence of the station had been a running sore for supporters of a neutral Germany without nuclear armaments. Today the site is intriguing, the Belgian troops that manned it have gone, but the bunkers, sheds and control tower remain, surrounded by fields and orchards. In the right season, large hares can be seen leaping through the fields.

The purchase of the rocket station gave Müller the opportunity to extend his interests beyond Hombroich Insel, where space is rather limited, and to develop a community of artists. In this sense the station has a different mandate, no longer displaying his collection but encouraging a wider range of activities. The two sites balance one another, the island gentle and concealed, the rocket station rough and exposed. With his usual enthusiasm—and finance—buildings were renovated, bunkers cleaned out, and specific artists, musicians, even scientists invited in to use the site. As an inveterate property developer, Müller saw a building crane as an indicator of life, and developed an ambitious architectural programme. Heerich was again invited to produce a number of buildings, this time four structures, including the *Archiv*, originally designed for use by visiting scientists; the *Fontana Pavillon*, containing artwork by Lucio Fontana; *Wohnhaus*, a three-storey seminar building; and, with his architect-son, the *Kloster*, a cloistered guesthouse. Each is interesting, but up here on the rocket station the buildings appear exposed, unable to shelter within Korte's carefully planned marshy landscape. Yet still Müller wanted more—and this is where he perhaps began to overextend himself, indulging his old fondness for buying in bulk. A series of celebrated architects were invited to produce additional buildings. Per Kirkby produced three modest and rather delightful vernacular buildings on the path down to the island; Raimund Abraham designed a very sculptural house for a musician, oriented directly towards the control tower, with a large circular concrete roof—like some kind of symbolic millstone; and there is a pleasant but rather uncertain gallery by Alvaro Siza. The Langen Foundation, another private arts foundation, separate from the Müller enterprise but sharing the same site, then commissioned Tadao Ando to design a museum, rather banal and corporate in appearance, the antithesis of Heerich's modest but formally inventive structures. Late in life, Müller made considerable efforts to bring in other celebrity architects, such as Peter Zumthor (who reportedly demanded that the site be cleared of all the other buildings) and Daniel Libeskind, but fortunately nothing came of this; the last thing Hombroich needs is the vanity of star architects. In 2004 he was still thinking big, inviting numerous artists and architects to produce a vast project for an art colony extending far across the surrounding fields, but his death three years later meant his 'HombroichRaumOrtLabor' never happened.

Seeing Müller's approach to the rocket station one might recall the parable cited by Kahmen, of the tale of the Fisherman and his Wife, always demanding more. At what point is there too much art? At what point are there too many galleries? At what point are there too many languages? Up here something has been lost of the mystery and subtlety of the ideal world below. Perhaps this is necessary; Hombroich Island, with its art separated out from the everyday world, is too perfect, too detached, the creation of the art paradise has its limits. However, the best thing about the rocket station is not the new buildings but the wild location on the plain, the industrial quality of the bunkers and tower, the wind, the fields, the creatures, the unexpected.

die grauen bienenaugen scannen
hier die wiese ab, die graue wiese
ein rechtes wachsrest-gedächtnis
wachsrest-diktaphon,
formt wies, tal und blöcke ab,
das ganze landschaftsding in
knete.

the grey beeeyes scan
here the meadow, the grey meadow
proper waxrest memory
a waxrest-dictaphone
forms meadows, valley and blocks
the whole landscapething in
clay

At the centre of the rocket station is a control tower, its raised operation room looking out over the landscape. Müller invited the poet Thomas Kling to live at the station and rather unexpectedly he chose the tower as his home, renaming it the *Dichterturm* (poet's tower). Unexpectedly, because one might not expect a poet to occupy the central position in a rocket base, making lyrical expression, rather than highly aggressive missiles, the hub around which it revolved. Born in 1957 in Bingen, further up the Rhine, Kling became one of the preeminent German poets of his generation, celebrated both for his verse and his biting putdowns of other more conventional poets. Through connected to Düsseldorf, and formerly part of the city's arts scene, Kling travelled widely, writing about the many places he visited—New York, St Petersburg, Finland, Vienna. But he retained a particular feeling for the Rhineland, its long history, its people, its ways of speaking, its fauna and flora.

die bienen, von den graugesehenen wiesen,
heimwärtsbretternd, zu der bienenbude
dort einlaßkontrolle zu passieren, um
tänze auszuführen, was bienensprächlich,
honigalphabetisch etwas übermitteln soll.

the bees from the grey-seen meadows,
homewards-speeding to the beehome
to pass by the entrycontrol, to
perform dances, in beelanguage,
honeyalphabetical, should convey something.

From early on Kling's writing was characterised by its disruption of the comfortable grammatical forms of German, mixing slang, ancient forms, invented compound words and imports from other languages as much as from geological and zoological phrases, following but reaching beyond the experiments of 1920s Dada poets like Hugo Ball, and the linguistic games of Austrian poets such as Ernst Jandl and Friederike Mayröcker towards the poetry of Paul Celan with its hefty invented compound nouns, and his love of words from botany and geology. A Kling poem often lacks any consistent syntax, usually has no clear grammatical subject or object, produces unanticipated repetitions and line-breaks, and requires several readings to determine its sense. Behind Kling's poetry lies the idea that the world is not as it seems, and therefore needs other forms of language to describe it. These forms cannot be a private language, which would not be understood, but might be linked to older forms of German, before it became a single unified language. His work is both an attempt at a kind of alternative German, and also what he described as *Spracharchäologie*, language archaeology, bringing out and resurrecting words that had been forgotten. A slender parallel can be drawn with those litanies of rediscovered plant names dug out of the dead tributaries of the Erft by Bernhard Korte, an ancient botany excavated and reused for contemporary purposes. In his younger days Kling would compound the complexity of his language by reading his poems out aloud in a mix of considered tones and angry shouts—sessions he termed *Sprachinstallationen*. Later he became less theatrical, more measured, but sounds and syntax remain central. His work, often difficult enough in German, is hard, perhaps even impossible to properly translate into English, where invented compound nouns have little sense, and where the particular sound of the German language is lost.

Heerich, who belonged to the island, and Kling, who was at the centre of the rocket station, can be compared. They are different but not opposed, both are concerned with the material world but also the immaterial, both are attached to the landscape of the Rhine, to its history, but each looks much further afield. Heerich believed in clarity of form, in what at first appears simple, but his work quickly becomes mysterious, baffling, deliberately labyrinthine. Kling starts off looking intimidatingly complex, almost nonsensical, but is often conveying a straightforward idea, with a deep, sometimes dark relationship to a people, animals and landscape. Both have a particular relationship to the Hombroich landscape, Heerich's buildings, though abstract, must be in their political position on the island, Kling's *Sondagen* poems refer to this particular Hombroich location.

This concern for the landscape and its creatures finds its way into other Rhineland art. Joseph Beuys famously carried a dead hare into one of his performances to allow this corpse perched on his arm to 'explain' his artwork. In Beuys's former studio in the Kunstakademie, now redecorated, there still a rectangular patch of the old paintwork, high on the wall on which Beuys wrote the word *Hasenpfote*—hare's foot.

in seitenlage, eben noch
ein junger hase
biegsam, ganz, noch
völlig flauschig
auf beiden seiten
ohne wunde
sonne scheint ihm rosa
durchs ohr
die uhr laüft drei
goldene fliegen und
eine wespe sonnengelb
erscheinen wortlos
auf wuscheligem
sommeraas

on its side, still
a young hare
flexible, whole, still

fully fluffy
on each side
without wounds
sun shines on it pink
through the ear
the time is three
golden flies and
a sungold wasp
appear without words
on furry
summercarcass

Kling's *Eine-Hombroich-Elegie,* published in his 2002 collection *Sondagen* (Soundings), is a long poem broken down into 21 individual fragments. The poem never mentions the Müller enterprise, the artworks or the buildings, but concentrates instead on the site's animals, birds and insects, especially the wasp, which became Kling's own emblem, appearing at the death of the hare. As in folktales, the animals may prove wiser than the humans, but their wisdom is unfortunately non-transferable, it remains in the animal world. The fragments of poems express a disturbing sensibility: the landscape and its inhabitants are slightly threatening, and death is just a step away, but life continues to buzz and chirrup in a language the poet cannot fully understand. The language of the poems, reduced down from the baroque complexity of his earlier work, displays the typical Kling inventiveness—waxrestmemory, honeyalphabetical, ochredepth—and syntactical disruption. The elegy, as a literary form, looks back to Virgil, whose *Georgics* dealt with the life of bees and other insects, but also to English poems of the eighteenth century, such as *Elegy in a Churchyard* by Thomas Gray or *Elegy on Death* by John Keats, which turned these pastoral requiems into sweet meditations on landscape and death. Where better in Germany to find possible allusions to this lyricism than in a wild English garden beside the Erft?

Navigating the rocket station you walk through the rather confused configuration of bunkers and towers before heading out onto the plain. Amid long grass you approach a square-shaped building, again sheathed in clinker brick, but unusually for Heerich it integrates a strip of utilitarian windows and, doubly different, is arranged over two storeys, the lower floor being cut away so that the upper level canters out in a rather disturbing fashion. You enter into a small shaft, open to the sky, but blank, revealing nothing, leading nowhere. A small door in one of the walls leads you to an interior room, and then up a simple dog-legged stair to the main space running around the upper storey, which contains rows of shelves with books, some of which appear to be organised by the colour of their spines. This was formerly a research space where a team of biophysicists led by Fritz Albert Popp experimented with biophotons and bioluminescence—one of Müller's wilder attempts to add science to Hombroich's arts-oriented programme. Now the building is an archive for the Müller project. Some researchers work quietly at a table, an unexpected outcrop of focused human beings in these often empty buildings. From the windows you look out across the plain. You walk around the perimeter of the archive, arriving at a second stair, identical to the first, leading downstairs to another identical exit. Once again this building is a miniature labyrinth, elegant, reduced, giving nothing away, the visitor orienting himself only by the windows which give onto different views.

The Hombroich project, utopian, highly aesthetic, hermetic, seems to have no fixed end. 'Its quality', Müller said in a 1992 interview, 'is that it will never be complete, and remains a living space, where the diversity of art meets the diversity of nature'. But how does such a project remain alive once its founder has gone? In the early 2000s the community of Hombroich began to thin out. Heerich died in 2004; Kling followed him a year later, at the early age of 48; Müller died unexpectedly in 2007; Graubner in 2013, Volker Kahmen in 2017. Within just over ten years Hombroich Insel had lost all of its main protagonists. By then Müller had spent most of his fortune, with comparatively little remaining to continue the ambitious scale of his project. Some of the pavilions now require substantial and expensive repair work, a necessary but ironic task, considering that Müller emphasised the transitory nature of his collection, and that Heerich was originally attracted to fragility and an emphasis on the idea rather than its material realisation. Wandering across the island now is a strange, almost hallucinatory experience, as if one had assumed the ghostly identity of a character in Lensing's photographs. In the Heerich atelier, for example, everything remains just as he left it, his books on the shelves, artworks set out on a podium, his bedroom behind with its bed still in position, the coffee percolators lined up on the shelves. There is on the island a certain weight from the past, as though the generation of the 1970s and 1980s were the giants, and all that came after existed on a smaller scale.

A foundation, Stiftung Insel Hombroich, was already set up in 1996, derogating responsibility for the administration of the entire Müller enterprise to the state of Nord-Rhein-Westfalen, the district of Neuss, and Karl-Heinz Müller himself. Transferring Müller's collection to the state solved some of his then considerable tax problems, and gave the island access to national and regional sources of funding.

Other members of the community remain, and various new artists continue to arrive. The poet Oswald Egger, born near Meran in Südtirol, came in 2002. Though rather different from Kling, his background Alpine rather than Rhineland, Egger is also a highly individual, mathematically inclined, poet of nature. Egger poems are often accompanied illustrations suggesting botanical forms. The wasps, as ever, are ever the smartest.

Mit der ersten
Biene, die ich fing,
in diesem Sommer
biss mich die Wespe

With the first
bee, that I caught,
this summer,
the wasp bit me

Like the religious order it rather resembles, the Hombroich community develops and evolves. Where once Müller and his friends made decisions and simply carried them out, now committee members engage in the usual endless discussions, each claiming to channel the wishes of the departed patron. The locust has achieved a kind of saintly status.

Müller once said 'I believe that art is a self-sufficient living entity'. Self-sufficient? Then perhaps it will look after itself. Müller certainly felt that art should be nourished but not coddled. Hombroich Island isn't really an island, rather a landscape of undefined marshy land, known in German as *Broich*, through which a number of small streams flow. It was by restoring and recreating the flow of these streams that the land was brought back to life. A sodden Arcadia? Time now for another leap to the east, to another river, away from the Rhine to the Neiße. Paradise enough for now.

Silesian Scenes
Görlitz–Zgorzelec

Görlitz and Zgorzelec are twin cities, lying on opposite sides of the river Neiße. Görlitz is in Germany, in the province of Oberlausitz, formerly in Silesia, now part of Saxony. Zgorzelec is in Poland, in the Lower Silesian voivodeship. The land Zgorzelec occupies was once part of Görlitz, but was handed over to Poland in 1945, as part of the postwar settlement, when the border between the two countries was moved west, along the line of the rivers Oder and Neiße.

The mystic Jakob Böhme (1574–1624) was living in Görlitz when he had a vision of a ray of sunlight passing across a pewter plate and realised, in that moment, that God revealed himself in simple objects. In his book *De signatura rerum* Böhme writes that each object has a signature which reveals its inner nature. His writing is bafflingly complex, and leads to much mental muttering.

Wes Anderson's *The Grand Budapest Hotel* (2014) uses as its principal location the vacant department store in Görlitz, transformed into a grand hotel. The film is set in a fictitious country, Zubrowka, apparently a land of snowy peaks, ski runs and isolated mountain monasteries—rather different from the gentle hills of Lausitz. It stars Ralph Fiennes as the eccentric hotel concierge Monsieur Gustave H, Toni Revolori as his charming assistant Zero, and numerous stalwarts from other Anderson films. A black comedy, with absurd conversations, family conspiracies, a stolen painting and a prison escape, *The Grand Budapest Hotel* presents the tale of the gradual loss of an idealised interior world.

Running up from Görlitz railway station, Berlinerstraße seems like any other street in an East German town, with its small stores, news kiosks and kebab shops, all very busy with shoppers. It gives way to the long rectangular space of Elisabethstraße, with Polish stalls selling eggs, blueberries, honey and bunches of herbs, the department store beside the small church of Unserer Lieben Frau, the odd round tower, the little streets, the trams, the marketplace, the Dreifältigkeitskirche, the shop selling maps and books of German Silesia, the nearby Silesian Museum, the downward curve of Neißestraße. All perhaps just a little too charming, but saved by a pleasantly tatty feel, a theatre set where elements might fall over to reveal some props and stagehands. And in Görlitz the merely picturesque sometimes mutates into the extraordinary. Beyond Neißestraße is the vast late medieval church of St Peter and Paul. Some curved steps lead up to the entrance. Inside is a fantastic vaulted space, the vaulting stretching out in all directions, seemingly weightless, with minimal solids and extensive voids. The effect is of a building that hardly exists, and which speaks in some language we no longer quite understand. Just below the terrace beside the church runs the river Neiße, remarkably narrow for such an important border. A small pedestrian bridge leads across the river, without any border controls, to the city of Zgorzelec.

Gustav H, in a train compartment, drinking champagne.

—You see? There are still faint glimmers of civilisation left in this barbaric slaughterhouse that was once known as humanity. Indeed that's what we provide in our own modest, humble, insignificant—(*sighs deeply*). Oh, fuck it.

The artist Giorgio de Chirico, painter of deserted classical cities, once stated that every object has two aspects: 'the normal one which all men can see, and another which is spectral or metaphysical and seen only by rare individuals in moments of clairvoyance'. At certain moments, Görlitz has just this feel, that something else lies just below its visible surface, about to be revealed.

Görlitz has belonged at varying times to Bohemia, Austria, the Electorate of Saxony, Prussian Silesia, the German Democratic Republic—and now to reunited Germany. Its stable unchanging feel hides the fact that it has always shifted with no great anxiety between different powers. Of course it remains in the same location, but this location changes its nature according to its orientation.

Among historic German towns the city is remarkable in that its fabric was left almost untouched by the events of the Second World War. It was beyond the easy range of the RAF (who gave it the code name Nautilus) and thus not subject to the devastating firebombing meted out to other German cities. Nor was it fought over in the final days of the war, as the Germans had no chance to make a disastrous last stand, and the Red Army simply bypassed the town on their way to Berlin. In a completely pointless action on the last day of the war, the Wehrmacht blew up the seven bridges over the Neiße river—only the small pedestrian bridge in the town and the road bridge to the south have since been rebuilt. In May 1945 the Red Army entered—it preferred to say 'liberated'—a perfectly preserved city.

Görlitz has the air of the perfect miniature city, furnished with a variety of building types, many seemingly borrowed from somewhere else but reduced in scale—the railway station with its vaulted duck-egg ceiling, the crenelated post office that looks like a toy castle, the diminutive natural history museum with its collection of local snakes and reptiles, the full-scale reproduction of the Holy Tomb in Jerusalem, the baroque house with the Oberlausitzische Bibliothek der Wissenschaften, or Upperlausitz Library of Science, with its collection of scientific books and early electrical experiments. The Kaufhaus, used by Wes Anderson for his film, is a version of one in Berlin. Görlitz has various other Jugendstil buildings, dating from its boom years in the early twentieth century, including the only surviving Jugendstil synagogue, the large Stadthalle by the river, and various large residences such as the exotic Villa Ephraim in Goethestraße.

The Görlitz synagogue stands a few streets from the Kaufhaus, built at a similar time with a similarly monumental Jugendstil exterior, capped by a large square tower and imposing dome. Jugendstil, as opposed to the more traditional oriental styles, was deliberately chosen as a sign that the Jews were part of modern German culture. The synagogue and the Kaufhaus were the last grand buildings constructed in the centre of Görlitz, signs of an optimistic culture which was in fact reaching its end. The synagogue, which was set on fire during Kristallnacht 1938, but saved by the local fire brigade, remained vacant for decades. Now restored to its original condition, it belongs to the city and is used as a cultural centre, with a small room for Jewish religious gatherings. A young man with a cap stands in the interior, explaining to visitors the history and significance of the building.

> —Almost all the Jews of Görlitz emigrated in the 1930s or were murdered by the Nazis. There is now a small Jewish community in Görlitz, we use one of the rooms here for religious purposes. You know the problems in Görlitz did not begin in 1945, as some people say, with the arrival of the Soviets. They began long before. And you see, the synagogue cannot just be considered a cultural centre, considering its history. It is different because of what happened to the culture to which it belonged, and still belongs.

The city's wealth was originally founded on cloth production and its location on the Via Regia trade route linking Western and

Eastern Europe. In the nineteenth century, as part of Prussia, it was both the base for various industries and a pleasant retirement town for affluent pensioners from the large German cities. This quiet affluence continued into the twentieth century, even with the rise to power of the Nazis. But after the Second World War things changed, as Görlitz became part of socialist East Germany. The population was swollen by large numbers of emigrants from Silesia, which had been handed over to Poland, who settled temporarily in the border town, hoping to go back home one day—in vain. Silesia would become their lost homeland, a source of often invented memories.

From being *bürgerlich* and right-wing, Görlitz acquired its very own Karl-Marx-Platz and Leninplatz. The East German authorities attempted to turn it into a workers' city, with factories producing railway carriages, optical instruments and manufacturing equipment. A large-scale lignite-fired power plant, optimistically named *Völkerfreundschaft* (Friendship Between Peoples), was constructed just to the south. Extensive housing blocks were built on the northern and southern outskirts, and as in many socialist cities these suburbs became the most attractive areas to live, preferable to the older buildings, which often lacked basic facilities. The German Democratic Republic, driven by a genuine concern to construct factories, schools, housing and hospitals for the workers, but overseen by a seedy regime devoted to spying on its own citizens, had difficulty finding any appropriate identity for the historic city. The socialist vision of the architecture of Görlitz is shown in posters in the graphic style of the period. Ignoring the churches and the Kaufhaus—presumably since they were tainted with religion and capitalism—they instead show the old houses, the city towers, then socialist housing, factories and power plants, all typically peopled with groups of contented workers. Görlitz was to become a new workers' city for a new age, but in the absence of an economic base to achieve this the inhabitants slowly seeped away. The old centre was gradually deserted, and many of the historic buildings decayed and were boarded up. In the final years of the East German regime the attitude to the old town became even more confused. At the same time as certain buildings were carefully restored as a celebration of an acceptable craftsman culture, it was proposed to raze a substantial portion of historic fabric and build in its place a centre worthy of the ideals of the socialist state. Fortunately this plan was never carried out—more from a lack of means than a lack of intent. Yet, the failure of the socialist state to produce any consistent attitude to the historic city was in fact instrumental in conserving it. Buildings survive through neglect as much as through care. Whereas many cities in West Germany were energetically reconstructed and lost much of their past, Görlitz slept, and in sleeping remained itself.

There is little left today of Görlitz's socialist industry, as state-subsidised factories have been asset-stripped and closed. The population has dropped to half its prewar figure, from 94,000 in 1938, to 78,000 in 1989, to 50,000 today, plus another 33,000 in Zgorzelec. Since 1989 many of the younger inhabitants have moved west for education and employment. However others have arrived from the west, particularly pensioners looking for cheap accommodation in a pleasant climate, and more recently those working in the digital industry.

To the west of the inner city lie the streets of high brick apartment blocks built in the second half of the nineteenth century for the pensioners who moved to the city from Prussia, for the warmer weather and easy atmosphere. The street names are a list of the cities and towns of Oberlausitz and Saxony—Dresdenerstraße, Bautzenerstraße, Lobauerstraße, Leipzigerstraße. In appearance, these streets resemble areas of nineteenth-century Berlin which are now fashionable and expensive—Kreuzberg, Prenzlauerberg—but here they are often empty, vacated by their previous owners.

An apartment on the third floor, large rooms with high ceilings. Laptops, big screens, tech equipment, Ikea tables and chairs, refrigerator. Two children watching an animation of large cats, mildly quarrelling. Young woman in shorts and t-shirt, talking very fast and sipping from a bottle of Fritzicola.

> —It doesn't really matter today where you are. We could be in the countryside, on a mountain, in a forest. But we like it here. The towns in the west are too expensive now. So we moved here, where the rents are cheap and there is plenty of space, with the countryside all around. Now we run a fashion site, it's quite complicated, but we know what

we're doing, there's money to be made. And in the summer we go swimming in the lake, the one they made from the former quarry.

A scene to the south of the city centre. Just past Johann-Sebastian-Bach-Straße, an extensive open area of allotments, in the suburb of Biesnitz. Cabbages, spinach, carrots, potatoes, various types of berries. Beside a large shed, a few plastic tables and chairs, a sun umbrella, gardening instruments and buckets. A general air of not a lot happening. A woman walks slowly, pushing a child in a pram.

—My father worked in the optical works, the factory did well, it made precision equipment. Then it was taken over and closed. It was easier to make the same products elsewhere. What to do? Why should we move? So we have the allotment here, we never go into the town, we grow everything. It's like being in the countryside, even the hares come in sometimes and eat the lettuce and the tops of the carrots. Here, try some redcurrants. They are excellent with a sip of homemade Holunderschnapps.

Görlitz—or, as it is sometimes termed, Görliwood—has frequently been used as a film location. Able without too many cosmetic additions to transform itself into various other cities, it has stood in for Paris in *Around the World in Eighty Days*, for Berlin in *Alone in Berlin* and *Fabian*, for a Sicilian town in Tarantino's *Inglourious Basterds*, and for any number of other German cities in *The Reader*, *The Bookthief* and various TV films. As much as asserting its individual identity, Görlitz is content to be a perpetual stand-in for other places—more people have seen glimpses of Görlitz in films than have ever visited the city itself.

Among these films is Anderson's film, *The Grand Budapest Hotel*, which creates its own world by combining actual locations with models at various scales and mixing conventional recording or scenes and stop-motion. While the grandiose interior of the large department store was adapted to become the set for the hotel lobby, other Görlitz sites were used for additional film locations.

Scene from above, camera tracking slowly: member of staff walks across bright red carpet in hotel lobby.

Scene with camera static: concierge desk in grand hotel lobby, staff in brightly coloured uniforms, waiting for guests.

Scene with camera static then moving fast: again inside hotel lobby, chandeliers, tables, chairs, grand stair in background, fascist police in absurd uniforms arrest concierge, who runs away.

Hotel lobbies tend to be compartmented; they are rarely large open-plan spaces leading straight onto hotel bedrooms. But the lobby of the Grand Budapest is a cinematic hotel lobby, so it can do what it likes. The architecture of the interior of the Kaufhaus remains much as it is: the big space, the stairs, the marble columns, the chandeliers. Red carpets now cover the floor, a reception desk is installed, potted plants and hotel sofas are dotted around. The horizontal open-plan layout of the Kaufhaus ground floor is closed off from view and pieces of sets are inserted along the sides, such as barber's shops, lobbies and lounges, suggesting that the interior is only one part of a much larger ensemble of spaces. Occasionally we are shown these other spaces, such as the great dining room, baths, guest suites, servants' quarters and corridors, which give the impression of being linked by a door to the lobby, but are in fact either constructed as sets or filmed in completely different locations. Since Anderson tends to shoot sequences of individual scenes rather than a continuous narrative, the audience never need to grasp the overall layout of the hotel, but only imagine how the various spaces might fit together.

Only the interior of the Kaufhaus exists in the film. The actual exterior is irrelevant and in the wrong location, being in the middle of a city rather than in a wild mountainous landscape as required by the script. The main facade of the Grand Budapest, an extraordinary fantasia in pink baroque, with turrets, an illuminated sign, a terrace and a funicular, is seen near the beginning of the film. This facade was constructed as a model almost 5m long and over 2m high, shot in front of a green screen in the

Babelsberg Studios in Berlin. The magnificent Alpine backdrop, a painting in the style of Caspar David Friedrich, was produced by the artist Michael Lenz and then digitally composited behind the image of the model. The funicular moves jerkily across the model, filmed in stop-motion. Model and painting create a disquieting, almost fairytale image, of the *Schloß* lost up in the mountains, with a touch of Joseph Cornell's collage box containing a large spooky house in the woods, appropriately titled *Pink Palace*.

These two worlds—that of the model and the real interior of the Kaufhaus—are matched to one another in such a way that the spectator who knows nothing of the Görlitz Kaufhaus might believe them to be one location. Sequences shift rapidly from an external set resembling part of the model to a tracking shot through the interior of the Kaufhaus to a scene in another set, without the viewer noticing the sleight of hand which has moved the characters from one location to another. The camera loves to show off the interior of the Kaufhaus: it pans horizontally across a line of maids on an upper balcony, then plummets vertically to look down at the red carpet, with a few figures moving around on it, as though an abstract painting has come to life. At the end of the film, in the final shoot-out, Anderson's camera whip-pans amongst the decorated Kaufhaus columns on the third floor, before following Zero down the stairs for one last view of the atrium.

The counter to all the grandness of the hotel interior are the views we get of the rooms inhabited by the hotel staff: the cluttered storeroom with a small spyhole looking down into the lobby, the cramped dining space, Gustave H's own room, a minute interior with a metal bed, hidden away somewhere in the back passages of the hotel. The film is shot almost entirely from the viewpoint of the servants rather than the guests, but Gustave H, for all his showy public demeanour, hardly exists as a private person.

The use of the interior space of the Kaufhaus is made more complicated by the fact that the hotel lobby is seen at various different periods. It mostly appears in its 1920s heyday, but it is also shown briefly after the fascist take-over, with the luxury fittings for the guests cleared out and the interior filled with swastika-like banners and men in military uniforms. The beginning and the end of the film take us from the narrator's present, 1985, to the mid-1960s, the austere period of Eastern European socialism. Gone is the glamour of the palm trees and red carpet, the grand interior space is concealed by a false ceiling, the concierge's desk is bland and neutral, functional chairs have replaced the expensive furniture and the elaborate metalwork of the lift-shaft is enclosed by flat panels. The walls are also painted the curious shade of orange loved by middle European countries of the period, and bear large signs in an ugly script instructing guests how to behave. We are also briefly shown a model of the 1960s exterior: the pink baroque facade has disappeared and the building has been reduced to a drab, utilitarian, soon-to-be demolished block. The transformation between the various states of the lobby is clever and moving. Anyone who has visited a similar hotel in an Eastern Bloc country in the 1960s or 1970s—or certain hotels in the West that were every bit as dismal—will recall the strange feeling of dislocation, of some exotic interior covered up with pieces of plasterboard and cheap panelling, as though a diminished way of living could not bear to reveal the better times of the past, but also could not quite conceal its own mediocrity.

This gradual dissolving of the glamour of the hotel mirrors that of the actual Kaufhaus, from grand empire style, to fascist store, to drab socialist box, to its rather utilitarian capitalist reincarnation. The interiors of department stores and hotels have changed in similar ways, reflecting the mentality of the culture that creates them. Perhaps Anderson discovered the grand hotel that was always lurking within the Kaufhaus interior, its desire to be something better than a store selling goods. Liberated from having to sell knick-knacks to the Görlitz bourgeoisie, in Anderson's film it assumes the role for which it was always destined. After all, the Kaufhaus sat on the site of the old coaching inn, Zum Strauss, and in creating *The Grand Budapest Hotel* Anderson was merely taking this Görlitz location back to its former use and glory.

For Anderson's film, the city provided a series of locations both for the interior rooms of the hotel and for parts of Lutz, the supposed capital of Zubrowka. A visitor to Görlitz would find these film locations in unexpected sites, and try with difficulty to match them to any topography within the film. The sequence of locations rarely matches the actual layout of the town. The very first image, supposedly of Old Lutz cemetery, already shows the contradiction. The view is very clearly of the towers and spires of Görlitz—the actual location is in Steinweg near the real Nikolai cemetery—but there's now a brick wall, built for the film, and the writing on it clearly says Lutz. Similarly, the lower station of the fanciful funicular connecting the town of Lutz with the terrace of the hotel up above is located beside the curving Renaissance stairway to the town hall, but any funicular from here would ascend only into the heavens. Turn around, and you find the arcade just opposite this stairway has shifted in the film to become the entrance to a cloister on distant mountaintop. Walk a few hundred yards down Obermarkt and you come to the aisle of the remarkable gothic Trinity Church that poses as the interior of this mountain cloister. The exterior of the Mendl patisserie is in a nearby Görlitz street, but the interior, where the ornate gastronomic creations are prepared and placed in the elegant folding cardboard boxes, is that of the equally exuberant Pfund Molkerie, a creamery located in Dresden Neustadt 90km away.

Other sites scattered around Görlitz become part of the interior of the Grand Budapest hotel. The cavernous dining room of the film, only seen in its rather reduced 1965 socialist condition, is actually the interior of the Görlitz Stadthalle, the impressive Jugendstil building by the distinguished theatre architect Bernhardt Sehring. The largest concert hall between Berlin and Wroclaw, it was used first for Silesian music festivals, then communist show trials and socialist boxing championships, but is today sadly empty. In the film the dining room is hung with another large landscape by the painter Michael Lenz, rather like a theatre backdrop, with mountains, a waterfall and a chamois standing on a peak. A full-scale mock-up of the hotel entrance, in bright pink with a Jugendstil canopy, was constructed against the side wall of the Stadthalle, at a remove of 1km from the Kaufhaus. For the military putsch scenes, with the memorable image of Patisserie Mendl's pink delivery van surrounded by soldiers and tanks, the Stadthalle was also decked with mock Nazi banners. Probably nobody quite recalls today Joseph Goebbels taking the stage there in the final days of the war to call, forlornly, for a last-ditch stand against the approaching Red Army. The minute bedrooms used by Zero and Gustave H are in the Brauner Hirsch Hotel. The hotel sauna, with its antiquated baths and tile-lined walls, is the nineteenth-century Freisebad in the affluent Dr-Karlbaum-Allee just south of the city centre, an institution once proudly boasting salt, pine-needle, steam and mud baths as a cure for any number of ailments, which survived the decades of socialism only to close in 1996. These twin topographies of film and town overlay one another, delight in failing to match up, two systems of locations, internally consistent but mutually irreconcilable.

Oberlausitz stands in well enough for the country of Zubrowka, despite having a very different kind of landscape. The train that carries Gustave H and Zero on their adventures passes through flat snowy fields and hilly forests, halting only for confrontations with small bands of militia. Various former palaces and castles, sometimes with grim backgrounds, act as locations in the film. The exterior of Schloß Hainwalde, a small palace near Zittau on the Czech border in which the Nazis interred political prisoners, becomes Schloß Lutz, but with its interior supplied by Schloß Waldenburg, west of Dresden, which was used as a medical facility during the communist period. Schloß Osterstein, where the writer of German westerns Karl May and later also the revolutionary communist Rosa Luxemburg were once confined, becomes in turn a prison for Gustave H. Today many of these palaces and castles, after long years of neglect, are being rehabilitated as tourist sites—or film locations.

Dr A, engineer and historian and conservation consultant, dressed in a casual suit, slightly uncertain, standing by the rear entrance door.

—Aha, there you are. Yes, let's start the tour.

The Görlitz Kaufhaus is the only surviving Jugendstil department store in Germany. It stands on Demianiplatz just outside the line of the medieval city walls, a massive building in granite with a determined urban feel rather different from the smaller buildings around it, as though it were the first step in some grand metropolitan plan which was never quite followed up. The site was previously occupied by a large coaching inn, Zum Strauss ('The Ostrich', an unusual ornithological choice for Oberlausitz), which for 200 years had provided accommodation for travellers before they entered the town. Just to the south is the late gothic Church of Our Lady, providing succour for the souls of the town's inhabitants, just as the Kaufhaus provided for their material needs.

By the late nineteenth century German department stores had become highly fashionable and profitable. They were seen both as a step up from trailing around a series of shops selling individual goods and as a symbol of a more exotic lifestyle. Ever larger and more glamorous stores were constructed to entice customers away from rival enterprises. Here, a rapidly growing provincial town like Görlitz could in its own way be as stylish as Munich, Breslau or Berlin. The Kaufhaus is modelled directly on the magnificent Wertheim department store in Leipzigerplatz, Berlin, designed in 1896 by Alfred Messel, but the Görlitz version is 26 times smaller in area than its Berlin inspiration. Designed by the Potsdam architect Carl Schmans for the entrepreneurs Hermann Ploschitski and Leopold Lindemann from Berlin-Charlottenburg, who already owned department stores in various German towns, it opened its doors to the public in 1913. The front elevation has a certain swagger. A two-storey arcade decorated with allegorical Jugendstil sculptures represents worthy themes such as work, determination and domestic bliss, as though the department store had taken over the medieval church front's function of providing moral values for its visitors. On the two long side elevations, great vertical windows follow the Berlin precedent in defying the horizontal floor structure of the interior to produce a monumental effect, dark by day but in the evening highly illuminated, advertising the goods for sale within. At the time of its opening the Kaufhaus proudly advertised a large range of goods for sale, including textiles, clothing, gramophones, books, musical instruments, furniture and foodstuffs. In addition, it offered a saloon for tea, a lending library, a writing room, a telephone exchange, a barber's and a beauty salon. It suggested a new way of life, a new miniature version of services mostly available elsewhere in the city, but now combined together in one special building. Public life in Görlitz, which up to then had principally been confined to military parades and churchgoing, must suddenly have looked rather more attractive.

The history of the Kaufhaus reflects the extreme political changes in Germany over the course of the twentieth century.

The store was built by a flourishing pre-First World War *bürgerlich* society, conservative and hierarchical but with time and money to spare. It seems to have weathered the economic troubles of the Weimar Republic in the 1920s: a photo shows the interior decked out during the 1928 *Weisse Woche* (White Week), with theatrical lighting effects and decorations. In the early Nazi period of the 1930s Görlitz became militarised, its socialists and Jews were rounded up, the streets hung with swastikas, but business at the Kaufhaus was still good and it remained a family-owned business. But after the war, when Görlitz became part of the German Democratic Republic, a client state of the Soviet Union, the Kaufhaus was first left empty, then nationalised. Renamed HO and then Centrum, it became an outlet for the now rather less stylish state-produced goods. The interior grew increasingly shabby—the state presumably had little interest in maintaining a symbol of the bourgeoisie that had supposedly died out in the class struggle—until 1984, when the glass ceiling and other features unexpectedly underwent a comprehensive renovation. During the 1970s the Kaufhaus became a shopping destination for large numbers of Poles who came across the border to buy East German goods that were of higher quality and greater variety than those produced at home. A special path was marked out for these Polish shoppers, so they could walk from the Zgorzelec bridge to the Kaufhaus without actually going through the town, avoiding any undesired encounters between the two populations. After the collapse of the socialist state in 1989 and the unification of the two Germanies, the Kaufhaus was returned to its prewar owners, Karlstadt, and run unconvincingly by a succession of capitalist enterprises including the UK conglomerate Dawnie Day. It still emphasised its cross-border appeal, training its staff to speak Polish as well as German, and accepting both the zloty and the deutschmark, then the euro. However, the early optimism of reunification faded, as East German cities lost their industries and their state welfare. The declining population of Görlitz could not support a department store and the Kaufhaus closed in 2009. But closure made it available for other uses, and it was discovered by a film team scouting for hotel locations rather than department stores.

Dr A, as we stand in the large space of the Kaufhaus:

—No, no, I haven't seen the film. I don't often go to the cinema. But it doesn't matter, I'm only here to show you the building. There's really not much left now of the film sets.

Walking around the building produced a strange confrontation of memories of seeing it as a film set, alive, filled with actors, part of a story, compared to both its current state, deserted, without any action, and then also to other ideas of how it might have been as a department store, again full of people. These three different conditions—film, present experience and imagination—flickered around each other. The interior of the building, four floors of potential sales space around a high narrow atrium, is slightly over the top, showy but now silent and a little sad. The bases of the columns around the atrium are clad in a pinkish marble, a grand staircase leads up to the first level and another stair ambitiously spans across the atrium, two large chandeliers like sea creatures from an undersea movie hang down from above. The large barrel-vaulted rooflight is constructed of squares of yellow and brown glass, some with geometrical patterns, and lets through a slightly tinted light. The effect is a little reminiscent of some palace—a Jugendstil palace of the people, or one of those metro stations in Moscow or St Petersburg, glamorous but uneasy. A small stair leads up from the fourth-level gallery to a large horizontal space between the atrium and the exterior, supported by a lattice of timber beams, a little like those spaces found in churches between the vaulting and the sky. The upper surface of the atrium rooflight rises up into the space, below another, clear and rectilinear rooflight.

Dr A, up on the roof:

—Yes, it's a little like a theatre, a consumer theatre, the great space where the action takes place. And then here in the roof space, and also in the basement, it's the backstage, where goods are stored and the performers, the people in the store, take a rest.

Dr A, in the attic space:

—Nobody knows when the show will resume. It depends on the investor.

Dr A, descending the stairs:

—The inner city of Görlitz has survived because for decades no one cared for it, it became empty, but nothing happened, no one tried to build anything new. Now many of the buildings are being renovated, there has been a lot of money spent on the town, which is of course good business for us conservationists, we have work and grow rich recreating the past.

We stand again beside the rear doors, in a small street. We enter a small self-service restaurant. We settle for some large rolls filled with unspecified ingredients and small cups of strong espresso. Dr A, in the self-service restaurant:

—Görlitz never really had a modernist period in the 1920s and 1930s, compared to Wrocłow, formerly Breslau, to the west, with its fantastic modernist buildings built in the last years of the German possession of the city and now immaculately restored by the Poles. Think of the wonderful Wertheim Kaufhaus in Wrocłow, from the late 1920s, with its horizontal lines of windows, the floors spreading outwards as they rise up, a classic of the time. Or Löbau, just a few miles to the west, with the Haus Schminke, the modernist villa designed by Hans Scharoun. Here the city never developed a modernist culture, it has never quite known how to move into the contemporary world.

Dr A, in the street, bidding farewell:

—And Zgorzelec? Yes, a very different kind of town. But of course you will have to go there and see for yourself.

The name Zgorzelec derives from the same root as Görlitz, Zhorjelc, given by the original inhabitants of the town, the Slavic tribe known as the Sorbs. So the names Görlitz and Zgorzelec are really a mirror image, the same town in different languages. The Sorbs call themselves Serbja, and are related to the Poles and also to the Balkan Serbs, whom they call southern Serbja, naturally considering themselves to be the real Serbja and the others merely a family offshoot. The Sorbs now inhabit the area to the west of Görlitz, some still use the Sorb language, which is recognised as an official minority language. Sorbish is one of three surviving creole mix languages, the others being Kashubian around Gdansk and Silesian in Silesia, barely surviving traces of a successful cohabitation between the Slavs and the Germans. The Sorbs were despised by the Nazis, who suspected them of not being German enough, but admired by the Russians for being Slavic, and providing a not entirely convincing claim that the land was and had always been really Slavic.

The two halves of Görlitz–Zgorzelec, the largest city in Europe spread over two nations, eye each other awkwardly across the river Neiße. On many German maps Zgorzelec is shown simply as a blank zone marked 'Polen'. Guidebooks hardly mention the Polish town, except as a vague memory of a now vanished location. For what is now Zgorzelec was once a suburb of Görlitz, containing barracks, a few houses by the river, some villas for the well-to-do, a grand memorial hall, woods and fields. In the last days of the war, all the bridges across the river were blown up, the eastern bank of the Neiße was ceded to Poland and the German inhabitants were expelled. This caused lasting antagonism, as the Germans felt that that the Poles had stolen their homes, while the Poles lived for a long time in a state of apprehension, expecting the border to be revised at any moment. For some years Zgorzelec remained almost empty. The area along the border was lined with barbed wire and patrolled by armed guards, while many of the houses beside the river were pulled down to prevent illegal cross-border traffic. A few former occupants of the grim Stalag VIII-A POW camp, located a few kilometres to the south, moved into the ones that remained standing. In 1950 the Polish and East German authorities signed a formal treaty, known as the Görlitz Agreement, guaranteeing each other's borders, but no one knew how long this accord would hold, given the uneasy relations between the two socialist republics. The single road bridge connecting the two parts of town, but avoiding their centres, was reconstructed in the late 1950s, but it was often closed. Only in the 1970s did relations between the countries improve to the point where ordinary citizens could cross the border if they had a visa. Poles were brought in to work in the East German factories. They also began to come over the border to shop in the Kaufhaus. However, the border became more difficult to cross in the 1980s, as Poland under Solidarity began to break away from the socialist system, and again in the 1990s, after reunification, when Germany was part of the EU while Poland remained outside until 2004. Now the border is open—there is hardly even a sign to say that one is moving from one country to the other—and the footbridge, constructed in 2004, connects the two centres.

Zgorzelec is today the more modern of the two towns, with a population largely under the age of 30. It sits on the edge of the lands once German but now Polish. The whole zone on the Polish side of the border, stretching from Szczecin on the Baltic coast down to the border with the Czech Republic, became known in the 1950s as *Dziki Zachid*, the Wild West, a new frontier for uprooted people trying to make a new life for their families. Although the new inhabitants of Zgorzelec inherited some housing stock, they essentially had to construct the community from nothing. During the early 1950s the town also became home to 10,000 Greek communists, rehoused by the Polish government after the civil war in Greece. It still has a Greek district with its own schools and restaurants, and even a recently constructed timber Greek Orthodox church. Since the Neiße is comparatively shallow and lightly guarded, Zgorzelec was a well-known crossing point for those attempting to flee to the more affluent West. It gained the nickname 'Little Chicago', as a border town run by 'businessmen' skilled in accommodating smugglers, drug dealers, would-be migrants, prostitutes and chop shops doing quick resprays of stolen vehicles—an edge city with little connection to the rest of Poland and a dubious reputation in Germany. But the city has proved to be a success, with large housing blocks and commercial centres, local power plants that offer reasonable employment prospects and a population of 33,000 that is gradually approaching that of Görlitz. Just as Anderson shows interest in creating an American version of a European city, so Zgorzelec has ambitions to being American. In addition to the rather confused geography of Wild West and Little Chicago, it has a ten-storey housing block known optimistically as Manhattan or Little America. Its reputation as a wild city seems rather misjudged, though. This is a quiet town of streets and housing blocks, semi-rural in that it is built on heathland and rapidly drifts into small paths through woods and fields.

In Zgorzelec there are strange reminders of its former existence. The vast and lugubrious Dom Kultury—the Hall of Fame built in 1900, originally equipped with oversize statues of German Kaisers in military uniforms—now stands isolated in a riverside park. A few of the nineteenth-century villas of the Görlitz bourgeoisie remain beside socialist housing blocks of the 1970s and 1980s. There are traces of the German city plan—avenues that run nowhere in particular, a long green strip that was once part of a garden suburb. However, Zgorzelec is clearly a modern Polish city, filled with young couples and kids, its main street lined with small supermarkets, nail shops, beauty salons, fashion outlets, minuscule bars, car salesrooms. Many of its inhabitants make a living from working over the border, but they very much have their own lifestyle here. Apart from certain older buildings, it seems refreshingly Polish.

The town's most distinguished building is the church of Jozefá Robotnika, St Joseph the Worker, by the architects Wojciech Kurowski, Alina Niedźwiedzka-Kurowska and Jan Niedźwiedzki. Located in Ulitsa Jana Kasaka, on the northern outskirts, it was begun in 1980 but only completed and consecrated in 2000. The church has a bold structure of three intersecting frames and curving walls. Outside stands a funky freestanding bell tower. The interior is filled with large images of saints, both modern in its design and traditional in its usage, typical of the churches built all over Poland in the wake of Solidarity's challenge to the socialist regime.

Two well-dressed women outside the church, speaking in English:

> —It took many years to raise the funds for the church, and then to construct it. It wasn't easy at the time to raise money for a church. But it is a sign of a new life here in Zgorzelec, a life for us the Polish people. And although the church was originally named St Joseph the Worker, now it the church of St Joseph and St Barbara. Which is certainly more balanced.

On the eastern outskirts of Zgorzelec, between the main road and the open fields, is a collection of mostly foreign-owned hypermarkets, including Carrefour, Lidl, Kaufland and Real, surrounded by car parks and open all hours. The best known of these, Real, is a vast shed filled with row upon row of consumer goods, some resembling well-known brands but with slightly altered packaging, manufactured in the factories and food production sheds of Eastern Europe. These hypermarkets attract large numbers of German customers from over the border, who come for the cheaper goods and the longer shopping hours. If Görlitz Kaufhaus once stood for a certain kind of traditional quality and lifestyle, Real and the other sheds are where the combined mass consumerism of Oberlausitz and the province of Silesia finds its appropriate location.

Both halves of this twin city are therefore highly individual, each inhabited largely by people who have come from somewhere else, each on the edge of their nation, each thriving on very different kinds of urban life, the one historic, conservative and ageing, the other new, uncertain, youthful. They remain very individual, but since Poland joined the Schengen Area in 2003 they have begun to make joint decisions. In 2006 Görlitz and Zgorzelec made a combined but ultimately unsuccessful bid to become the 2010 European City of Culture, a sign that the two halves can also imagine themselves to be a whole. There are bilingual kindergartens on either side of the border that take both German and Polish kids. And while Zgorzelec supplies the workforce for the tourist industry across the river, its nightclubs and cut-price hypermarkets lure over Görlitz inhabitants and visitors. A vision is evolving of a city that is both fragmented and combined.

At the main border crossing between the twin cities Marshal Jósefa Piłudskego street, named after the prominent Polish nationalist general of the 1920s and 1930s, runs down for a rather unlikely meeting with Pope John Paul II bridge, named after the celebrated Polish pope. Cars come by in each direction, the drivers sometimes calling out a greeting to those standing on the bridge. Just before the border are a few shops selling beer spirits and cigarettes at attractive prices. Cars stop and load up with a few crates.

Woman standing outside the shop, in basic German:

—Well it is often very busy here. Now it's quieter, people go the big supermarkets on the edge of town. But we are important, we are at the point where the two countries meet. Look what we have—Żubr, Tysekie, Lech, Żywiec, even some Becks and Carlsberg. And good prices. Just one can? Żubrówka vodka? Why not take two bottles, the second comes cheaper. Yes, we are always open, we are businesspeople.

Shoe lathes, leather, hammers, piles of shoes. Just wait a while, just be patient, it may take some time. Don't pay too much attention, and the inner essence of each thing will be revealed. Jakob Böhme, thin face, slight goatee beard, long hair, sitting in his shoemaker's workshop. And from his visionary book *De signatura rerum*:

> Nature gave every thing its own language (according to its essence and inner form). Each thing has its own mouth for revelation and this is the language of Nature, each thing speaks of its individuality and always reveals itself.

Jakob Böhme, the seventeenth-century Görlitz shoemaker and mystic philosopher lived, appropriately enough for a man who always steered a course away from the accepted centre, on the eastern, now Polish, side of the Neiße. In his lifetime, Oberlausitz was a refuge for numerous individualistic religious sects, quarrelling with one another about their beliefs, each claiming to know the truth. Even among the unorthodox, Böhme stood out for his radical redefinition of a personal religion, with a divinity who does not sit on judgement on high, but is to be found in every particle of the physical world around us. He was an autodidact, and claimed to derive his knowledge from a vision of light emerging from a metal bowl, the divine manifesting itself through a banal object. 'And the visible world', he wrote in his best-known work, *De signatura rerum*, 'is a manifestation of the inner spiritual world'. All that we see around us is therefore in essence a sign of this other world, which lies very near to us, but which can only be accessed through the spirit. His books are filled with delirious imagery.

Light emerges from darkness, qualities and flavours and planetary courses provide a basis for his self-created universe in systems of dazzling complexity. Illustrations of his works show his extraordinary ideas depicted as interlocking circles and geometric figures, another version of a delicate watch mechanism. Unsurprisingly, Böhme ran into trouble with the religious authorities of his time, but he would become an important inspiration for later thinkers and poets, finding his way into the works of countless mystical groups famous and obscure, such as the Rosicrucians, the Gichtelians, the Quakers, the Society of Women in the Wilderness (yes!) and also to individuals such as Goethe, Schopenhauer and Hegel, the Königsberg philosopher Imannuel Kant, the English poet William Blake, the Russian Nikolaï Berdyaev and the Armenian Georges Gurdjieff, even reaching as far as the US badlands of Cormac McCarthy and the musings on flavours of the Leningrad poet Elena Schvarts. Böhme's beliefs anticipate the statement by de Chirico mentioned earlier, that there is the normal visible world, and then also a spectral or metaphysical world that is only revealed at particular moments. James Joyce had a copy of *De signatura rerum* in his study in Trieste and Böhme found his way into *Ulysses* as Stephen wanders on the Sandymount Strand: 'Ineluctable modality of the visible, at least that if no more, thought through my eyes. Signature of all things I am here to read, seaspawn and searack, the nearing tide ...'

The attraction of Jakob Böhme is that his feet are firmly on the earth, in the natural realm, but everything has changed, all is infused with the spirit. And wandering through this twin city, one might hope to experience that signature, that moment of revelation. But one also knows that expecting or hoping is just what prevents it appearing. Only by not looking directly is there any chance of that ray of sunshine reflecting off the metal dish.

Böhme was buried on the edge of the Nikolai cemetery, just to the north of the city centre, which features briefly at the beginning of *The Grand Budapest Hotel* as Old Lutz cemetery. His tomb is simple but appropriate for a man who did not aspire to wealth, in contrast to the bizarre baroque funerary houses of the Görlitz bourgeoisie; too simple, in fact, for the nineteenth-century municipality, who placed a large statue of him, wearing robes and looking more like a grandee than a shoemaker, beside the Stadthalle, its back to the town and facing the river. When the postwar border was put in place this statue looked out at the huts of the German and Polish guards, and would have been an unlikely first figure to be seen by those crossing over from Poland. In the early 1970s, since a religious esoteric was hardly the appropriate person to welcome visitors to a socialist republic, the statue was relocated to the woods of the nearby Stadtpark, where it remains today. However, the socialists on either side of the border gradually remade Böhme in their own image, as a member of the proto-proletariat and as an early class warrior in the struggle against the hierarchies of the church and aristocracy. Jakob-Böhme-Straße in Görlitz old town is a 1980s creation of the socialist city authorities. Böhme remained popular after German reunification, and has today been adopted both as the town's favourite son and as a guiding spirit for its small counterculture, his books prominently displayed in various shops. His diminutive house, largely reconstructed and painted an unusual shade of orange, stands not far from the footbridge connecting the two halves of the town, beside the cut-price cigarette shops, restaurants and nightclubs. Though now marketed as a tourist destination, it evades any of the qualities of grandness and style presented by the grander buildings of the two towns.

Böhme's concept of the origins of the Divine Being, the *Ungrund*—the 'un-ground', relating to the Gnostic idea of the abyss (*Abgrund* in German)—refers to the locationless and indeterminate state of all being before the arrival of the world we know, and puts into question standard ideas of historical time. Böhme's *Ungrund*, before the beginning of time, links tenuously to the French composer Olivier Messiaen's mysterious *Quartet for the End of Time*, whose movements include *The Abyss of Birds*, composed and first performed in 1941 in the Stalag VIII-A POW camp. Messiaen in the sheds of the camp unconsciously balances, three centuries apart, Böhme in his room in the small house. 'The *Ungrund*', Böhme states with his customary baffling mode of expression, 'is an eternal nothing, but makes an eternal beginning as a desire for this nothing is a desire after something'. This nothing is a desire? One struggles to keep up with Böhme, but can't help being enticed in by his tumultuous spirit.

Move eastwards. Move beyond Görlitz, beyond Zgorzelec, into the lands which are now part of Poland. Keep the scenery much the same but change the names and the actors.

In the summer months Görlitz attracts large numbers of German visitors, passing through on their way to visit the towns and villages where their families had lived before 1945, in what was then Silesia. The Silesian shop and the very interesting and impartial Silesian Museum in Brüderstraße provide a historical background for these tourists tracing their family origins. But just under the pleasure of such visits lies considerable trauma, derived both from the German and the Polish experiences of the time. Small, charming Görlitz opens up to a geography and history which reaches out ever further.

Holger Bunk, German born in Essen, living in Amsterdam, longstanding personal acquaintance, in an extended email letter about his family, who fled Silesia in 1945:

> I have to work hard to get myself to think about Silesia. My mother was born in Liegnitz/Legnica, to the west, and my father in Oppeln/Opole, in the south. These towns were part of our childhood in countless stories and led to constant emotional demands. What should children, who knew nothing about these distant places way behind the Iron Curtain, say about the traumatic and loss-inspired stories of their parents? We were living in a West German town, but we weren't really at home. We went for a family trip to Silesia, our old German map was confiscated at the border, so we drove without a map, trying to find our way with the unfamiliar Polish names, stopping at the untended German graveyards. But the anger of my parents at the neglect, dilapidation and poverty was unbearable. I can still hear the crying of my mother and the bitterness of my father. I remember the landscapes, the rivers and the craggy hills and the battered town with beautiful churches and palaces. But you know there is also a Silesian humour, which I experienced from my aunts and uncles. My mother said the Silesians could move very easily between correct German and their own dialect (*Mundart*). Our family conversations were

filled with word games and speech which streamed in all directions, almost like Dada. I feel this very special humour, which I have inherited, lies within me.

The Silesian language—or dialect or lect or ethnilect, depending on the familiar and extended argument as to what is a language and what is a dialect—had numerous subdivisions, according to geographical location. The speaking of Silesian was banned in Poland after the Second World War, most of its native speakers were driven out or fled to Germany. Their children and their children's children all now speak standard German. Silesian is now almost a dead tongue. Only around Görlitz is it still spoken, in the countryside, but as a traditional mix of Saxon and Silesian, reflecting the status of the area around Görlitz.

Silesian: Dau—was haut's'n dau? Mau! Und dau? Au Mau! Nu dau, dau, lauter Mau. Mau!
Standard German: Du was hat's denn dort? Mohn! Und dort? Auch Mohn! Nu da, lauter Mohn. Mohn!
English: What is there? Poppies? And there? Poppies. Then, nothing but poppies. Poppies!

A small self-service restaurant beside the Wrockław market hall with its remarkable reinforced concrete construction, designed by Richard Plüdermann back in 1906. Meeting with Felix Wozniak, Polish language teacher, whose family had moved to Wrockław in 1945 from further east. Conversation over bowls of pierogi, mushroom and spicy sauerkraut filling:

—But of course you tend to look from one point of view. From the west. From the Germans, from the people you happen to know. But everything is very different when seen from the other direction, from the east. Our story is also about people who were forced to move to a new location, about which they knew nothing. The ethnic cleansing of the German-speakers was wrong but it followed the ethnic cleansing of the Poles and Jews and many other nationalities. It is a story not just about an end but about a new beginning. Or perhaps another chapter in a long story, which began a long while ago, of movements backwards and forwards, and which has many different strands within it.

Before the first half of the last century the population of the lands to the east of Görlitz–Zgorzelec was a very diverse ethnic mix. Silesia was a land for settlers, brought in from medieval times by its sequence of controlling powers, including Germans, Poles, Sorbs, Ukrainians, even Walloons and Dutch and, surprisingly, Scots. The former Prussian provinces of Upper and Lower Silesia stretched from around Görlitz to what is now the Slovakian border. Mostly open countryside, fertile and reasonably easy to farm, with crops of wheat, rye, oats and all manner of beets, it also has large areas of now controversial coalmining in the east. There various large towns have been progressive, often with a modernist culture, such as Wrockław–Breslau, with its mix of baroque and 1920s modern, and Katowice–Kattowitz, once a major centre for coalmining and the steel industry, now a lively contemporary town. After the First World War the eastern part of Upper Silesia went by plebiscite to Poland, but its population mix of Poles and Germans at first remained much the same, there was no great pressure on German-speakers to emigrate. However during the Second World War the Silesia provinces became just one part of the Central European disaster zone, with the extermination of a large part of the Jewish population, the eviction of the Poles and others, then the fighting as the German army retreated and the Red Army arrived. At the end of war the borders of Ukraine, Belarus and Poland were all shifted west. The German-speaking population, estimated at around 4.5 million in Upper and lower Silesia, either emigrated or was forced out across the line of the Oder and Neiße rivers, and had to find new homes in the new states of East and West Germany.

Görlitz was one of the crossing points. One of its residents at the time, Richard Süssmuth, reported almost medieval scenes that are difficult to reconcile now with the fine streets of the town.

> Beaten-down, half-starved people dragged themselves through the streets. They pulled handcarts and pushed prams with paltry possessions. I saw a cart without a horse, pulled by six children, and pushed by a pregnant woman.

> I saw seven-year-olds who dragged a handcart ... the inhabitants of Görlitz look like wandering corpses, wax-pale, hollowed out, and starved to skeletons.

Görlitz became a border city, divided in two, with a sizeable population of emigrants in what was now the last surviving part of German Silesia. The East German state agreed to the new borders in 1950, with the treaty signed in Zgorzelec. The West German state disputed the border, with varying levels of conviction, until 1990, with the fall of the Soviet Union and the reunification of Germany.

In 1945 many of the German emigrants had thought the new borders would be temporary and they would return to the ancient homelands. Over the years they came to realise this would not happen. Görlitz remains as a last location for fading memories of German Silesia. On Brüderstraße there is the Silesian Museum and a shop selling Silesian souvenirs, photos, books, maps. In the marketplace there are stalls selling traditional Silesian pottery, plates, cups and pots with rather elegant geometrical patterns—now mostly made in Poland. There is both a charm and also a certain unease to all this, an edginess to the city which is at odds with its quiet retro feel. There still exists in Germany the remnants of once very active revanchist societies, calling for the return of Silesia and other lost lands. Fortunately these societies are gradually declining, as their members die out.

The Polish population who arrived post-1945 in Silesia had been displaced from their homelands in what is now western Ukraine and Belarus, several hundred kilometres to the east, and had to set up a new life in the towns of the displaced Germans, not knowing whether the arrangement was permanent or temporary. As decades have passed the arrangement has indeed become permanent, with minimal questioning of the border along the Oder–Neiße line. The faultline of Central Europe has since moved further east, to the north–south line running down from the Baltic states through eastern Ukraine, with the disputes over the Donbas region and Crimea.

To the east, the borderline along the southern edge of Silesia, with its original mix of Polish-, Czech-, Slovak- and German-speakers, was for many postwar years uneasy and filled with physical memories of the past. The area is described by the Polish novelist Olga Tokarczuk in her novels *Dom dzienny dom nocny (House of Day, House of Night)* and *Prowadź swój pług przez kości umarłych (Drive Your Plough over the Bones of the Dead*) both set in towns along the border with the Czech Republic. *House of Day, House of Night* tells of the lives of the new Polish inhabitants of Nowa Ruda (formerly Neurode), many of whom moved into the homes of the vanished Germans:

> The German houses grew more willing to surrender their contents to their new Polish owners—pots, plates, handles, bedding and clothes that were almost like new, some of them truly elegant ... the cellars were full of jars of jam, puree and apple wine, berries preserved in sugar with juice as thick as ink, yellow chunks of melon that they didn't much like the taste of, and pickled mushrooms ...

The Poles try on the clothes of the Germans, use their crockery, search for valuables amongst the drawers and cupboards and dig in the gardens for suspected treasures. The Germans occasionally return and try and remember the villages where they used to live:

> It all seemed darker and smaller, as if they were on the inside of a shabby photograph ... the worst moment of that day came when Peter didn't recognise his own village. It had shrunk to the size of a hamlet, with houses, backyards, lanes and bridges missing. Only a skeleton of the original village remained. They left the car beside a padlocked church behind which Peter's home used to be.

Tokarzuk's tales are very bizarre, of a world where past and present are mixed up. They are not so much about Poles and Germans, as they are about a whole society which drifts between dreams and actual life, which is never quite sure what is real.

Traces of the original German culture exist further to the east in Upper Silesia, particularly around Opole. Some German inhabitants remained here, in spite of the land being granted to Poland after the First World War, and still speak a form of Silesian, or

Slůnsko Godka, a German-Polish creole, which is now recognised by Poland as a minority language. There is even now a movement for autonomy for Silesia, with claims for its individual culture and history. In these lands no culture ever quite disappears, traces always remain to disturb and also enrich the lives of those who arrive and occupy the land.

Felix Wozniak again. Part of the same conversation in the self-service restaurant. Black tea, pineapple-flavoured cream cakes.

—Too far? Don't you see, you always need to go further. You start off with something simple. A small journey. An amusing American film made in a little German town. Americans—what did they ever understand? All too comfortable. Then you cross the river. You have a beer. And another. Then you move through the landscape. Already it's different. It's all Polish. The names of the lands have changed, their borders no longer match the old borders. Dolnośląskie, Opolskie, Śląskie and so on. Already many different peoples, reaching across the borders. Who knows where they are all from. My family also lives here, and they came from far to the east, from Tarnopol, now Ternopil, in Ukraine.

—Ah, where now?

—Keep going in your head. Look at the map. Read some books. Andrzej Stasiuk. Olga Tokarczuk. The great Polish poet Adam Zagajewski, whose family had to move from Lviv to a little Silesian town. Histories, parahistories.

—Such names ... wait, talk slower, my heart is beating too fast, it is all too much ...

—Now into the mountains. Isn't your American film set in the mountains? But now, the Carpathians. So you are almost in Ukraine, but it also used to be part of Poland and before that it was Austrian, and before that.... well. To Galicia. It was once a Hapsburg culture, another of your German-speaking places. Then in the bad years of last century everybody killed or evicted the people they considered their enemies. Poles, Soviets, Germans, Jews, Ukrainians.

—Aha.

—And this all affects what you see in Görlitz and Zgorzelec, for the movement of different peoples begins around here, and results in the two twin towns with different populations beside the little river Neiße.

—Where is all this? Galicia? How far from Görlitz and Zgorzelec, which already seem a long way east to me.

—750km or 8 hours by road according to Google. A point in Galicia is officially the middle of Europe. The Hapsburgs even built a monument to mark the spot. Halfway from the west coast of Ireland to whatever it is that lies far to the east beyond Europe. They knew.

—What did they know?

—Wonderful geography. Just here the rivers to the north flow up to the Baltic. To the south they flow down to the Black Sea. You know nothing about all this. Nobody in your country knows much about this. You just sit on your little island. And then ...

—Well, yes. You are talking much too fast. I am trying to catch up with all this. Yes. No. I hardly understand. All this about the middle of Europe being right over there. Maybe. But it must wait for another day.

—My friend, always another day. Another year. Maybe soon we can meet and try the classic Ruski pierogi, with quark, fried potatoes and onions. Or the Varenky version, with sour cherries, which really need to be eaten at the time of the full moon.

Jakob Böhme never stops writing, here are final words of *De signatura rerum*:

> It is now a time of seeking; for a lily blossoms over the mountain and the valley, and in all the ends of the earth: who seeks shall find. Hallelujah!

The Kaufhaus was scheduled to reopen as a department store in 2016 under the name of Kaufhaus der Oberlausitz (KadeO), matching and perhaps rivalling the well-known Berlin department store, Kaufhaus des Westens (KadeW). Great hopes had been pinned on the reopening as a sign that Görlitz is once more a fully functioning city, with the potential to again attract customers not only from Germany but from across the borders with Poland and the Czech Republic. However at the time of writing the project has not advanced, the interior is not even a construction site, the building remains empty. Perhaps the vacant building will find other uses.

In Görlitz politics remains uneasy. In the 2019 mayoral election the candidate for the AfD, the hard-right anti-immigration party, gained the most votes in the first round, but lost out in the second round to the candidate for the centre-right CDU. The AfD, a highly popular party in the east of Germany, holds the highest number of seats on the council. However as one wanders through Görlitz one sees few obvious immigrants, it appears solidly German.

In Polish *przeszłość* means the past, *przyszłość* the future. One letter separates the two. Zgorzelec and Görlitz, really the same name in different languages, continue to follow their individual but overlapping ways. From March to June 2020 all the bridges across the border were closed by order of the Polish government, on account of the high coronavirus infection rates in Saxony. All interchange between the twin cities was halted, and the situation returned to the bad days of the quarrels between the two governments in the time of communism, when the Neiße was a hard border. Large numbers of Poles and Germans who usually crossed the border everyday for work or study were unable to travel. The reopening of the bridges was marked by a small celebration on the pedestrian bridge, attended by the two mayors. The economies and social life of the two towns are now so completely interlinked they are considered a unity by most inhabitants.

The landscape around Görlitz is known as a fine location for electrical storms, as the flat countryside to the north rises up into the mountains of the Riesengebirge to the south and two weather systems encounter one another. One evening in May, a bus drives south through the remarkably optimistic socialist housing blocks built on the outskirts of the city for the power station workers. The main road runs alongside the meanders of the river, by the meadows on the Polish side of the border, down through the open countryside to the shores of the Berzdorfersee, created from the quarry that supplied the lignite for the Hagenwerder power station. A great technical achievement by the East

German state, generating electricity for the town and its factories for decades, the power station had the unfortunate side effect of drenching the surrounding area in pollution. The site of the now-demolished plant is marked by a construction that would sit happily in an ambitious 1920s science-fiction film—a large mining excavator, with multiple mechanical arms and grabs and devices for moving bucket-loads of lignite, an impressive monument to the scale and technological ingenuity of the people's project. The quarry, 4,000m long and 70m deep, has now been filled with water, a process that took several years. A new addition to Görlitz, the lake provides leisure activities, boating, scuba diving, swimming, its shores lined with sunbathers in summer —Görlitz as a lakeside resort.

On this May day the air is filled with the sounds of distant thunder, and grey clouds hang in the sky. The leaves shimmer with a strange electricity, dust drifts up from the path, the waters of the lake seem tense, expectant. Groups of teenagers by the shore appear excited by the charge in the air, and run in groups beside the water. Suddenly the storm breaks out, rain pours down, forming a grey aquatic curtain, reducing visibility across the lake. It is as though the known visual world has disappeared, to be replaced by an electrical haze. Small flashes of lightning skitter out of the clouds towards the surface of the water, almost bouncing off the surface. The storm, with the meeting of fire, air, land and water would surely be appreciated by Jakob Böhme, who devotedly listed elements, planets and moods, believing that if he kept going long enough everything would join up. The rain and the electricity bring a sense of freshness, a clearing out of the old, something hidden is revealed, a visible signature of things at last, even if only for a few moments.

The aged Zero speaking of the former concierge Gustave H, at the end of the film:

> —His world had vanished before he ever entered it. But he certainly sustained the illusion with a marvellous grace.

Some years after my last visit to Görlitz, Dr A mailed me a picture of his giant white owl, a beautiful but slightly disturbing creature, 70cm tall, with red eyes. It stood on his owner's shoulder, almost dwarfing the man. The photo was taken outside Dr A's house in the countryside south of the Berzdorfersee. There might just be some undeclared link between the great owl and the towns. Giant owls are a threatened species, in need of care and conservation, but they have a wild hunting nature. Owl, please, just one short moment, before a zick or zack back again to beside the Baltic, for some very different scenes. Then call out great owl, in your own language, open wide your sleepy eyes and reveal your true nature.

Hop Rayuela Backstein

Lübeck–Wismar–Stralsund

To play the game of hopscotch, a set of lines, usually in the shape of an elongated cross, is drawn with chalk on the ground. The players hop from one square to another, in varying sequences, throwing or kicking a stone from box to box. In Spanish hopscotch is called *rayuela* (little line). In German it is known, amongst many other regional names, as *Himmel und Hölle* (heaven and hell), *Hupfspiel* (hopping-game), *Hasehoppeln* (harehop), *Paradiesspiel* (paradise-game) or *Tempelspiel* (temple-game). Hopscotch has many other names across the world—*Mèo bắt chuột* in Vietnamese, *Kithi* or *Stapu* in Hindi. The aim in hopscotch is to arrive in heaven—but by hopping, rather than following a conventional line.

Backsteingotik (brick gothic) is the German name for the style of churches constructed in Germany in the late medieval period. Many of these churches were built in the Hansa ports, the league of trading cities around the southern coast of the Baltic, among them Bremen, Hamburg, Lübeck, Wismar, Rostock, Stralsund, Danzig

(Gdansk) and Königsberg (Kaliningrad). The Hanseatic League had links in the west to England, in the north into Scandinavia, and in the east to Reval (Tallinn), Riga and even Novgorod.

The Ukrainian writer Juri Andruchowytsch claims in his essay 'The Town-ship' that ships from the Hansa league sailed deep inland into what is now western Ukraine, to Lviv (German: Lemberg):

> Four hundred years ago sailing ships from Gdansk and Lübeck reached here, and you could catch with your bare hands snake-like Atlantic eels from the Saragossa sea ... these eels still survive today in the sewer-system.

If the Baltic now seems peripheral, it was once central to European trade and prosperity, its ports providing immense wealth that displayed itself in the building of extraordinary churches.

The game of hopscotch with churches, as explored in this text, has two potential levels. First, at a small scale, the individual internal vaulting system of the churches produces variations of a gridded plan, sets of squares, rectangles and other less regular forms. The visitor to the church moves from square to square, aware also of being within a complex three-dimensional system. Second, at a larger scale, one can consider the churches as individual squares in an architectural game that stretches out along the southern Baltic shore. One hops from one church or square to another, from town to town, but in no predefined order, sometimes moving backwards or sideways. The game will finish, after various encounters with vampires, sea creatures, fakers, Latin American novels and extended families, with three final ascents into the heavens.

There are some 70 *Backsteinkirchen*, brick churches along the southern Baltic, running east from Lübeck along the coastlines of Germany and Poland to the three Baltic states. There are of course many others in varying styles inland and also, with a rather different tradition, in locations over much of Europe. However the concern here is with three cities: Lübeck and two towns to the east, Wismar and Stralsund, all Hanseatic ports. Each has a medieval centre surrounded by a sprawl of later developments. Lübeck and Wismar lie about 40km apart, on either side of the former border between the East and West German states. Lübeck is the larger and richer city, Wismar rather smaller. Stralsund, once with the largest merchant fleet along the coast and still with a ship-building industry, lies a little further on, beyond the industrial port of Rostock. Lübeck is linked to the Baltic by the river Trave, while Wismar sits directly on a shallow bay, and Stralsund is separated by a narrow channel from the island of Rügen.

These cities are on located on the flat coastal landscape of dunes and small hills, as the land slopes down into the shallow waters of the Baltic, then rises slowly on the opposite coasts of Denmark and southern Sweden. All along this coastline lie areas of sandbanks, almost-islands just below the surface of the water, shallow bays that may silt up, channels that might lead nowhere, thin strips of seashore protecting saltwater lagoons, lakes that might become, or have been, part of the sea, a landscape as left by the retreating glaciers, at the end of the last ice-age. A small change in altitude distinguishes sea and land, the sea level is slowly rising, so that over time the coastline will develop a very different profile. Sven Talaron, in his book on Rügen and the Baltic coast describes how the coastline is in a constant state of change:

> The material that the glaciers of thousands of years ago scraped and eroded from the deeper layers of the terrain, have since been reformed by wind, weather and currents. The geological dynamics along the coastline operate not only during heavy seas, but are continually active. Heavy storms and floods accelerate the changes. Erosion, frost and floods wear away the shoreline and carry off chalk, clay and sand. This material is taken by the currents and deposited elsewhere. At the edges of the currents, in what are called current-shadows, this material mixes with the beaches or forms sandbanks. When these sandbanks become stable, often through attracting adequate vegetation, then from these deposits are formed spits, which enclose areas of the sea, link islands and create the typical shallow coastal bays.

The construction of the vast *Backstein* churches along the coast was perhaps partly a hope of keeping things the same, of building something fixed and eternal, the vertical forms of the churches contrasting with the horizontal lines of the land and the sea. Constructing on the unstable ground entailed deep timber piles reaching down into the mud and sand, foundations which in some cases have over the centuries shifted or rotted away, causing the buildings above to distort. The churches were built from the material of the land, from mud and earth dug out in quarries and turned to brick via a process of baking in large-scale kilns. *Backstein*—baked stone. The quarries that were excavated have themselves become ponds and lakes, adding to those existing naturally.

Each of these towns has changed hands several times. All were originally founded by Slavic tribes and their names stem from Slavic words—*liubice*, *wyszemir*, *strale*. Lübeck was for long periods a Free and Hanseatic City, but was also in turn the possession of Denmark, Saxony and Prussia, was temporarily French during the Napoleonic wars, before being finally absorbed by the German Empire. In the years after the Second World War Lübeck lay right on the border between West and East Germany, between capitalism and communism, the border running along the small Wakenitz river, hardly 3m wide, to the east of the city, with Schlutup, a northern suburb, offering the most northerly crossing point over the border. Both Wismar and Stralsund were Swedish cities for a long period in the seventeenth and eighteenth centuries, Stralsund was also Danish for a while. Both were in East Germany following the Second World War. The language of the inhabitants of these cities was known, in the complex terminology of the very diverse German world, as Middle Low German, once spoken all along the southern Baltic coastline controlled by the Hansa cities, right up to Estonia. It is similar to Dutch, Frisian and to some extent English. All these cities have therefore been located on, and sometimes beyond, the edge of the Germanic world, and like most ports have very mixed cultural influences. They existed at a time before the modern state of Germany, and its single unified language, came into existence, and therefore reflect a very different kind of culture.

A pause for breath. A narrow street in Lübeck, Große Gröpelgrube, busy people rushing by. A woman with a large shopping bag:

—Yes, there are so many churches. A church on every corner. Which one are you looking for? Aha that one. It must be around here, maybe at the end of the next street. Or maybe that way. Really there are too many churches in this town, we need more supermarkets, with cheaper prices.

Another pause: Dr Krogger, a retired doctor living in a fine villa just outside the centre:

—All these churches used to be connected by secret underground passages. Many of them led from the cloisters only for men to the cloisters only for women. Don't believe anything the clergy say, they have minds and bodies like the rest of us.

Confusingly, the names of the *Backstein* churches are often repeated, part of the litany of saints' names strung along the Baltic coast. Lübeck has five large *Backsteinkirchen*, Wismar and Stralsund each three.

In Lübeck:

1. the Marienkirche, begun in 1250, with its two towers, badly damaged in the Second World War and now restored
2. the Dom (cathedral), begun in 1173, also badly damaged, and also restored
3. the Jakobikirche, begun in 1300, much of it still in its original state
4. the small Aegidienkirche, begun in 1227, also still largely in its original state
5. the Petrikirche, begun in 1227, largely destroyed by bombing, but now reconstructed

In Wismar:

1. the Georgenkirche, begun in 1404, badly damaged by bombing, left empty for half a century and now reconstructed

2. the Marienkirche, begun in 1310, bombed and then, apart from the tower, controversially dynamited by the socialist government in the 1960s so that now only the tower remains
3. the Nikolaikirche, begun in 1381, and remaining in its original state

In Stralsund:

1. the Jakobikirche, begun in 1303, badly damaged in the bombing but since restored
2. the Marienkirche, begun in 1278, with its original spire the tallest building in the world from 1495 to 1647, this spire destroyed by lightning
3. the Nikolaikirche, begun in 1276, for the most part in its original state

But to use the word 'begun' for such buildings is almost meaningless. These churches have been rebuilt many times, and many of the same sites were sacred places even in pre-Christian times. The churches derive their forms from one another, a development in one affecting another. They have no real beginning, just as they now have no real end. Because of this, *Backsteinkirchen* are forever restless: continually reconstructed, pulled down, changing their form, partly destroyed only to reappear rather altered. For instance, the Petrikirche in Lübeck had various forms as it grew almost organically, expanding out from an ancient building. The Dom expanded longitudinally over centuries to become an elongated sequence of spaces. Some churches were left unfinished for many years due to a lack of funds, remaining as not-quite-buildings. Work on the Wismar Georgenkirche paused for almost 30 years before starting up again with a completely different group of people with competing ideas as to the form the building should now take.

Backsteinkirchen are instantly recognisable, great structures in brick, usually with a tower or towers, their size dwarfing the houses around them. Architectural historians tend to view them as a linear sequence, constructed one after another over a specific period, evolving in complexity. Certain recognised types emerge, such as the *Basilika*, where the exterior of the nave rises above the side aisles, the intermediate *Staffelkirche*, still a staggered section, but the clerestory is abandoned, and then the *Hallenkirche*, or hall church, where the whole of the interior is under one roof. A church can start as one type but transit to another. From this point of view one can construct highly ordered evolutionary paths, forever refining but never arriving at any definitive solution. However, one might also choose the hopscotch route, encountering these buildings in no predetermined sequence, by the chance visits made to these towns, where one church becomes overlaid in memory on another, where their individual forms become intermixed, where they coalesce into one large protean building. From either point of view, historical or chance visits, the aim of the whole *Backstein* project along the Baltic shore can be understood not only as the production of individual buildings, but as the evolution of a building type with an ever-changing form.

Some further hopscotch considerations, from the Argentinian writer Julio Cortázar's novel, *Rayuela* (*Hopscotch*), 1963:

> Hopscotch is played with a pebble that you move with the tip of your toe. The things you need: a pavement, a pebble, a toe and a pretty chalk drawing, preferably in colours. On top is heaven, on the bottom is earth, it is very hard to get the pebble up to heaven, you almost always miscalculate and the stone goes off the drawing. But little by little you get the knack of how to jump over the different squares (spiral hopscotch, rectangular hopscotch, fantasy hopscotch, not played very often) and then one day you learn how to leave earth and make the pebble climb up into heaven ... the worst part of it is that precisely at that moment, when practically no one has learned how to make the pebble climb into heaven, childhood is over and you are into reading novels, into the anguish of the senseless divine trajectory, into the speculation about another heaven that you have to reach too. And since you have come out of childhood, you forget that in order to get to heaven you need a pebble and a toe.

Julio Cortázar used the idea of hopscotch to write a novel in which the reader can hop from one chapter to another in two very different sequences. *Rayuela* can be read either as a linear narrative with a discernible story or as a compilation of individual moments without immediately obvious interrelationships and without any particular resolution. The narrative sequence is easier to read, but the second, disrupted sequence is ultimately more satisfying, for it allows the material to be seen freshly, bringing into play new elements such as extraneous bits of narrative, philosophical comments, pataphysical leaps and extracts from completely different books—all added seemingly at random, but actually with great care, the novelist always staying just ahead of the reader. The interrelationships between the parts are thus gradually built up into a more complex pattern, traversed through leaps and jumps, without any definitive end. *Rayuela* is really several books, which happen to exist within one cover. There might also be many other versions of *Rayuela*, just as there are an infinite number of variations on the hopscotch game—or *Backsteinkirchen*.

From the exterior the churches appear to be simple enough, compared to the extravagance of French or English cathedrals: a big brick box, with the expected external additions of buttresses, occasionally flying buttresses of modest engineering daring, chapels, towers, gables. The main effect is of size, compared to the small scale of the surrounding houses, and of the addition over time of various elements with different shapes but all built of the same material, brown-red brick. The Nikolaikirche in Wismar, for instance, is neither delicate nor elegant, nor particularly original, but it has a wonderful presence, a massive brick block occasionally broken up by pieces of decoration. Similarly the Lübeck Marienkiche, seen from beside the exterior of the choir, is rather banal—a set of oversized elements that should not work together but somehow create an architectural effect of a building that is on the point of metamorphosing into something else. There is something direct and basic about these exteriors, assembled from small building elements to create a single massive form.

Entering one of these churches, and moving through the regular three-dimensional geometry within the box, one gradually becomes aware of the quality of the interior, so different from the additive forms of the exterior. The aim of much European church architecture is to take the visitor, or worshipper, into a space deliberately different from the exterior, a divine space removed from everyday life. French churches such as the cathedral at Beauvais, with its very high nave, thin out the structure, elongate the forms, making distance and location hard to read, so that the visitor is first dislocated and then gradually discovers him/herself in relation to a divine order. Such techniques for constructing church interiors later become more and more refined as ideas are passed on from one church to another, until in Italian or south German baroque—as in the churches of Borromini or the Asam brothers—one is surrounded by forms which seem in perpetual movement, defying gravity, deliberately avoiding the creation of any single identifiable space. However within the Baltic *Backstein* churches this game is played out more slowly, without the showiness of the south. The effect is both sober and deceptive. While the exteriors are usually solid and massive, the interior vaulting, which at first seems regular, gradually appears to vary, the lines of the ribs on the ceiling creating an extraordinary mesmerising pattern that changes according to where one is standing.

Pause again. Thuggish-looking young man, smartly dressed, carrying leather briefcase, standing beside the Lübeck *Kant und Katze* bar, finishing a cigarette and leafing through the weekly offers in the Lidl supermarket magazine. He seems to know a great deal:

> —Don't visit too many churches. You become uncertain if you have been in this particular church before. Various parts seem familiar, but slightly altered. The ratio of width to length to height seems particularly unstable, never the same on a second visit as on the first. Consider, hop, deduce.

Lübeck. The centre of the town is a plump, slightly elongated island, surrounded by different strands of the river Trave. The streets on this island are mostly narrow, left over from medieval times. All five *Backstein* churches are on the island, their spires and towers standing up above the skyline. The centre is plush, internalised, edging on self-satisfied, with teashops and marzipan shops. It is a relief to step outside the centre, which is ringed by a muddle of later developments, fine nineteenth-century villas, housing blocks, industry, wharves, university buildings. All of these buildings are placed within a landscape of small rivers and ponds, allotments, fields, woods.

Fish, ships, churches. The Schiffergesellschaft is located in Lübeck's Breitestraße, in a *Backstein* Renaissance house. The exterior has an extraordinary set of diminishing gables, all in brick. The dimly lit interior space, once used as the headquarters for shipping guilds and sailors' brotherhoods, is now a restaurant. Diners sit on benches at long tables of dark wood. The entire ceiling is hung with numerous models of Lübeck sailing ships, from small single-masted boats, to trading vessels, to men-of-war with their rows of protruding cannons. A small family of four, mother, father, daughter, son, are ordering their meal from a respectful waiter. The mother is in charge.

—I love the immaculate construction and complex curves of the timber hulls. Seen from here, from below, from the viewpoint of a sea creature looking up at the ships on the surface.

—Would the distinguished society care to place an order?

—Ah yes, of course. For me the large North Sea plaice, fried with bacon, and boiled potatoes.

—For me the fried cod fillet on mustard sauce, spinach and parsley potatoes.

—Ah, for me the pike fillet, fried on the skin, with crayfish cream sauce, spinach leaves and boiled potatoes.

—And then for me sweet and sour pickled herring with onion rings and fried potatoes. And of course the mayo and the ketchup.

—Excellent. And to drink?

—As usual. Four large glasses of Haake Kraüser Pils.

—The sea creatures look up at the ships. The humans are in the ships, fishing the creatures. Compare this to the churches, it's all now inverted, the humans are in the churches, they look up towards the skies, towards paradise, where their souls, they hope, will be rewarded. The sky and the deep sea reflect one another.

—Four more beers please.

The simplicity of materials used in the construction of the churches adds to the impression of being simultaneously stable and unstable. The clay of the surrounding land provides the constant construction material of brown-red brick; stone was in short supply along the coast. To build in stone is to cut and shape the individual pieces so that they fit together. To build in brick is to cast out of the soft clay hundreds of identical rectangular pieces and to bake them until they are hard. This was a major enterprise on an industrial scale. The construction of Stralsund Marienkirche, for instance, required over three million bricks, which were placed in ovens, gradually heated up over several weeks, baked at high temperature, then cooled for several weeks. The ingenuity of the bricklayers was to take this simple standardised construction module, the brick, and use it to create forms of considerable plasticity. Out of this multitude of individual elements arose a single complex form. The colour of the bricks changes from church to church according to the source of the clay, the baking technique, and certain additives, such as ox blood, which gives a dark, almost black hue. Since the ground on which the churches stand is often marshy and unstable, and the whole area is coastline with an uncertain relationship to the water, the clay for the bricks also belongs to the sea. The churches are assembled piece by piece from the land and the sea, baked in fire, and rise up into the sky.

The aim of the *Backsteinkirchen* is of course religious, to aid the citizens to communicate with the Christian god, and to assist their souls in the move from terrestrial existence to paradise above. But their massive forms are also part of an architectural system of power. The German princes had forcibly colonised these Baltic lands, evicting or absorbing the original Slavic population, an action repeated in various forms by various political powers over centuries. The Hansa cities were proud of gaining a measure of autonomy, based on wealth built up through trade. Each church represents a particular political force within the city. The Lübeck Marienkirche was the church of the traders, the Jakobikirche was where the sailors and fishermen gathered, the small Aegidienkirche was for the craftsmen. The Dom, the cathedral, belonged to the city bishop and the religious authorities, who struggled without success to make it as large and as bold as the buildings of the rich lay authorities. There is something mournfully earthbound about this cathedral. Its entrance is called Paradies, indicating that one has arrived at heaven, but the building straggles out horizontally, attempting to cover a lot of ground while failing to get very far vertically: height and elegance belonged to the enterprising Baltic ship owners rather than to the Almighty's official representatives.

The uneasy relationship of the church spires to the skies has continued since their construction. Amongst other celestial acts of destruction:

> In 1539 lightning destroyed the spire of the Wismar Marienkirche. Its replacement was destroyed in a great storm in 1661.
>
> In 1647 lightning destroyed the spire of the Stralsund Marienkirche
>
> In 1703 the spire of the Wismar Nikolaikirche was blown off in a great storm and fell through the vaults into the nave. Due to lack of funds, the damage to the interior was not repaired until the late nineteenth century.
>
> In 1942 the roof and spire of the Lübeck Marienkirche caught fire during a bombing raid and descended burning through the roof, setting fire to the interior of the nave.
>
> In 1942 the twin towers of Lübeck Cathedral were hit, caught fire and blazed like twin flares.

Imagine a sheet on which are set out the plans of many *Backsteinkirchen*. The plans appear like a collection of insects, all laid together, at first sight rather similar and then developing into ever more complex variations. Usually they are laid out horizontally, but if turned 90 degrees they appear like towers or rockets or curious figures which grow stumpy limbs. These plans are drawn in the conventional way, showing the horizontal cut through the building at ground level, but also the pattern of the vaulting at roof level. One sees a remarkable ability to keep to a generic plan, composed of the grid of vaults, but then to riff on this basic layout, to add side chapels, to distort the vaulting, to carve into the solids with stairways and rooms. The beauty of these plans lies in the way they adopt a simple additive system and then, over an extended timescale, play with it in an almost light-hearted way, always finding new possibilities within the same basic set of rules. They are based on symmetry, but then introduce any number of minor asymmetries.

The plan of the Lübeck Marienkirche is typical: it sets out a nave and two aisles, but performs ingenious geometrical tricks with the external east wall as it winds its way around a set of chapels, while the west end is a massive brick construction forming the base of the towers. The two types of construction—minimal wall and massive towers—hardly belong in the same building. Then, as though not content with what has been achieved, the nave ends in a chapel that suddenly pushes its way out like a miniature head, while the south wall swells to give birth to the Briefkapelle, a perfect miniature church in itself, with two central columns and some extraordinary vaulting. The Marienkirche is organic, in the sense that it grows extra organs, beginning in a fairly mundane way and then gradually transforming itself into another creature.

The Dutch historian of the middle ages, Johan Huizinga, wrote on the nature of play, and on how games are based on the creation of a particular space, in his book *Homo Ludens: A Study of the Play Element in Culture* (1938):

> Formally speaking there is no difference between marking out a space for a sacred purpose and marking it out for the purposes of sheer play. The turf, the tennis court, the chessboard, and the pavement hopscotch cannot be formally distinguished from the temple or the magic circle.

Huizinga proposed that play be considered as something separate from everyday life, whether as a kind of performance which can take place anywhere but is controlled by certain make-believe rules, or as an activity which follows rules but in a particular location, marked out as being different from the surrounding world. If one follows Huizinga's lead, then the laying out of the plans of churches relates to the laying out of a court or pitch for a game, the demarcation of a particular space for a specific activity, whether sacred or ludic. Within this space different codes of behaviour are specified. The space is created as much by the acknowledgement that it is special, by the effect of make-believe, as it is by the physical means of its construction—chalk on pavement, bricks and mortar. All those participating need to acknowledge the rules: breaking these rules implies the necessity of eviction (penalty, excommunication) from the sacred or ludic space, and possibly from the society that creates the space.

One might object, however, that games are not entirely separate, that elements of the everyday world—competitiveness, desire, ambition, personal emotions—are carried back and forth across the little line dividing the imaginary world of play from actual life. Those within the church, or the hopscotch game, are within a special space and are subject to particular codes of behaviour, but they also still retain in part their everyday personalities and ways of behaving. The players know they are playing a game.

Does the game precede the church—or is the church based on the game? The ludologist Roger Caillois' *Les jeux et les hommes* (1958), a criticism of Huizinga's text, makes clearer the link between hopscotch and religion:

> In antiquity hopscotch was a labyrinth where one pushed the stone—that is to say the soul—towards the exit. With Christianity, the drawing was stretched out and became simpler. It reproduced the plan of a basilica, it was a question of pushing the soul—ie of pushing the stone—to Paradise, to the crown or to the glory, which coincided with the high altar of the church, schematically represented on the ground by a sequence of rectangles.

Caillois plays down the idea of the separate space and links games to a pagan past, directly transferred into Christianity. The stone is now not just a piece of game equipment, but represents the soul. The soul/stone can't move of its own accord—it needs to be kicked through the labyrinth or hopscotch pitch—but the body can, or must, hop, following the soul. We walk today through Caillois' sequences of rectangles, through the plan of the church, unaware of the serious kicking and hopping we need to do in order to arrive at paradise.

Wismar. Bright sunny day in March. Beside the harbour. Smell of grilled fish. Young woman with bright yellow apron, metal spatula, fork:

> —It really depends on what you are searching for. Complicated thoughts, no. But the boats come straight in here from the sea. Whatever the weather. With the fresh fish. Eels. Plaice. Herrings, grilled or fried. Excellent in a bread roll.

Like many ports along the Baltic coast Wismar is a mix of different nationalities. Lübeck lies a little inland, but Wismar always looked outward to the Baltic and belonged for almost two hundred years to the Swedes, who gave its architecture a Scandinavian feel. It was even occupied for a short time in 1945 by the British, who were surprised to find the city full of all kinds of refugees from the east, fleeing the Russian Army. In the postwar period the socialist authorities attempted to recreate Wismar as a ship-building city for the Eastern Bloc, with links in particular to the ice-free city of Kaliningrad. The socialists reconstructed the quays, and built a series of finely engineered dockside cranes. Out on the flat landscape around the city they built large colonies of *Plattenbau*, the typical socialist housing of the 1970s and 1980s. They dynamited the walls of the Marienkirche, but in this action they were perhaps distantly following the lead of north German Lutherans who had whitewashed the images in the churches and replaced the idea of entry to paradise through saintliness with a reward in the afterlife based on hard work—a considerable amount of kicking the stone would be required. In DDR Wismar there was no particular need either for churches or for an afterlife, since paradise would now be created by the workers, in the present, in this city by the Baltic. Wismar has an air of detachment from the surrounding world which made this unlikely dream seem more credible. The housing colonies of Seebad and Wendorf, just to the northeast of the centre, have that undefined immaterial quality sometimes produced by the DDR, mass housing by the shallow Baltic seaside. The streets along the coast are still named after socialist martyrs, victims of the Nazi terror: Rudolph Breitscheid (Reichstag deputy), Ernst Scheel (Wismar sailor–musician), Liselotte Herrmann (known as Lilo, a resistance fighter) and their comrades. They balance well enough the Christian saints St Anna Selbdritt (with a ball and a child), St Johannes (book and knife) and St Barbara (red brick tower), all charmingly innocent, sculpted in wood and located back on the altar screen in the Wismar Nikolaikirche.

When the DDR collapsed in 1990, the new political authorities took over and proceeded to remove many of the buildings put up by the socialists in the centre of Wismar, such as the taxation office, attempting to eradicate any sign that the banal dreamworld of German socialism had once been proposed here. The new political forces had their own vision of the future of the city, as part of a revived Baltic region freed from the divisions of the previous decades. By far the largest structure today is the great blue and white shipbuilding shed on the wharf to the west of the centre. At over 400m long it exists at another scale to both the medieval *Backsteinkirchen* and the socialist harbour facilities, and is now filled with the massive motor yachts of Hamburg businessmen and Russian oligarchs, a sign of the use of the Baltic changing from trading to leisure. This wharf is currently owned by a conglomerate of Russian investors who sort out their business affairs in the traditional way. In September 2011 the head of this dubious organisation, Andrei Burlakov, another man who seemed keen to invent his own way of overleaping rules, was shot in a Moscow restaurant by a contract killer, under circumstances yet to be fully explained. Wismar is today only a short hop away from the field of operations of the Russian mafiosi, so the dreamy otherworldliness of the sacred *Backstein* city is liable to sudden incursions of violent reality.

Wismar is closely linked to Lübeck through F W Murnau's film *Nosferatu: A Symphony of Horror* (1922). In this film the two cities were used to form a composite, Wisbourg. The opening shot, made from the tower of the Marienkirche in Wismar, looks down on the red roofs spread around the marketplace with its baroque fountain. The viewer gets the notion of a city from a fairytale. The courtyard of the Wismar Heilig-Geist-Kirche, a small *Backstein* church not far from the Marienkirche, stands in for the home of the film's narrator, Thomas Hutter.

The progress of the vampire can be traced as a series of leaps across the twin cities. Nosferatu travels out of the Carpathian forests, following the course of those eels mentioned at the start of this piece, but in reverse. The death-ship *Demeter* approaches Wismar harbour, carrying the vampire's coffin from his castle in Transylvania, its crew all dead, the dead steersman bound to the helm, the ship overrun by rats, the symbol of the plague. As the ship arrives, the tower of the Marienkirche can be seen in the background, the body of the church still intact. Beside the Wismar city gate, near the harbour, we see the fiend carrying his coffin, moving furtively. He stalks purposefully in the twilight outside the Wismar Georgenkirche. Always mindful of the necessary equipment for travelling, he is still clutching his coffin. He is next seen in Lübeck, in a boat beside the Salzspeicher, a series of brick buildings once used for storing salt. The vampire makes the Salzspeicher his home. The churchyard of the Lübeck Aegidienkirche features briefly, as part of Hutter's home.

Actually some 40km apart, the two cities make a reasonable cinematic match. Untouched by the First World War, these cities must have appeared in 1922 as towns out of a northern fairytale, with their oversize *Backstein* churches and diminutive houses, and *Nosferatu* is indeed a kind of dark fairytale, a story which seems straightforward but then makes one wonder about the darkness it reveals. Today Lübeck, marzipan city, seems almost too sweet, too self-satisfied. Wismar is less homogeneous, more clearly disjointed. Although both have now become tourist cities, they have a strange uneasy edge to them, a feeling of innocence but also a sense that all is not quite well, not quite as simple as it seems. In the decades following 1922 there were clearly reasons to doubt the innocence of Germanic homeliness; the effect of these decades still remains today, so we look on both the film and the cities differently.

The Murnau vampire is a curious figure: rat-like, but delicate, almost fragile, moving with a certain elegance. He is no ironic Hollywood upper-class fiend, but slightly tatty, almost ludicrous. The critic Siegfried Kracauer saw the vampire, and other 20s cinematic nasties such as Dr Caligari, as forerunners of the Nazis, harbingers of the destruction of German *bürgerlich* society. The vampire seeks eternal life, but brings the rats and the plague that will destroy the inhabitants of Wisbourg. He comes from the outside, apparently from the heathland to the east, he is *heidenisch*, heathen, a threat to the churches and a kind of joker in the pack, playing by his own rules, which no human understands, rules that are transmitted through infection. But he is also from the inside, the sign of excessive imagination and psychological disturbance, brought to life by the fears and anxieties of the inhabitants of Wisbourg.

The Hanseatic cities, which had survived reasonably intact any number of political changes over the centuries, suffered major destruction during the Second World War. In revenge for the Luftwaffe's bombing of Coventry cathedral, Lübeck, which had little strategic value, was chosen as the first city to be area-bombed with incendiaries by the RAF in March 1942. Eighty per cent of the timber-framed houses in the inner city caught fire and burned down. The brick walls of the houses remained, but were pulled down by the Nazi authorities, who didn't want any ruins to be seen in German cities. The great timber roofs of the Marienkirche, the Petrikirche and the cathedral caught fire and collapsed, the burning timber spires descending through the roofs to crash into the brick floors. The interiors of these three churches were largely burnt out. The retaliatory raids by the Luftwaffe on British cities, in particular on Bath, Exeter and Canterbury, were known as the Baedeker raids, the deliberate and pointless destruction of the cultural artefacts of the enemy. This vicious tit-for-tat continued: Rostock's Petrikirche and Nikolaikirche were near-destroyed in April 1942, the city centre was also bombed once again in 1945. Hansa cities such as Hamburg were bombed with great loss of civilian life and almost to the elimination of the material fabric in a series of firestorms. Much of the centre of Stralsund was destroyed by the USAF in October 1944, in part because the aircraft had missed their real targets, the V2 rocket sites in Peenemunde, and needed to dump their bombs. Wismar, also of little military value, was bombed in April 1945, a few weeks before the end of the war, at a time when the city was filled with refuges from the east. The city's Marienkirche and Georgenkirche were reduced to shells. In a few years, from 1942 to 1945, much of the *Backstein* fabric of the southern Baltic coast, which had lasted from the middle ages, was reduced to ruins.

Rainy day, a walk through the reedbeds along the river Trave, at Gothmund, just outside Lübeck. Single-storey houses, brick walls, roofs of reed. Three women of various ages, wearing green coats and jeans, large boots. Along the river the reeds are too high to see over. The women walk carefully, uncertain of the way forward. Each woman speaks in turn.

—All this talk of destruction from the skies depresses me. Lübeck is concerned with the water, the rivers, the sea. The Baltic is a very special sea, almost a lake, for it is only connected to the North Sea through the narrow channels in the Danish islands. It is almost an inland sea, with its own culture. Sail down the Trave from here and out to the Baltic, to Stockholm, Helsinki, up the Gulf of Finland to St Petersburg. Or past the Aland Archipelago and right up the Gulf of Bothnia, to the far North, almost to the Arctic circle.

—Forget about the sea. Too wild, too far. Better to remain at home and read. You know that the writer Günter Grass, originally from Danzig, now of course Gdansk, lived in Lübeck. Perhaps because Lübeck is a little like Gdansk, they are both Hansa towns. And of course Thomas Mann wrote his great novel *Buddenbrooks* about a Lübeck family, trading with the Baltic and the North Sea. And Thomas Mann didn't care much about churches, he was modern. Maybe not as modern as Julio Cortázar, no leaps, no hopscotch, no strange hopping movements in time. But he described the vanishing of the old, the not-quite-birth of the new.

—Forget about seas and all this literary stuff. I understand little of what either of you say. Aha, here we are finally out of the reeds. Somewhere around here there's a small café, with cakes of rhubarb and strawberry, and sticky buns filled with caramel.

Back in the centre of Lübeck. Just opposite the northern entrance to the Marienkirche, at Mengstraße 4, is an eighteenth-century merchant's house with an elegant baroque facade, high windows and a fine gable. This is the 'Buddenbrookhaus', the former family home of Thomas Mann and the setting for many of the scenes in his wonderful novel, *Buddenbrooks* (1901), which tells the story of the long decline of the Buddenbrooks family, from successful grain merchants through poor marriages, business errors, dubious loans and erratic family members up to the sale of the great house in the 1870s. The Buddenbrooks are strict Lutherans, but seem to spend little time in Lübeck churches, preferring to invite the pastors around to perform ceremonies in the hall of their house. Despite the downward trend, the opening scenes of the novel relate a grand Christmas dinner and there are remarkable descriptions of long conversations, of thoughts about music. Like an early Dickens novel, it is filled with strange eccentric people who flitter in and out of the story, their characteristics and clothing described in great detail, Lübeck is never actually named, but the churches, streets and houses are clearly from the Baltic town, and many of the characters were based—at the time controversially—on people Mann had known during his childhood in Lübeck. This is a Germanic world before the formation of the German state, where the characters are at home in a very mixed culture. The opening words, a conversation between a child and her grandfather, are already in three languages:

—Was ist das.—Was—ist das ...
—Je, den Düwel ook, c'est la question, ma chère demoiselle.

Or translated but losing something of the feel:

—What is that.—What—is that ...
—Jesus, the devil as well, that's the question, miss!

The first sentence is in Schriftdeutsch, ie what would become standard German. The second begins in the local version of German, Plattdeutsch, and then shifts to French, the language of the educated middle classes. The servants and lower classes tend to speak Platt, but so too on occasions do the Buddenbrooks family, who also display a certain nostalgia for the polite formality of the French language. As the novel progresses, standard German becomes more dominant, provincial life less distinct.

Buddenbrooks is a traditional novel. It proceeds in a linear narrative, concerned with a very material world, with trade, with money, with how much people are worth. But it is also disquieting: the stability of the known world is increasingly put in doubt, the characters are often shifty, uncertain.

The last of the Buddenbrook family, the little son, Johann, lives in a self-created world of music and games:

> Little Johann, with his soft wavy hair and his pleated pinafores, quietly and innocently plays beside the fountain in his garden or up on the balcony, created especially for him by the addition of a little row of columns on the third-floor landing—a four-year-old at play. His games have a deeper meaning and fascination that adults can no longer fathom and require nothing more than three pebbles, or a piece of wood with a dandelion helmet, perhaps; but above all they require only the pure, strong, passionate, chaste, still-untroubled fantasy of those happy years when life still hesitates to touch us, when neither duty nor guilt dares lay a hand upon us, when we are allowed to see, hear, laugh, wonder and dream without the world's demanding anything in return, when the impatience of those whom we want so much to love has not yet begun to torment us for evidence, some early token, that we will diligently fulfil our duties.

The playing of such fantasy games extends to the current Buddenbrookhaus. The Lübeck house, with its dining room, hall of columns, salon, landscape room, bedchambers, is in fact a reconstruction, a fake. The visitor moves through the rooms and recalls the scenes in the novel, and how these rooms were described by

Thomas Mann. But a fictitious family can hardly have inhabited a real house. In addition, all that remained of the original Mann family home, after the bombing raids of 1942, were some elements of that fine facade. The house was reconstructed after the war, not exactly how it used to be, but improved to make it more like the novel. It is highly popular with visitors, so much so that is currently being doubled in size, a fictitious home requiring more space than a real one. This feel, of things being not quite real, pervades Lübeck, largely destroyed and then reconstructed, jumping between old and comparatively new, time muddled up, sometimes spiritual, close to revelation, sometimes banal and material.

A very different story of a fake. The fires from the bombing destroyed most of the interior of the Lübeck Marienkirche. The layers of sixteenth-century Lutheran limewash peeled away, revealing in some areas long-hidden medieval paintings. In the 1950s a programme of restoration of these paintings was put into place, led by an art professor, Dietrich Fey, and a mural restorer, Lothar Malskat. Originally from Königsberg, the most easterly of the Germanic cities—and since 1945 the Russian enclave renamed Kaliningrad—Malskat was already famous for his restoration of the medieval paintings of Schleswig cathedral in the 1930s. His discovery there of a medieval image of a turkey, previously thought to have been brought back from America by Columbus, caused the early history of contacts with the New World to be rewritten—Teutonic Norsemen now being given the credit for introducing the fowl to Europe. In the postwar years Malskat began work high up on scaffolding in the choir of the Lübeck Marienkirche, scraping away at the limewash, and soon revealed some astonishing medieval artwork—friezes, decorative animals, the Virgin and Child and some 21 saints, to add to the many figures already discovered in the main aisle. Malskat's discoveries became known as the 'Miracle of Lübeck'. The church was visited by the West German Chancellor, Konrad Adenauer, religious visitors poured in, the state granted generous funds for more work by the restorer. Postage stamps were printed with images of an angel found in the nave. Art experts hypothesised on links between Chartres and Lübeck, and speculated on the itinerant painters of the thirteenth century. The colours of this artwork—reds, greens and ochres—were remarkable, given that one might have expected the tones to have oxidised in the heat of the fire, but this was really part of the miracle.

The story soon took an unanticipated turn. Annoyed by the fact that Fey had claimed all the credit for these discoveries, Malskat revealed that none of the images in the choir of the Marienkirche were actually medieval: he had painted them all himself. When asked about his skills, he commented:

> For the artists of that time the reference to creative ability was seen as a mortal sin, worthy of being burned at the stake, since the attribute of 'creativity' belonged until well into the eighteenth century to the Almighty alone. They would have considered it wholly legitimate that, in the extreme need of the postwar period, I decorated the church nave in God's name, in their style, for the piety of the believers.

The famous Virgin, featured on the cover of at least one learned work on medieval art, was in fact a 1930s film star, Hansi Knoteck, for whom Malskat had developed a certain passion in his youth. Art experts insisted Malskat was lying, and produced as evidence other artworks, very similar in style to those in the Marienkirche, on the walls of various medieval buildings in Lübeck. Malskat morosely declared that he had painted these images too, and in addition had invented the celebrated Schleswig turkey. To Malskat's own satisfaction he was imprisoned for a short while, together with Fey, but the deluded art experts remained at liberty. This whole tale, with certain novelistic exaggerations, is to be found in Günter Grass's book *The Rat*. Grass, long-time inhabitant of Lübeck, wrote that Malskat was really a medieval painter who had somehow moved a square too far, operating in the wrong time: 'when I say the middle ages were his time, I see him in flesh high up on the scaffolding, seven hundred years ago, his woollen hat pulled down over his ears'. Grass concluded that Malskat 'bridged over centuries, so through him the fury of the last war was brought to nothing, so he triumphed over time'.

In the game of art and history being played out high in the choir of the Marienkirche, Malskat, like the vampire, was the joker, or perhaps the cheat, who recognises the rules but does not abide by them. The cheat demolishes the rules of the game but sets up other rules. Malskat's work was declared valueless and painted out—a long strip of greyish whitewash is still visible on the wall just below the high windows of the choir. Without his confession, the deception might never have been discovered. His mocking deceptions achieved, as Grass suggests, a sudden jump in time, where images that are supposedly very old reappear and distort the whole of history, which is revealed as just so many stories. Better, then, to accept that past times are mostly inventions, and use this as a way of finding a path forward to a new, open society. The last remaining—acknowledged—painting by Lothar Malskat in the Marienkirche is the great figure of St Christopher, on one of the columns of the nave.

Guide, overheard:

> —We have left this picture, even though we suspect it is not quite correct, because a church is not a museum—and because we like the picture.

If one looks at these churches in the light of the Malskat tale, then one begins to question, in great uncertainty, what is original and what a recreation. One looks at the extraordinary, coloured vaulting of the Briefkapelle on the side of the Marienkirche and questions whether a sympathiser of Malskat didn't have something to do with this pop art colouring, and if it isn't also better so. If the German middle ages needed to be reimagined, then why not recreate them as boldly as possible? And if, in contrast, one stands in the absolutely white space of the nearby Petrikirche, which seems almost completely modern, then one realises that this isn't so much a medieval church as a contemporary creation, a bauhausisation of the original interior, a repeat of the actions of the earlier Lutherans who had so disliked the colours and images of the medieval world. The Petrikirche has been reconstructed, but without its interior fittings, so that it resembles a set of open plan modernist spaces, the medieval period reinvented as adjoining the early modern, hopping over the tedium of nineteenth-century reconstructions. The effect is however very interesting, the original plan of five-by-five vaults providing an almost square space, surrounded by an irregular exterior wall. The Petrikirche now hovers intriguingly between its old form and something new. In comparison, the recently restored Georgenkirche of Wismar, its roof and vaulting now rebuilt, has retrieved its original form, but is still just a shell. In spite of the effort and expense of the restoration, there is something missing: the body is there well enough, but somehow the building has yet to rediscover its soul—perhaps because soul is not a matter of form, but depends on belief. To find a *Backsteinkirche* with some sense of an earlier atmosphere, one has to visit the Lübeck Aegidienkirche, with its clutter of timber benches and its odd bits of timber construction, such as the unusual bridge within which the choir sometimes sing. The Aegidienkirche has no grand idea, but this church is more than a pure form, it contains contradictions, layers of addition and change.

There was once another painting in the Lübeck Marienkirche with a complicated ancestry. In one of the side chapels of the north side hung the magnificent *Totentanz*, the dance of death, produced in the mid-fifteenth century during the ravages of the plague. This 30m-long painting has often been attributed to a painter called Bernt Nolke, but he is a shadowy figure who may just have acquired the attribution because he was around in Lübeck at the time; it is more likely that the painting, like the church, was by various hands. The *Totentanz* showed 24 life-sized figures, arranged in a social hierarchy from an emperor and a pope through to a monk and a knight to a hand-worker and a hermit, each matched to one of 24 skeletal corpses. These cadavers seemed to represent those already dead, but perhaps also the living in a future state, dancing with their own skeleton in all that remained of their finery. The two groups pranced and swayed merrily enough together, the dead rather more lively than the living. Only a baby in a cradle was spared the dance, at least for the moment. Behind the dancers stretched the familiar Lübeck landscape with the towers and spires of the city, the *Backsteinkirchen* easily identifiable. One of the cadavers, in cheerful anticipation of F W Murnau's *Nosferatu*, carried his own coffin. A text beneath the images, also altered at various periods, celebrated the dance of death, each character speaking in turn. Death calls out in the old Lower German language:

To dussem dantse rope ik al gemene
Pawes keiser unn alle creature
Arm rijke groet vnn kleine ...

I call everybody to this dance
pope, emperor and all creatures,
poor, rich, great and small.
Step forward, because grieving doesn't help you!
But consider well, at all times,
that you bring good works with you
and become free of your sins,
because you must dance to my pipe.

At various periods the original medieval painting deteriorated into such a poor condition that it needed to be repainted or restored, in particular in 1701 and 1853, each repainting no doubt varying the original vision of the *Totentanz* to conform to the contemporary image of the medieval period. The *Totentanz* was completely destroyed in the firebombing of the Marienkirche on Palm Sunday 1942, flames finally bringing the dance to an end. A very similar and equally wonderful *Totentanz* still exists in the *Nikolaikirche* in Tallin (German—Reval) in Estonia. The Lübeck version survives today largely through the black-and-white photographs of city photographer Wilhelm Castelli, who carefully documented the painting in the 1930s. Castelli, who ran an apothecary in Lübeck but specialised in photography, had the good luck to survive the wartime bombing of the city, though much of his archive was destroyed. He shows the *Totentanz* winding around what looks like a dim and dusty room, surrounded by ancient wooden confessional benches, a painting that was already becoming its own ghost. Castelli also recorded numerous Lübeck landmarks, interiors and exteriors, all photographed in the clear black-and-white style of *Neue Sachlichkeit*—immaculately focused modernist images reinterpreting a medieval city which would be largely destroyed a few years later. The massive brick forms seem surprisingly modern in Castelli's photographs, very similar to the north German brick buildings produced in the 1920s and 30s.

In the mid-1950s two large stained-glass windows were installed in this same chapel, designed by Alfred Mahlau, a graphic designer who had worked with Castelli. These windows show the figures from the original *Totentanz*, arranged vertically rather than horizontally, but now with the humans decreased in number to 18 and the cadavers upped to 26. Death had clearly made progress in Germany since the medieval period. However, in one image two skeletal figures are shown kneeling before a standing child, a symbol perhaps of the triumph of birth over death, as though the child in the original frieze had proved more powerful than death. At the bottom of the stained-glass windows are images of the Lübeck churches in flames, the original cityscape of the *Totentanz* separated from the figures and in a process of destruction. Mahlau himself was another unusual Lübeck personality, the product of his family's own contradictory mix of spiritual and political concerns, blending anthroposophic communism with a kind of ultra Catholicism. To some extent Mahlau invented the contemporary image of medieval Lübeck. He had designed the *Eiergeld*, or emergency money, issued by the city in 1921 when the official German currency was in collapse, along with the wrappers for the well-known Niederegger marzipan featuring images of the seven spires of the city's churches, and in 1926 organised a large-scale street parade with figures in medieval costume and locals dressed as skeletons leading the dance. This parade seems to reflect both back, to the loss of life of the First World War, and forward, to what was to come. In 1942 Mahlau designed postage stamps to celebrate the 800th anniversary of the city the following year, at the request of the extreme Nazi mayor, Hans Böhmker, a zealous organiser of campaigns for the extermination of the Dutch Jews. He was recognised by Adolf Hitler as one of the Third Reich's leading graphic designers. It is not that Mahlau held fascist opinions, but from marzipan wrappers to associating with Nazis might seem one long hop in the wrong direction. At the time of this octocentenary the town lay in ruins but the Mahlau stamps showed the churches in their original state, as though the medieval period still continued, untouched by the contemporary world. Mahlau's graphic work is elegant and simple, reducing the world to bold, almost childlike forms emanating an inner beauty and sense of innocence. In one image he shows all the Lübeck churches lined up like building blocks, the city reduced back to a compacted island, the houses compressed into that ideal German home of the simple form with the pitched roof. *Backstein* has become a kind of game of children's wooden blocks, all the later accretions on the city stripped away to reveal the city in some primal state. In this sense, Mahlau's simplifications are both pleasing and deeply disturbing, with the graphic reduction of German culture being easily appropriated by those who wished to use such medieval images to support dubious, and ultimately poisonous, notions of German racial identity. Something of this worrying linkage continues unintentionally into Mahlau's windows: the original *Totentanz* reflected on the destruction caused in Germany by the plague, while the stained-glass windows of Mahlau seem to portray the world of the 1950s seen through a screen of medieval iconography. As one gazes at his version of the *Totentanz* in coloured glass one might wonder just who is represented by the figures being carried off to their death, and who exactly are the cadavers doing the carrying.

Meanwhile the vampire is involved in a rather different dance of death. He is afraid of the rays of sunlight, which can destroy him. In any game of paradise he needs to play by other rules than the humans. In his version of the game he must at all costs avoid reaching heaven, and must remain in the shadow world of the undead.

Further sunlight and hopscotch considerations. According to the German writer Friedrich Hirsch in his book *Der Sonnwendbogen* (1965), the game of hopscotch derives from pre-Christian beliefs and links back both to the labyrinths of classical times and to pagan rituals around the rising and the setting of the sun. Hirsch researched many versions of the game, from inside and outside Germany. He proposes that the movement though the hopscotch squares from earth to heaven, and the kicking of the stone, are derived from the practices of devotees of sun religions, and in particular the orientation through systems of stones to the position, at specific times of the year, of the rising sun. This idea could be extended to a further comparison between the game and the *Backsteinkirchen*. The layout of many churches defines movement from the entrance in the west, through a series of spaces, finishing towards the east, where the sun rises and where the altar is located.

The many patterns of hopscotch games, from circles to rectangles to extended lines, give an endless variety derived from a simple set of squares. Of course this does not mean that the plans of hopscotch and churches are the same, but the resemblance is at least suggestive of the idea that they may have a common origin.

Move eastwards. Medieval scenes carved onto wooden panels in the Stralsund Nikolaikiche. Russians with long beards go hunting and gather honey and resin. They arrive in Riga and trade their goods with Stralsund merchants, with shorter beards, who carry large bags of money.

The further one moves east, away from the rather self-satisfied atmosphere of Lübeck and the uncertainties of Wismar, the more the churches, ignored by the communist state, are left in a decayed condition. Stralsund lies well to the east of Wismar, the other side of the large port of Rostock. The medieval town centre is almost an island, cut off from the land by a series of brackish ponds, part of a series of islands and half-islands that includes Rügen, which is as much archipelago as island, and also Hiddensee, a wonderful spit of land that can't quite decide what it is and which used to be hiding place for dissidents and other renegades in DDR times. To the east of Stralsund is an almost-bay, of the type known in German as *Bodden*, surrounded by sandbanks. This is land/seascape, forever changing, held together in part by man-made bridges, dykes, dredging to keep channels open, which only delay the inevitable advance of nature.

The churches of Stralsund form part of this man-made effort, but are also part of a system of constant change. The Nikolaikirche, which like much of the medieval centre was almost abandoned in the DDR period, is magnificent, with two great towers, one surmounted by a spire, the second left uncapped—like the Strasbourg Munster. The interior is filled with timber screens, bits of chapels, half constructions which no one has quite finished, all added in an ad-hoc way to the regular system of columns and vaults. The walls of the Nikolaikirche are still painted with medieval images, as though neither Lutherans nor socialists ever came here, as though it never made it past the Reformation and even remained semi-pagan. The plan of the Stralsund Nikolaikirche reveals that this indecision had already set in at the time of its construction; the outer wall of chapels at the eastern end was never completed, as though the builders ran out of energy at the last moment, giving the whole a pleasing asymmetry. In comparison, the Stralsund Marienkirche, along with the church of the same name in Gdansk, is the largest *Backsteinkirche* along the Baltic coast. As already mentioned, its spire was the tallest in the world until it was destroyed by lightning. Now the tower is topped by a large baroque cupola, which evolves into an onion dome and small spire, hardly traditional *Backstein* but solid and individual. Inside the church are remarkable decorations, including an extraordinary early eighteenth-century altar designed by the baroque sculptor Andreas Schlüter, responsible for the Amber room in Königsberg. The altar has a rather wild *Last Supper*, with Jesus and his disciples dressed in luminous gold suits, all the bodies in a state of excited motion, as though animated by some unseen force. Clearly Stralsund kept out of the medieval period and adapted to a later period of art. To balance this, outside the north entrance is a large obelisk of red granite, erected in 1967 to the soldiers of the Red Army who fell in the liberation of the city. On the front face of the obelisk a solidly built Red Army soldier greets a thankful Stralsund resident. The third great church in Stralsund, the Jakobikirche, badly damaged by bombing in 1944, was also hit by cannon balls in earlier wars, struck by lightning, used as stables by Napoleon's troops and as a garage and materials store by the Russians. Finally restored in the late 1950s, its interior is plain and elegant, with little sign of centuries of trauma.

The socialist regime of the DDR, with little interest in religion, had no clear idea what to do with the remarkable array of Stralsund *Backsteinkirchen* that had fallen into its hands. They were distant remnants of the old German society, which had just ended in war and disaster, and which was now to be replaced by a better world. Mostly the regime just quietly ignored them, constructing new housing blocks outside the medieval centres, shipyards, factories. Sometimes it found some alternative purpose, particularly when it lacked funds to construct new buildings. The Stralsund Katherinenkirche, once part of a much larger cloister, lies in a small street. In 1951 it became a natural history museum, on the principle that a disused church should be put some practical use. In 1973 it was converted to a marine museum. Hanging in the nave, as if to confirm a suspected deepsea–*Backstein* link, is the skeleton of a young fin whale, 15m long with a large skull and the ribs strung from the spine. The skeleton was found in the 1825 on the island of Hiddensee, north of Rügen. Arranged around the fin whale, like worshippers at a shrine, are parts of other whales discovered in the Baltic. On a new floor inserted into the nave are the remains, and also recreations, of other sea creatures. Alongside are wonderful ship models, a fantastic Atlantic trawler from socialist times, and another of the bathyscaphe *Trieste*, which in 1960 descended 10,911m to the deepest point of the oceans, at the bottom of the Mariana Trench. Downstairs in the basement are aquariums with turtles and seahorses. Up in the roof space, not accessible to the public, are rows of jars with preserved marine specimens, barely recognisable fish eels and other life rather creepily preserved in glass. The Katharinenkirche has grown too small for its contents, as interest in the seas has grown. Nearby, on the waterfront, is the brand new Ozeaneum, with a more contemporary display, including the skeletons of a fin whale, sperm whale, and common minke whale. There are fine glass models of jewel squids, mantra rays, oarfish, sunfish. But it is the Katherinenkirche which sticks in the mind, linking the tradition of the medieval *Backstein* church to the technology of the ships to the ever-unknowable creatures of the undersea.

Two Stralsund boys stare at a full-size model of a giant octopus with arms covered in suckers, reaching upwards:

> —It's the Kraken, he was god long ago. I read a story about him, he lived under the sea for thousands of years. He could sink ships by pulling them down underwater with his arms. He was a god, people worshipped him. He can never die, he is still there under the sea.

Man, in his fifties, Prof Mats Makler, in slightly old-fashioned suit and hat, horn-rimmed glasses, in the long road beside the rail lines, Auf der Werft, to the south of the medieval town.

> —Just follow me. Nowadays people despise the socialist state and its lack of attention to the churches of Stralsund.

But along here in the 1950s they built a new town, with housing blocks for the workers. And here are the great shipyards where they built the ocean-going trawlers, and where more than 8,000 people were employed.

—What kind of ships?

—First the ships were built for the Soviet Union, then for our own fishing fleet. This was to be a new world, with new hopes, moving on from the old discredited past. And then in the 1990s, after the fall of socialism, private companies built this vast shipbuilding shed, coloured bright blue, for the construction of container ships, then cruise ships and even today wind turbines. The hall is 300m long, 100m wide and 75m high, one of the largest in the world. And with the largest ship lift in the world, a fantastic machine. So here they can build ships almost 300m long! Just think the Marienkirche nave is 100m long and 40m wide, so you could fit more than five of them into this shed, three along and two across, sadly without the tower. Or all the *Backsteinkirchen* in Stralsund, churches instead of ships.

—But to get back to the ships ...

—The ships would be towed out to the wharfs, where they were finished off. You could stand here and see the great hulls being assembled. The ships were sometimes taller than the buildings in the town. *Erstaunlich!*

—And the money?

—The old Stralsund, of the Hansa league, used the money from the ships to build the churches, to create something for the town. Now where does the money go? To offshore owners, who knows where. But still, what a fine bold shed, a balance and contrast to the medieval buildings.

Sea creatures, ships, churches. German makes explicit the equation of church with ship: where English uses the Latin-mediated 'nave' (from *navis* or ship—hence navy) to describe the approach to the altar, the German word is *Schiff*. The Hansa ports were trading cities, operating fleets of ships as part of an early capitalist economic system, the ships conceived almost as floating extensions to the wharves and buildings of the city. The churches were also constructed as inverted ships, fixed in place, but reaching up vertically to heaven. It is in the extraordinary spaces of the timber roofs, above the actual naves, that the skill of the ship's carpenters can be seen, the ribbed ship's hull rotated vertically 180 degrees and raised up into the sky. These roof spaces above the brick vaulting are not normally seen by visitors to the church, but if one ascends by the spiral stairs set into the walls one emerges into a wondrous space, far bigger than expected, formed by the great inverted V of the roof trusses, and with a floor of convex shapes, the usually invisible topsides of the vaults below. These roof spaces are dimly lit, a hidden penumbral world between the light-filled churches and the actual sky. If the vaults below represent the sky, one has somehow penetrated into a location beyond the sky, almost like the backstage of a theatre, where the material construction of the illusion is revealed. There is a link between the forms of the ships sailing across the Baltic from one Hansa city to another, containing their valuable cargos of cloth and wool, sometimes also using as ballast the bricks used for the churches, and the forms of these church roofs, repeating from one city to another, always placed in the most prominent location, visible from all over the city as well as out at sea.

But the real elegance of the *Backsteinkirchen* lies in the immaculate construction of the vaults. These vaults have little structural effect—when they collapsed under the bombing, the walls of the churches remained in place. Their construction technique is simple and ingenious. The great roof was erected, over the walls and columns, giving the craftsmen shelter while they worked on the vaults. The four ribs between the columns, which usually form a square, and also the diagonal ribs dividing this square into four spaces, triangular in plan, were erected by means of movable scaffolding. Then, without the use of any internal scaffolding, the vaults were built up with bricks, usually in fishbone bond, the curvature of the bricks creating a cohesive structural shell that held everything in place. The undersides of the vaults were then usually painted white, or thinly plastered, to contrast with the pure brick of the columns. The ribs of the vaults appear to transmit the forces down through the columns to the ground, but actually it's the structure of the curved brick shells, pressing out on the ribs, which holds the vaults together. There is thus a *spielerisch*—playful—difference between what the vaults appear to do and what they are actually doing, the production of an architecture which deliberately defies the elegance of its own structural logic. The ribs are sometimes picked out in red or green to emphasise the structure of the lines. Occasionally the vaults use shapes other than the simple square, evolving into pentagons and more complex patterns, where the lines of the ribs seem to defy structural logic, so that the vaults appear to be weightless, to float like a great net of lines and planes above the interior. As one moves to the churches of the east, to Wismar and then to Rostock and Stralsund, the quality of the vaults becomes clearer, often as yet unrestored, sometimes slightly tatty, reflecting the light from the windows below, an archaic religious architecture which is also both direct and effective today. One hardly knows what to make of the extraordinary vaults of the Marienkirche in Stralsund, painted in a yellowing white, with ribs of pale blue and red, which make no attempt at showy engineering complexity, but which leave one with the impression of effortless, almost dreamy, architecture, created by the subdued, seemingly ever-changing linear pattern of the ribs and the curved planes of the vaults. Such an architecture produces a meditative, emotive, condition in the viewer, which is impossible to record through photography because it is a matter of a mental and emotional state, rather than a mechanical image.

Over the centuries the churches have of course deteriorated and required constant repair. The lime used in the mortar of the period allows *Backstein* buildings to slowly distort over time, so that the walls bend rather than break apart and collapse. The weakness of this mortar became a strength, allowing the brickwork to adapt to the forces around it. The massive *Backstein* city gate of Lübeck wobbles and bends, sinking irregularly according to the varying lack of firmness of its foundations in the muddy soil. In the Salzspeicher of Lübeck—the abode of the vampire—the gables have twisted and the foundations slipped so that the forms of the individual buildings stand at various angles to one another. The towers of the Lübeck Marienkirche are distinctly off vertical, and many of the columns in the church seem distinctly out of true.

A similar disregard for the orthogonal appears in many of the plans of the churches. As already mentioned, the grid of the columns of the Petrikirche gradually disintegrates at the east end, creating an irregular pattern which defies any conventional notion of a grid—whether by deliberate intention of the architects or through movement over time it is difficult to say. The floors of many of the churches, too, are allowed to slope or step down according to the original lie of the land, rather than attempting some ideal horizontal plane. In the Lübeck Marienkirche the floor slopes steeply downwards away from the choir, and in the Wismar Nikolaikirche it seems to move around almost like a gentle landscape. It appears as though the builders attempted some kind of perfection in those parts which belonged to the air, but were happy enough to allow the earthbound elements to take their own form.

Pause, stand in the side-aisle, under the wooden model of a warship, sails down, cannons pointing through the openings in the hull. An old man in the Wismar Nikolaikirche:

> —I was born here in Wismar and was a child at the time of the bombing. National Socialist gangsters destroyed our pride. The Allied bombers destroyed the churches, simply because they needed to dump their bombs on some German city, but they missed the Nikolaikirche. The socialists then tried to destroy the town by moving everyone out of the centre. Here in the Nikolaikirche nothing happened for almost half a century, everything remained the way it was. Since then there has been little money for the church, so no great restoration has been carried out. We have lived through extreme times when we might have expected to be obliterated, but have been saved by neglect and poverty.

Ah yes, the Wismar Nikolaikirche, a personal favourite. The church is pure *Backsteingotik*, built as one piece, brick exterior and interior. It sits beside a small undistinguished street, lined with cropped trees. The exterior is simple, almost plain, with warm red bricks for the walls and bright red roofs, a solid three-dimensional mass with the buttresses of the nave, also in the same brick, poking up through the roves of the aisles. The gable above the entrance is in blue glazed terracotta, laid out in a complex pattern, and the top of the tower is similarly picked out in a pattern of limestone, with diagonal patterns of brick. One might even see it as a distant ancestor of German brick architecture of the 1930s, undemonstrative, trusting in the materials of its construction, concerned with the play of forms, but somehow also mysterious. Inside, the nave is the highest in Germany in proportion to its width, its bright columns faceted to break down their volume, the vaults plain in white with red ribs. Placed in the squares of the plan of the church are various large objects including a relief in plain grey wood, several meters high, with almost surreal montages of naked women, foliage, symbolic objects of some cult whose meaning has long been forgotten. Hanging from the vaults in the side chapels are various models of ships, including the fully rigged three-master *Friedrich Franz* with its black hull, red below the waterline. Books, mostly leftovers from the time of the DDR, are piled up on timber shelves. The Nikolaikirche has a rough feel, everything is on display, there is no place for elegant deception. Even on a dull autumn afternoon, and in spite of the fact that the brick colour is rather dark, the light coming in through the windows of the aisles and the clerestory of the nave illuminates the space and dematerialises the weight of the bricks.

As to the characters in the *Backstein* story, they reach their final squares one by one—heaven, hell or some neutral location, as appropriate.

Murnau's Nosferatu vanishes, or rather evaporates with a certain decisive elegance. We see a window with the sunlight dawning on the gables of a mock-up of the Lübeck Salzspeicher. The vampire sucks the blood from Ellen, the beautiful woman of pure heart, who needs to sacrifice herself to defeat the evil one. He walks across the room, with his peculiar stiff movements, passes the window, is touched by the sunlight, turns and vanishes. A puff of smoke emerges from the floor. *Der Meister ... ist ... tot* reads the intertitle, but since the Meister has already long been one of the undead he can hardly die now.

But Nosferatu himself, of course, is by nature ever on the return. The undead have no easy means of moving on, but must repeat themselves in tireless cinematic remakes. Werner Herzog remade *Nosferatu* in 1979, with Klaus Kinski as the fiend and Bruno

Ganz as the narrator, Jonathan Harker. The socialist city authorities of Wismar declined to offer their city as a background for the film, so the rather un-German Delft stood in for Wisbourg. In Herzog's version, Harker also becomes a vampire and rides off in the last scene with the comment that he 'has things to do'—vampirism thus passing, following traditional Marxist tendencies, from the degenerate aristocracy to the bourgeois classes.

F W Murnau died in a road accident, in 1931, near Santa Barbara, in a car driven by his Filipino servant. His last film was *Tabu*, divided into two parts, *Paradise* and *Paradise Lost*.

Alfred Mahlau became a respected professor of fine art in Hamburg and died in 1967. The Mahlau font, based on his work for Lübeck marzipan wrappers, is named after him.

The painter Lothar Malskat died a natural death in 1978. He had lived contentedly just outside Lübeck, in Wulfsdorf, a hamlet near the river Trave, mainly inhabited by fishermen. The local paper announced in August 2011 that the Malskat house had burned down. A local resident claimed it was struck by a bolt of lightning.

Cortázar's *Rayuela* has no end, but as suits a novel which can be read in various ways it bounces forever back and forth between two final chapters, unwilling to decide how to resolve itself. We are left uncertain as to whether the main character dies or not.

Buddenbrooks ends with the family fortune completely lost and the great house sold. The daughter, Antonie, the last surviving Buddenbrook, wonders whether the family members may meet again in paradise.

Of the architect/builders of the Baltic *Backstein* only names remain, no personalities: Baumeister Johann Grote, Heinrich von Bremen, Hermann Münster, Hans Martens, Heinrich Plattensleger, Heidenreich Luckow, Peter Stolp. They follow on from one another as a chain, but are to be distinguished mainly by their remarkable architectural achievements.

Three ascents. First the 366 steps to the top of the tower of the St Marienkirche in Stralsund. From the platform, once the highest in the Baltic region, there is a view of the town, the sea and the flat lands of the island of Rügen to the north.

Then hop to the Petrikirche in Lübeck, with its modern white interior. Why climb the stairs—take the lift. Arrive finally at a small platform, high up in the tower, with windows open to the sky. Due to the uncertain Baltic weather this platform may be surrounded by clouds and drifting mist. But this time the weather is fine and clear. The visitor looks out over the red roofs of the town houses below, the banal suburbs, the countryside, the sea in the far distance to the north.

Finally, jump towns again, enter the tower of the Wismar Marienkirche, the only remaining part of that once great church. No lift here, but several flights of stairs through various rooms. At the top, just below the belfry, is a room with narrow vertical windows. From here one looks down at the marketplace and the baroque form of the city fountain, reprising the opening shot of Murnau's *Nosferatu*. One makes out the bay where the *Demeter* arrived, and just beyond it the long flat line of the Baltic coast. Ah, but time to move around to the other side of the tower, to look out to the south, to move on from the damp horizontals of the northern sea—and to go up into the mountains at last.

Olagaga in the Alps
Südtirol—Alto Adige

The train moves through the suburbs of Innsbruck, climbs up through the Austrian Alps and after an hour, around midday, arrives at the border on the Brenner Pass, once one of the more significant points in Europe, dividing the North and the lands reaching up to the Baltic from the South and the Mediterranean. The train pauses for a few minutes, but there is no control now. The formal border between Italy and Austria, for many years one of the most controversial in Europe, was removed in 1997, since both countries are within the European Union with its open borders. Lines of trucks still queue up to cross the pass amid a rather desultory collection of buildings, petrol stations, supermarkets, hotels, a few houses. The train begins to move through the mountains, now in Italy, with similar slopes, similar woods, similar buildings, similar cattle to the other side of the border.

The line is level at first, then descends into a long winding valley. In the train sit a small family, man, woman and daughter, a couple of years old. They chat away in some language, possibly Arabic, they eat some kind of rice and meat and pancakes, out of plastic boxes, the woman gives the daughter brightly coloured sweets. The daughter stands precariously on the metal shelf by the window and points at objects going past the window, exclaiming loudly in a language which sounds like childish nonsense, but which may mean something.

—Olagaga, olagaga. Ola ola ola.

Another woman, with a large number of bags and cases, sits opposite.

—Lei parla italiano?

There is a pause. The man is silent. The daughter waits. The mother speaks.

—Piccolo, piccolo ... no, ja, ein bissen, piccolo wir wohnen in Bozen.

—Ah, Bolzano, in Italia.

The daughter becomes very excited by something outside the window, she stands on the table and points and says the same word, ever louder, over and again:

—Olagaga, galala.

No one pays much attention. The mother looks out of the window, lost in thought, the sunshine is brighter here, and the train runs on though all those towns with double names: Sterzing–Vipiteno, Brixen–Bressanone, Klausen–Chiusa, signs of the double culture, where everything happens twice but in a slightly different way. The mountains are visible in the distance, two-dimensional forms hardly distinguished from the sky, their peaks brightly illuminated by the sun. When the train arrives in Bozen–Bolzano, we all walk together along the platform, carrying our baggage, and then through the underpass, illuminated by flickering fluorescent lamps, and we bid farewell to each other uncertainly in various languages.

A sunny day. Freiheitsstraße–Corso della Libertà, in a spacious arcade from the 1930s, with the feel of being in Milan or Turin. Avalon Officino del Gelo, small ice-cream bar. Neon ceiling lights, white and red in a geometrical zigzag pattern. Small frozen desserts in various bright colours, in paper cups. Short queue waiting

to be served. The man behind the counter waves his arms and talks very fast in Italian.
Woman, resident of Bozen–Bolzano:

—My grandfather came here from the Dolomites, to work in the transport system, he was a bus driver. Then he married my mother who was from here, but from further up the valley. My mother was a German-speaker but my grandfather's first language was Ladin. Of course not many people speak Ladin here in the town so we spoke it in the family as a secret language that nobody else could understand. My grandfather was born in 1919, just before the Italians took over, so really he was Austro-Hungarian though he always said he was just Ladin and that the Ladin people had been here long before the Austro-Hungarians, or the Italians, or anyone else. Well, now who cares, we shouldn't now worry too much about such things, just get on with our lives and making money. Ah yes, one Persia, with saffron and rosewater, and one Fior de Latte, in paper cups. Excellent.

The writer Claudio Magris, from Trieste, writes in his book *Microcosmi* of the many different peoples who have passed through Tirol:

> Carantanian Slavs, the Duke of Tassilo's Bavarians, Franks, Longobards, and before them remote peoples, Ligurians, Illyrians, Celts, Rhaeti and others who are pure names, Venosti, Saevantes, Laicianci, names that perhaps indicate the same peoples and their conflicts, their mingling, their destruction and their extinction ... there are borders running everywhere and one crosses them without realising: the ancient one between Rhaeticia and Noricum, the frontier between Bavarians and Alemanni, between Germans and Latins. All the Tirol is a frontier, dividing and uniting, the Brenner separates two states and yet is at the centre of a land that is felt to be a single entity.

In his book Magris describes how large areas of Northern Italy are composed of what he calls microcultures, existing within the dominant but often ineffective Italian state. He travels through the borderlands of Slovenia, Friuli, the lagoons, the mountains and of course Trieste itself. What one might in ignorance have simply assumed to be Northern Italy is inhabited by any number of intermingled ethnic groups, each still proudly maintaining its own identity. Magris loves these different cultures, sees them as beneficial, embodying an underlying individuality in an increasingly conformist monocultural world. The same applies to the neighbouring countries, Switzerland or Austria, where what seems to be a unified culture is also a collage of varying identities. Südtirol is one of these Italian microcultures, itself containing in turn a series of even smaller cultures, often hostile to one another in the past, now living peacefully but also slightly uneasily together. Magris considers it as both confused and inspired by its multiple identity, its writers 'Italian amongst the Germans and German amongst the Italians, eagerly awaiting the onslaught of the custodians of the homeland's memory, so as to be able to say, with ringing sincerity, that the pain is in not knowing to which world they belong.'

Bozen–Bolzano, like all other towns in Südtirol–Alto Adige, has two names, one German, one Italian. All its streets have also two names, in German and Italian. In theory these names are interchangeable and merely reflect the different languages, but also they have a political meaning. Bozen implies the town is German-speaking, Bolzano that it is Italian. Even which name comes first is a matter of linguistic orientation, implying main and subsidiary names. Occasionally a third language, Ladin, is added, but this is really only spoken in an eastern area of the province. In Ladin the town is Busan or sometimes, to confuse matters further, Bulsan. What is not in question is that Bozen–Bolzano was assessed by the newspaper *24 Ore Italia* as having the highest quality of life in all Italian cities—just as Südtirol–Alto Adige has been assessed as having the highest pro-capita income in the country.

All this is part of a history that tends to change according to who is telling the tale, when and why. Tirol was in medieval times an independent Alpine state belonging to the counts of Tirol, roughly the size of current Switzerland, stretching from the German border, south of Munich, across the Alps right down to just north of Verona, and from the Swiss canton of Grisons in the west to the Austrian province of Kärnten in the east. Its inhabitants spoke various languages, including German, Italian and Ladin, with innumerable barely mutually comprehensible dialects. Tirol had an identity as an Alpine culture—architecture, clothing, society, food—that it shared with its neighbours. In late medieval times it became part of the Hapsburg empire, where it remained, with various short interludes, until after the First World War. Between 1915 and 1918 fighting on the Alpine front, mainly in the mountains to the east, rather than on Tirol territory, left over 1.2 million dead. In 1920, with the break-up of the multi-ethnic Austro-Hungarian empire, Tirol was split up between Italy and Austria. The northern part, with its capital in Innsbruck, went to the new, and very fragile, republic of Austria. Below the Brenner Pass were formed two new provinces, both belonging to Italy, mainly German-speaking Südtirol–Alto Adige, capital Bozen–Bolzano, and Italian-speaking Trentino, capital Trento.

From Francesca Melandri's novel of a Südtirol family, *Eva dorme*:

> A joyful crowd saw off the first *Optanten*, pioneers of the new *Heimat*. Very blond children (chosen expressly for the colour of their hair) placed daisy chains on the heads of those leaving. The red, black and white of swastikas stood out against the deep blue sky, the whiteness of the glaciers, the dark gold of the larches in the fall.

The inhabitants of the new Italian province of Südtirol–Alto Adige would have preferred to remain with their fellow German-speakers to the north, and be part of Austria, or possibly even Germany, but the great power settlement cared little for their woes. In the 1920s the Italians began a process of Italianisation, which grew fiercer as the fascists under Mussolini took power and began to assert a largely invented Italian national identity. Towns and villages were renamed, mostly with translations from the original German, even family names were meant to be Italianised. The German language was strongly discouraged and was no longer taught in schools or used for government affairs. Mussolini encouraged large numbers of Italians to move to the province, mainly to the towns, to work in new industrial areas and live in new urban settlements. In 1938, in a dirty deal between Mussolini and the Hitler, the German-speaking inhabitants, who had been hoping their territory would join the Third Reich—perhaps a rather questionable desire—were given the option of integrating into Italian society or going into exile in some as yet undesignated place, yet to be Germanised, perhaps in Burgundy, or the Crimea, or further east in the Ukraine. The option was thus to become a German fascist somewhere else (an *Optant*) or an Italian fascist at home (*Dableiber*). Those who wanted to remain were castigated by Nazi politicians in words similar to those used to describe the Jews—'false Christians, old wives, egotists, whores, collaborators, Italian bastards, some with a few millions who gained their money through trickery ...' There was no option not to live in a fascist state. Many voted to move to Germany, fewer actually moved. This choice caused lasting divisions in the German-speaking population, each side claiming to be the true patriots, and accusing the other of being traitors. For a brief period in 1943–45, after the fall of Mussolini, Südtirol was a Nazi statelet, its Jews and dissidents removed to the camps and murdered, before returning to Italian control at the end of the war.

In the 1950s an independence movement gathered force, culminating in a mass demonstration in 1957, beneath Schloß Sigmundskron, led by the politician Silvius Magnano. After this, small militant groups, some linked to the nationalist hard-right in Austria, turned to terrorism to assert their claims. Italian monuments were bombed and on 19 June 1961, on the 'night of fire' (*Feuernacht*), large numbers of electricity pylons supplying power to Italian-owned industrial plants were blown up. At this stage, with the arrival of emergency troops, mass arrests, allegations of torture, Südtirol–Alto Adige appeared to be on a course towards civil war, paralleling other European autonomy movements such as those in Northern Ireland, the Basque country, Catalonia, Corsica. However, after extensive negotiations between Italy and Austria, a political compromise was reached in 1969, and the province was granted a gradually evolving autonomy. Initially, Trentino and Südtirol became a semi-autonomous province, but this was controversial as it gave a majority to the Italian speakers. In an agreement in 1972, language rights, schooling and a large measure of self-government were restored to Südtirol–Alto Adige. In

1995 Austria joined the EU and with the Schengen Agreement the border along the Brenner pass was dismantled. For the first time since 1920 there was freedom of travel between the two parts of former Tirol. In addition, all three parts of what had been Tirol, ie Italian Trentino and Südtirol–Alto Adige, together with Austrian Tirol, are now linked together to form a transnational entity, more cultural than administrative, with representation at the EU in Brussels.

Up in the Alps on the border between Austria and Italy, different groups of tourists judge the safety of an accessible sculpture:

> —Take care. If we all stand by the window, the weight will be too much and the whole thing will fall into the valley, into Italy.
>
> —It is designed by an engineer. It must be totally safe. But to be sure we'll stay here by the door, in Austria, while you go over to the window and look out.

Timmelsjoch pass, high in the Alps, beside the path running along the Austro-Italian border. A long, irregularly shaped concrete object, brown-grey in colour, cantilevered over the valley in what looks like a precarious way. The foundations are on the Austrian side, but half of the construction projects into Südtirol–Alto Adige. Visitors enter through a door in Austria, cross, rather anxiously, the invisible border within the interior space, gaze out through a window in Italy, looking out to the South. A little further along the path there are four other similar objects, two in Austria, two in Italy. Architect Werner Tscholl, born in the Vinschgau valley, in Latsch–Laces.

From almost a century of political and social strife, Südtirol–Alto Adige has emerged as a successful land, the richest province in Italy, and one of the richest in the EU. This wealth is based on agriculture, particularly fruit farms, wine, tourism, hydroelectricity and small environmental industries. Its problems, in particular the struggles between German- and Italian-speakers, have become an advantage, as it can profit from links to the richer parts of Italy, Austria and Germany—such as Milan, Innsbruck and Munich. All inhabitants now have to learn at least two languages in school, all government business is conducted in one of the three languages. There are certainly still autonomy-minded political groups, but the various political compromises have worked. The linguistic integration has proved so successful that various Ladin areas currently in the Veneto have voted to join Südtirol–Alto Adige. And indeed why not—who would not want to be part of a province with such natural advantages, an affluent easy-going mountain paradise, where there appear to be no great social issues to be resolved. The resulting smugness is perhaps just a little worrying—beautiful scenery, excellent cuisine, easy life creates a certain inward-looking self-satisfaction.

Standing on the complex double bridge for pedestrians, over the Talfer, beside the fine new Bozen–Bolzano museum of contemporary art, the Museion, a man, bearded, dressed in casual clothes, comments on Tirol languages:

—You've tried to be fair, I can see that. You've tried to include everyone and to be impartial. But you've completely forgotten Osttirol. It's where I come from. It's certainly the best part of Tirol with best mountains and the best cooking.

—Osttirol? You mean there is yet another Tirol?

—Of course. Osttirol is quite small, it is in Austria, it borders Südtirol north of Bruneck, and also the Veneto, but it does not have a border with Nordtirol, which is also in Austria.

—What language do you speak there?

—The Osttirolisch dialect of course. Or rather, dialects, for there are several.

Just above the Victory Arch in Bozen–Bolzano is the Via dei Combattenti–Frontkämpferstraße. In English something like partisan street. But who were these partisans—Italians fighting against fascism? Germans fighting against the Italian state? Fascists holding out against the advancing allies? Tirolers fighting against German fascists? On this bright Sunday morning the street seems quiet enough, not bothered by ideological details.

A small bar, in a 1960s-style building on Corso Italia, just up from the former Casa di Fascio. Two women, well dressed, smoking, one drinking an expresso, the other an aperitif of a dark brown colour, speaking Italian.

> —What do we think of these buildings? Why do you ask? Why ask us? Ask the waiter there, he studied architecture in the university, even though now he has gone straight and works in a bar. Aha, you're a foreigner, foreigners always ask questions, sometimes there are too many foreigners and too many questions. Well, these buildings were built by the fascists, a long time ago, the fascists built so much around here, and the buildings they put up were different from what had existed before. They were certainly misguided, but they gave to this very provincial town a certain style, a feeling of being part of a wider world. What happens in them now? There are lawyers and bureaucrats and politicians, as there always were, no not all of them good men and not all bad. Always the same. But here in the Plaza bar, it's Italy, the good things from Italy. Yes, I smoke too much, too much, too much.

Further down the Corso is a small church set back from the road. Chiesa Christo Re. It has a tall round tower and a brick facade. It appears to have been transported whole from a Tuscan hill village. The doors are locked. Some kids skateboard cheerfully around the small piazza.

A couple of streets away, by the river, lies Viale Venezia. Here the houses are pastel-coloured, yellow and pink, with overhanging roofs, decorated balconies and arched doorways. They also appear to have been transferred, this time from the Venetian lagoon, or perhaps some film set recreating the lagoon.

Up until the transfer of Südtirol to the Italian state, Bozen–Bolzano had been a small sleepy Hapsburg town, easy-going, charming, with some remarkable medieval churches, small streets, villas, the slightly retro Austro-Hungarian urban architecture of the nineteenth century. Mussolini and the fascist government decided to make an example of what the new owners of the land could achieve, to make the town clearly Italian, populated largely by Italians, living in an Italian way. It would become a showcase for the new fascist state. Today the town has more fascist-era buildings than any other city in Italy.

This ambitious enterprise raised the issue of just what Italian fascist architecture should look like. Should it represent the great historical past of Rome and of Italy, since the fascist government saw itself as restoring the power of the Roman empire and the glory of Italy? Should it attempt to recreate an Italian regional architecture, since no national style of architecture existed? Or should it be something new, relating to the architectural experiments being carried out in France and Germany, in the style the Italians came to call rationalism? The answer would somehow be a bit of everything, and evolved over two decades from the time the fascists took power in 1922 up to the last year of the regime in Südtirol, 1943—and beyond, for some of the larger projects were still being constructed in the 1950s. The effects of these decisions, and of the linking of certain kinds of modernism to Italian fascism, were to last much longer.

Some of the innovations were essentially cosmetic, making existing buildings look Italian. The main railway station facade, for instance, received a set of classical columns and two classical statues, dedicated to the female allegories of electricity and steam. The building that was to become the archaeology museum was deprived of its pointed roofs and gothic elements (some of which were restored in 1990 at the time of the arrival in the museum of Ötzi, the iceman). Other buildings were given grandiose classical entrances, columns, statues.

Much more ambitious was the urban planning to the west of the centre, across the river Talfer, in what had been the village of Gries. This was now planned as an Italian new town, effectively replacing the old centre with a contemporary urbanism. Urban competitions between Italian architects were held, grand projects were proposed, with avenues, squares, fine buildings. What was actually built was more modest but still in its own way impressive and surprisingly diverse.

Across the Talfer bridge was constructed the Monumento alla Vittoria, designed by Marcello Piacenti, leader of the classicist faction in the city, in the form of a classical Roman arch, but updated with sculptures of fascist symbols such as bundles of lictors, linking the new fascist power back to the Roman empire. On the facade an inscription includes the words '... from here we instruct the others in language, law and arts', making clear that a new force had arrived, the others being those whom the Romans had called barbarians, the Germanic tribes to the North, who would now have to learn a new language and new ways of living. The arch was inaugurated in 1928 by Victor Emmanuel III, in the presence of Il Duce and many fascist officials, all wearing fantasy military uniforms and with appropriate military ceremonies. It was both a memorial to Italians who had been executed by the Austrians during the First World War, and a celebration of the rather dubious victory of the Italian army in 1918, which resulted in the Italians annexing Südtirol. The arch is not particularly grandiose, seen against the scale of the mountains in the distance, and is a little tumbledown, parts currently fenced off with railings. Under the arch there is a gloomy basement that now hosts a permanent exhibition about Italian fascism, an uncertain warning about the evils of dictatorship that the arch was originally intended to celebrate—the arch remains to proclaim its message, the counter argument is hidden away. One might have expected the arch to be removed in the postwar years as a symbol of a rotten regime, and there were various attempts by separatists to blow it up. But Bozen–Bolzano has a majority of Italian speakers, for whom the arch is a sign of their right to be in Südtirol–Alto Adige, and of Bozen–Bolzano being an Italian town, so it remains. Even the proposal to change the name of the surrounding square from the antagonistic Piazza Vittoria–Siegesplatz to a neutral Piazza della Pace–Friedensplatz was decisively rejected in a referendum in 2002.

Sitting in the Piazza Quattro Novembre, a small square beside a rather elegant fascist era housing block. The sun shines, some women push prams, an old man sits on a bench reading the paper. It seems pleasantly Italian, calm, as though nothing has ever happened here. Woman in jeans and yellow raincoat:

> —My family came up here after the war, from the south. Life is much harder down there. My husband is also Italian. Here I have a job in the city administration, I am well enough off and we have a flat in the housing block. And I speak

both Italian and German quite well. But nobody seems to understand my German and when I go back down south they think I speak a strange Italian.

—Happiness?

—Yes, a kind of happiness. And confusion.

A man pulls up in a dark car, an Audi. He waits for a minute or so. Suddenly, with a brief wave, the woman gets into the car, which drives off.

Running south is the large traffic-filled Corso Italia–Italienallee. Here the fascist strategy grows beyond simply producing imitations of historical Italian architecture. The remarkable Piazza del Tribunale–Gerichtsplatz is squeezed between two massive stone buildings, originally the Casa Littoria, or Casa del Fascio, the headquarters of the fascist party, and the Tribunale, the law court, ie the two centres of power for the new state based on the fascist party and the rule of Italian law. The latter building was not completed until the mid-50s. The square itself is rather awkward, not large enough to accommodate the two massive buildings to the north and south, and is bounded to the west by village streets, as though it does not have the authority to assert itself on the surrounding area. The Casa del Fascio, which dates from 1938–42 and is by the architects Guido Pelizzari, Luis Plattner and Francesco Rossi, has a monumental, slightly convex facade, with a massive 35m-long frieze dedicated to the achievements of fascism, including the march on Rome and the conquest of Libya and Ethiopia. In the centre is a large bas relief of Il Duce himself, on horseback, one arm raised in salute, surrounded by figures in Roman dress, and the words *credere obeddire combattere*, believe obey fight. The general effect is of a widescreen cinema made in stone, crowded with large numbers of marching figures out of some epic 30s movie. In front of this massive relief is a long balcony, conceived as a platform from which the fascist leaders would speak to the loyal masses below.

The frieze, by the sculptor Hans Piffrader, who conveniently changed his first name to Giovanni and his style from Viennese modern to classical monumental, was not actually completed until well after the death of Il Duce. It thus serves as a belated memorial as well as a celebration. The square today, remodelled to accommodate an underground car park, feels rather empty, as though something happened but has now gone. A few bored *carabinieri* loiter, checking that no outrage to the spirit of the past takes place. For what is to be done with such a vast building dedicated to a regime which is now—largely, though by no means totally, since there are neo-fascist parties in the current Italian parliament—disgraced? The problem is similar to the one currently engaging various cities in the US and UK. What is to be done with sculptures that celebrate unacceptable historic events—slavery, empire—but which are still seen to have some kind of cultural value? Should we remove them and eradicate the past, or let them remain as artefacts that have become part of our cities? The question, difficult enough with an individual statue, becomes almost unsolvable with a 35m-long stone frieze. The resolution for the former Casa del Fascio has been to leave the frieze but alter the message. In front of the frieze, in neon letters designed by the artists Arnold Holzknecht and Michele Bernardi, is now inscribed:

> *Deguni ne à l dërt de ulghé*
> *Kein Mensch hat das Recht zu gehorchen*
> *Nessuno ha il diritto di obbedire*

'No one has the right to obey', in Ladin, German and Italian. The phrase is taken from Hannah Arendt, derived from the Königsberg philosopher Immanuel Kant—whose attitude to obedience to regimes was actually rather more nuanced. The new inscription, about which there has been considerable discussion, is intended to subvert the injunction to obey on the original freeze. No one can claim they have the right to carry out an order that may be considered unacceptable or immoral (as some of those who had followed fascist instructions later claimed); rather, obeying is an individual moral decision. The new inscription is ingenious, but like the anti-fascist exhibition in the basement of the Victory arch, the architecture remains more powerful than the attempt to negate its message.

Pause. Breathe in, and then out. Enough fascism. Enough of the past. Further down, in Via Roma. A small supermarket with a cluster of students outside, eating rolls and drinking from tins.

To the left of the supermarket, the vocational school, Scuola Professionale, as ever doubled, so Landesberufschule, 2005, architects Höller and Klotzner. Two long thin blocks of concrete and glass, with small rectangular windows, stretch back from the street, seeming to reach far into the distance, towards the mountains. The building is much larger than it appears from the street. The feel is modern, stylish, fresh, a little daunting. Some students are hanging around.

> —Yes, we like the building, though it is so long, it takes quite a while to get to the end, it feels like you're walking right out into the mountains. And there is a baseball court where we can practise in the evening. It's good because it has a feel of being new, there is too much old in Bolzano. Yes ,after graduating we want to leave here, perhaps go to Vienna, or to Milan or Venice, we are lucky to be both Italian and Austrian and to have lots of options.

At the bottom of the Via Roma, running along the river, are other less heavily loaded pieces of fascist architecture. To the east, in a network of streets named after Italian towns, Via Milano, Via Torino, Via Firenze and so on, is the last of the 1920s *case rusticale*, homes for the new arrivals from Italy, with gardens for growing vegetables that would allow them to maintain a relationship to the countryside while working in the factories.

Running west and back into town is the remarkable modernist lido by Ettore Sotsass and Willy Weyhenmeyer, with its long low buildings and extraordinary diving boards, a complete contrast to the political buildings already discussed. Sport and fitness were part of the message of the regime, but to be treated differently from politics. A little further up the Viale Trieste, which runs beside the river Eisak, is the Campo Sportivo Drusa (Drusus being a Roman general known for beating the German tribes), a stadium with a slightly surreal baroque archway leading to the grounds of the city's football team (FC Südtirol, firmly in the third league, kit colour white at home, red away, supported mostly by the Italians rather than the Tirolers, who are more interested in winter sports). And just beyond lies the elegant Pompeian red rotunda of the Casa del Giovane, its circular forms wrapping around one another, built for the encouragement of fascist youth and now, with a contemporary glazed extension, the seat of the European Academy, with an excellent bar. This group of buildings is unexpected. Apart from the football arch they have nothing of the retro-classicism of the Victory Arch or the Casa del Fascio; they still feel fresh and contemporary.

Finally, the Drusus bridge crosses the river Talfer, now shorn of now of its original heroic bundles of lictors surmounted by grumpy eagles, and thus a bit forlorn. An undated photograph by the Meran photographer Leo Bährendt, of whom more later, shows the bridge still with its eagles and lictors, with the mountains as ever in the background. A couple of pedestrians, dwarfed by the size of the birds, stand and chat in the road since clearly no traffic is passing by. The effect is once again of the remnants of some film set, perhaps of some low budget imperial sci-fi.

There are in Bozen–Bolzano many other interesting buildings from the fascist period, too many to list. They have long been absorbed into the fabric of the city. Stand on the Drusus bridge and look to the north along the Tafler river. It's easy enough to see the left bank as 1920s and 1930s Italian, the right as Hapsburg. The Italian and Hapsburg parts contrast, and even the various buildings by the fascists are in themselves a surreal mix, but out of these cultures emerges something unexpected, an uneasy composite. The new contemporary buildings of Bozen–Bolzano, such as the concrete and glass Museion gallery for contemporary art, visible to the right beside the river, and the long cool blocks of the Scuola Professionale Provinciale, just out of sight to the left, belong more to the inheritance of the rationalist buildings of the 1930s, such as the lido and the circular youth centre, than to any traditional culture of Südtirol. This culture, which appears at first to the visitor as affluent and calm, is really multiple, often contradictory, the various elements sitting happily enough together. The land needs this diversity, in order to move on, within its wonderful seemingly never-changing landscapes, where there is always the backdrop of the mountains, which appear to have always existed, but which of course are also in a state of gradual evolution, gradually revealing what has been concealed for millennia.

Along the outside of the archaeological museum a queue of several hundred people, including many families. On the other side, beside the river, a meeting of owners of classic sports cars. Fiat 124 Spider, orange, monocoque, rear drive, mid-1960s. Lancia Flaminia Super Sport Zagato, coupé, red, late 1960s. Chevrolet Corvette C2, pinkish red, cabriolet, mid-1960s. Gentle sounds of high-performance engines revving up.

On the walls of the archaeological museum a poster advertising an exhibition about Max Valier, born Bozen 1895, who became a pioneer of rocketry and author of *Der Vorstoß in den Weltraum* (*The Advance into Space*) 1923, proposing interplanetary flight. He worked in Germany on rocket-propelled cars, and in 1930 performed a test drive of the first liquid-fuelled rocket-propelled car, for the Opel company. He died shortly afterwards in a laboratory explosion. A small astronomical observatory in the Eggental–Val d'Ega to the east of Bozen–Bolzano is named after him.

Two children waiting by the side of the road.

> —The ice man, he had so many weapons, daggers and knives and arrows. He was wild. He could beat anyone.
>
> —But in the end he died. Somebody killed him. Nobody knows who.

Fire and ice. Rockets and glaciers. The Italian writer Mario Rigoni Stern, from Asiago in the Veneto, is author of many books about living in the mountains in northern Italy and of an extraordinary account of his experiences on the frozen Russian front, *Il sergente nella neve* (1953). He speaks about the iceman in the Trieste journalist Paulo Rumiz's book on the Italian mountains, *La leggenda dei monti naviganti*. Rigoni Stern considers the iceman as a contemporary, but with skills that have today almost disappeared:

> —You know I often think about Ötzi, the man from Similaun. Go and see him, I have been several times. I speak to him and he speaks to me. He is a modern man, like us, but much shorter, and more capable of getting by on a little.
>
> —Did he tell you something?
>
> —He made a long discourse, that man there. To understand him it is necessary to be alone with him ...

> and when you are alone, listen to what he says and pay attention to the things he has with him. His equipment is a masterwork. Shoes, arrows, shirt, the waterproof coat of straw from the marshes, the hunter's weapons. You see how he set up his bivouac, he protected himself from the cold ... and the wound in his back, you could write a novel about that ... why in the back? Why there? Why so far from the valley? Was he followed? Vendetta? War? A mistake while hunting? And the fire, everything necessary for the fire in his bag. A flint and dry tinder to light the twigs, the basic fuel for the fire of Prometheus. Tell me, who today knows how to light a fire in a wood in the rain? Almost nobody. You know if I didn't know how to light a fire I would be dead.

The most celebrated inhabitant of Südtirol is also one of the oldest, the man known as Ötzi, the iceman, born some 5,300 years ago. The mummified body of Ötzi was found by chance by hikers in September 1991, in Tisenjoch near the Similaun glacier in the Ötztal, and a mere 100m on the Italian side of the border with Austria. The body was lying in a shallow ravine and was revealed by the melting snow. He was still dressed in the clothes in which he had died. The age of the body was at first unknown, he was presumed to be a contemporary mountaineer. Rather crudely dug out of the ice with pneumatic drills, he was transported to the University Clinic in Innsbruck for examination, along with the remains of the remarkable grass coat and the leather jacket and shoes, and his bag containing various possessions. It was soon revealed that the mummy was actually from about 3300 BCE, from the period known as the Chalcolithic, the Copper Age.

Whatever the troubles that led to his violent death on the Alpine pass, his arrival in Innsbruck marked the beginning of Ötzi's second period of suffering. He was placed in a chamber with low-level lighting, at minus 6 degrees and 100 per cent air humidity—cold dark damp, imitating the conditions under which he had been preserved by nature. He was repeatedly thawed out for examination and then refrozen. Every centimetre of his corpse was examined using the most advanced techniques of contemporary science—radiology, computed tomography, endoscopy, microbiology, genetic investigation. He was cut, sawed, drilled, trepanned, investigated from every angle. His body became, as Walter Leitner, director of the Innsbruck Institute for Archaeology, has written, a Stone Age advent calendar, covered with small openings leading into his interior. It turned out that he was some 40 years old, 1.60m tall, had spent his youth in the Eisaktal near Brixen, and later lived in the Vinschgau in the upper Eschtal, below which he met his death. His DNA reveals that he is not related to the present inhabitants of northern Italy; his people must have been exterminated or driven out by the waves of other peoples who arrived later. Ten years after his discovery, a stone arrowhead was found in his shoulder, the shaft long broken off; he had been killed by a close-up shot from behind. The archaeological investigation also became a murder mystery, but the reasons for his killing—war, private quarrel, power struggle—will never be known. And even if the techniques of contemporary science have extracted every piece of information about the mummy, we still know little about the man himself, and fill in the vacuum with imagination and desire to make him rather like ourselves.

In 1998 the body was moved to Bozen–Bolzano, a ceremonial transfer from Austria to Italy, in a convoy accompanied by police cars and a helicopter. The iceman was welcomed by a large crowd in Bozen–Bolzano. His new residence was on the first floor of the archaeology museum in MuseumStraße, again in a special chamber with similar conditions to Innsbruck, lying on a large set of scales that recorded any weight loss, the main fear being that the mummy might dry out and disintegrate. Visitors, well over a quarter of a million a year on average, queue up for several hours to get a glimpse of the mummy through a small window. What they see is a definitively dead figure, brown-coloured, lying on his back, the left arm reaching out across his body, the right arm slightly stretched out, in an unnatural pose. However the museum has created a full-size version of Ötzi nearby that shows how he might have been when he lived, standing upright, bearded and longhaired, bear-chested, clutching his long bow, in action pose, an ageing but athletic figure, perhaps a new-age mountaineer, an idealised, very masculine Südtiroler, the kind of man one might meet on the mountain pass today. This figure, with its beard and long hair, bears even a resemblance to the other heroic masculine figure of the province, Reiner Messner, champion mountaineer and founder of the six Messner Mountain Museums.

The fame of the iceman has spread well beyond Südtirol. He features in tourist brochures, and also advertisements for refrigerators, ice shoes, drinks and sweets. Three-dimensional versions of his body and possessions have been created in many archaeological museums. A 4m stone pyramid now marks the place where his body lay in the Tisenjoch, regular groups of pilgrims visit the site. Tales of visions of the iceman and claims to be his reincarnation clutter the internet, he has received various offers of marriage but as yet has given no reply.

The iceman has become an important component of the local economy of Bozen–Bolzano, bringing in the tourists, who of course then spend their money in the restaurants and hotels. In 2019 proposals were made by an Austrian firm to create a new home for Ötzi on the Virgl mountain just south of the city. They envisaged the construction of a new cable car up to mountain, leading to a complete new museum based around the iceman, with a large shopping centre alongside it. An architectural competition for star architects was won by the Norwegian firm Snøhetta, who proposed a ring-shaped cable car station, a large piazza and various late-modernist buildings. The iceman himself would be provided with new improved accommodation and all the necessary technical support. The iceman has clearly grown too important for the city and now needs his own piece of exhibitionist architecture on his own mountain. The scheme is opposed by a substantial portion of the locals, who don't want to lose their star attraction.

The strange and unlikely rise of the iceman stretches from an ancient corpse covered in snow lying in a ditch on a mountain pass, to a contemporary figure subjected to the most modern scientific techniques, who inspires both dreams and visions of the distant past and who can also provide motivation for large architectural compositions and considerable investments. As temperatures continue to grow warmer, as glaciers and snow retreat from the mountains, every year brings the discovery of caves and shelters full of objects, of the bodies of First World War soldiers or long-lost mountaineers and walkers. One might wonder what, or who else, might emerge from the Alpine passes.

But there are other versions of the distant past, which is always open to reinvention. In her book *Die Frauen aus Fanis* (1992, produced with a parallel set of illustrations by the artist Markus Vallazza), Anita Pichler writes of the myths of the early female inhabitants of the Dolomites, half-human, half-goddess:

> The first people were of stone. They were called Croderes, those born on the rock, they sat hard on the earth and over the water. With their ice-hair they caressed the wind and with their feet pushed the rivers, now here now there, from their bed. Tanna was the queen of the Croderes. Her head stretched up towards the sun, until it warmed her; her ice-hair melted and flowed, dug valleys in the earth. Grass sprouted and flowers.

Further back. More fire, more ice. Certainly no men. Anita Pichler was born in 1948 in a small village near Meran–Merano, lived for varying periods in Trieste, Berlin and Vienna, and died at the age of 49 in Bozen–Bolzano. Pichler is often presented as a counterbalance to the conservative male-orientated culture of Südtirol, a female voice, lighter, more experimental, open to a more complex version of the province, concerned with both the visible and the invisible. The story of Ötzi is male and he has been integrated into the male history of the province. The legends Pichler recounts of the women of Fanis are from a time even more distant than that of the iceman and they are set in the territory of the Ladins, in the south of the region, which is very different to the Alpine passes to the north. Here, the mountain valleys are closed, difficult to cross, allowing Ladinian culture—the remnants of a much larger culture that once spread across north Italy—to survive by being hidden away. Their legends were published in the early twentieth century by the folklorist Karl Felix Wolff, who collected them by speaking to the local people, just as the Brothers Grimm did in Germany. There is no fixed form to the stories. Anita Pichler treated them as fragments of a culture that has now evolved and moved on, tales of a time before time, remains of a matriarchal society. She writes of Tanna, who emerged when people were stones; Moltina, who grew up and could speak to animals; Samblama, a winter goddess; Molta, a water spirit. Pichler was not interested in these tales as any kind of version of the world that evolved into what we now believe, but rather as the creation of a shifting and undefined female environment of creatures that emerged from nature but were somehow pre-human, still linked to the time of creation. It is not necessary to choose between the scientific version of the earliest times and this freer, poetic version; both can co-exist. As Pichler wrote:

> *Fanis* is a possible story, a possible version of the beginning. The stories from *Fanis* concern a knowledge that remains lost, whose truth we don't grasp, which needs no faith. One cannot believe in these stories ... nothing in them can be proven, but in all of them we can glimpse something true: true as hunger, thirst and food, as water and fear, as love and rejection, as the time which comes and comes and then will be gone.

Three ascents by cable car, in different locations around Bozen–Bolzano.

First ascent. In the Kohlern–Colle cable car, a genial old man in a rather well-worn suit:

> —I have worked all my life in the town. I came here in the 1950s, from Milan, after the war, when times were difficult all over Italy, and I worked for many years in the town hall as a civil servant. Now I live alone in my flat, it is comfortable, no one disturbs me. I like to come up here in the cable car in the evening, up out of the town into the beginning of the mountains, when it is quiet. I stay a while, drink a beer with friends and then I return.

Second ascent. In the Oberbozen–Soprabolzano cable car, travelling over several kilometres, as the light begins to fade. The car rises up and down, moving in and out of the shadow of the mountains. Two women, in their thirties, with a large suitcase, take photos of the landscape with their mobile phones:

> —Cable cars and hotels. That's why we're here. Like birds. We take the cable car, we see the beauty of the land,

we go to the hotel, but the cable car is best. We are from (… incomprehensible …).

Third ascent. From the window one can see the fields, the steep slope down, the station of the Jenesien cable car and then the cables leading down the slope. A woman around 40 years old, owner of the restaurant in Jenesien:

—I come from a family of five sisters, and one brother. Yes, that's a reasonable size family, our grandfather founded the hotel, then he left it to his daughter, our mother. And now we sisters run it, well actually just the two of us, no, we have mainly female cooks and even one who sings, no men are involved. Yes, we are a German-speaking family, most people here in the countryside are German-speaking. In the town below, in Bozen, there are mostly Italian-speakers, but really now there only a few problems, not like a while ago, not like the years when there were many arguments. What do we cook? A mixture of German and Italian food, always according to the seasons. We have meat from our farm, from our own foals, cattle, pigs. Dumplings and risotto with sage and pears. Asparagus in springtime. At Advent, chestnuts, sweet pastries. Herbs and vegetables we pick from the garden outside. Wine from our vineyard, with a slight mineral taste. I really don't know what more anyone might need. You see, here it's a kind of paradise, all run by us women.

A path through the woods leads steeply upwards, over small steams, often appearing to expire, dividing, turning back on itself, then continuing. It leads to some open meadows, grass a very lucid green, some cows, their bodies a pale grey, their heads black, some standing some lying. Ah, the cows, you cannot have Südtirol without cows. As ever in the distance, large mountains, the peaks, and below them vast areas of bare rock. The path of the cable car is just visible, the cabins swaying slowly across the landscape. Just here there is a large three-storey barn, with a pitched roof. Its timber construction is rural but immaculate: the front of dark brown wood, a long balcony on the first floor, the second floor partly open with timber grills. The side however is divided into three bays by the timber frame, the wall plastered, with three windows, and with a pair of small doors, unpainted and ragged. On the ground floor is a wide concrete ramp leading up into the interior. This construction appears to be part farmhouse, part barn, with some small living area along the side. The building is both elegant and rundown. Like the cows and the mountains, it is all very much how one might expect a Tirol building to appear. Seeing it here creates a feeling of happiness, an ease, an expectation fulfilled. Beside the building a young man is stacking hay with a long fork, he waves in a vague greeting.

Francesca Melandri again, in her novel *Eva dorme*:

> The doors closed behind them, the large wheels continued to turn with the roar of a furnace, there was a sudden increase in speed, almost a change of state, the cabin got off the ground ... when the cable passed through the small wheels of the pylons it produced for a few seconds a metallic screech which made the silence that followed even more intense. It was a silence reserved for the two of them. Gerda looked up at Hannes. This was the moment he seemed to be waiting for: he bent over her and kissed her.

Cable cars cross the landscape of Südtirol, providing easy access to the mountains from locations much lower down. The construction of the cable car systems was linked to the spread of tourism, particularly after the Second World War. Construct a cable car and an otherwise inaccessible location becomes more valuable, a good place to build a hotel or a restaurant.

The landscape of Südtirol–Alto Adige is a complex three-dimensional topography of mountains and valleys. Places that seem near on the map can in practice be far apart. The valleys, often former glacier beds, are farmed intensively. The line between these flat valleys and the slopes of the mountains is set out exactly, the houses run up to the edge of the mountains, then stop as the land rises and becomes inaccessible. But then there are also castles and other buildings, perched on top of small peaks, today appearing fanciful and almost absurd, but placed there for purely pragmatic reasons, defence and control. Today it is hard to look at the mountains, the valleys, the meadows, the glaciers, without seeing them as supremely aesthetic, inevitably picturesque. During the nineteenth century, as a romantic notion of the mountains developed, Südtirol–Alto Adige became a place to be visited for a certain kind of experience, a process which began slowly, proceeded at varying speeds, and has now resulted in the entire land being a location for mass tourism. The cable cars also provided a new way of looking at the landscape. As the visitor is slowly pulled up into the sky, above the tree line, they can see horizontally across the fields and woods, but also down, as though looking at a model of a landscape, viewing the roofs of the houses, the patterns of the tracks, the backs of the cows. Travelling in the cable car is like travelling in a balloon, the movement is slow and smooth, rather mysterious, with no sense of danger.

The idea of Tirol as part of popular visual culture, to be seen from a particular point of view, developed along with the spread of the cable car, aided by photography. While the cable car makes the mountains accessible to tourists, photography allows them to take away a memory of their experience. In the process, the views of specific locations become defined, become fixed and stylised. The visitors become part of the image, an inevitable part of the landscape they have come to see.

Some of the earliest photographers, in the 1860s, set up in Meran, to the north of Bozen, at the time a prime resort for Europeans of all classes wanting an experience of the Alps. Meran had 380 visitors in 1850, 9,000 by 1885, 40,000 by 1914 (today 1,150,000). Among the photographers with their large-format cameras and boxes of glass plates, which needed to be carried by horse or donkey, were Giovanni Battista Uterveger from Trentino, Anton Gratl from Innsbruck, Bernhard Johannes from Meran itself. These photographers responded to the increasing number of visitors, setting up studios selling original prints and then, increasingly, postcards. With their photos of folk wearing *Tracht*, mountain views, folk working in the fields, they created an image of Südtirol not just as it was but also as it should be, and as it should remain.

The most interesting of a later generation—or perhaps the one who had the good luck that a large archive of his work survived into the 1960s in a shop run by his niece—was Leo Bährendt

(1876–1957), originally from Marienwerder in Prussia. Leo had at first wanted to be a landscape painter but would follow the tradition of setting up as a photographer in Meran, together with his brother. Portraits taken by his brother show a stocky man dressed in knickerbockers, accompanied by his dog Chessy, standing by the roadside before his box-camera, mounted on a tripod. His open-topped car is parked nearby. The Bährendt brothers' photographs, mostly taken in the 1920s and 1930s, were particularly linked to tourism. Images of landscapes, mountains, castles and hotels usually feature a diminutive figure in the foreground, often leaning on a walking stick, gazing at the view. Increasingly, vehicles appear, first coaches pulled by horses, then large open-top touring vehicles, their passengers dressed up in special touring clothing and fashionable hats, often being admired by local kids. There are also images of the cable cars, the Kohlen–Colle system near Bozen–Bolzano as well as the system near Cortina d'Ampesso in the Dolomites. Judging by the angle of view, Bährendt took photographs from inside the cable cars as well. He also used a balloon for aerial photography. Bährendt produced wonderful images of Tirolers wearing *Tracht*, the men in dark suits and soft felt hats with tassels, the women in long white dresses with extraordinary floral constructions on their heads. A vast white horse pulls a highly decorated Christmas sleigh, occupied by a man and woman in elaborate costumes. An old man, with a white beard and wearing a conical hat, smoking a bizarre pipe, stares out at us, surprised and a little angry. This is almost a self-creating world, combining the reality of the past, when such clothing was normal, with a fantasy of how such figures could exist in the very different time of the present. Bährendt set up his studio in Freiheitsstraße to produce these images in almost industrial quantities. There were two large enlargers, running on tracks, for the large-format images, two other devices turning out the smaller images, lead developing trays, racks for drying the paper, and printers for printing the details on the reverse side. The studio also processed the films of amateur photographers, developing and printing overnight.

The division between the local world and the exterior was—and to some extent still remains—clear. Südtirol was ultra-conservative with a well-defined identity, which the increase in mass tourism threatened, both by introducing foreign customs and then by appropriating the very image of the landscape and the people. The historian Claus Gatterer, originally from Sexten in the east of the province, wrote:

> We children were at that time cocooned in our own world, which, I think today, seemed not really part of the outside world. Everything was simple, modest, ordered. Everything had its sense, every day its procedure, every week its order, year in year out. It would be difficult to say whether the sequence of weeks and months were decided more by centuries-old customs, or the immutability of the seasons prescribed them, as the final law of sun, rain, snow and ice ruled over everything.

Among Bährendt's photos are images of the many large hotels that were being constructed at the time. These buildings exist within an architectural taxonomy of their own. The long horizontal Grand Hotel Penegal, with its medieval turrets, the Hotel Auffinger and Hotel Bellevue, both in Meran, both classically stodgy, and the massive Hotel Belle Epoque in Karersee, southeast of Bozen, with its 500 beds, ballrooms and saunas, a meeting place for the wealthy of Europe, a Tirolean version of Wes Anderson's cinematic Grand Budapest Hotel. These vast hotels appear to be wayward descendants of the two previous large-scale Tirol building types, the monastery and the castle, placed in isolated locations, now adapted for commerce rather than prayer or defence. But their architecture has deliberately little to do with any local tradition; they are mostly simply large and brash and could be any grand tourist location of the period.

It was in the Belle Epoque that the Berlin-born actress Leni Riefenstahl made an early dramatic appearance, seducing the film director Arnold Frank, well known at the time for his rather macho mountaineering films, into making her first cinematic success, the 1927 *Das Große Sprung*, in which she plays a goatherd who swims lightly clad across the freezing Karersee and climbs a remarkably phallic mountain pinnacle barefoot to impress her tourist lover.

A few years later in *Das Blaue Licht*, filmed just north of Bozen, Riefenstahl would play another mysterious Tirol woman, inhabiting a mountain cave full of blue crystals. Such roles as adventurous if hardly believable women, combining peasant simplicity and bravura, sexy but not vampish, uncorrupted by the modern world—a slightly wayward model for what would later be projected as the Aryan female—were the first steps towards Riefenstahl's career as a celebrated Nazi filmmaker.

Walking in a meadow beside the Talfer. Conversation with Samanta Martens, resident of Bozen and speaker of both Italian and German:

> —How to think of these strange films about the women of Tirol. They are quite crazy women, who live a life outside the normal, wild, passionate, sexy. So, they are to be admired. They are not like the boring men in their old-fashioned clothes and their silly hats, always off wandering in the mountains. But they are hardly real. And also they tend to be early fascists, harbingers of a vile regime that treated women only as creatures for giving birth. Nothing here is so simple, it's not a simple case of good or bad. If I look at the films of Riefenstahl I feel both repelled and attracted.
>
> —And you?
>
> —Aha. Well, I live a quiet life.

Very different from these grand hotels, and also recorded by Bährendt, is the Sporthotel Valmartello Paradiso del Cevedale–Ortlergebiet, more simply Hotel Paradiso. Val Martello is to the west of Meran, one of the smaller valleys leading south off the Vinschtal. Bährendt shows the hotel in a simple shot, taken in winter, a five-storey building with an unusual curved facade, six horizontal balconies and an overhanging roof. The hotel is on a much more modest scale to those just mentioned. Only one figure is visible, a man dusting off his skis; other skis are stacked up against the facade.

The designer of the hotel was the Milanese architect and industrial designer Gio Ponti, later renowned for many buildings both in Italy and around the world, including the Pirelli Tower in Milan, and as editor of the influential *Domus* magazine. In the 1920s and 1930s Ponti's projects were often carried out for the fascist government, but as part of the modernist grouping, looking out towards what was happening elsewhere in Europe, rather than the retro-nationalistic style often used in fascist constructions. In the early 1930s Ponti was involved in a scheme to build an ambitious cable car system reaching through the southern Dolomites, linking Cortina on the border of the Veneto to Bozen–Bolzano, some 45km away. This cable car system would connect a series of new hotels placed in remote locations, and would also bind Südtirol–Alto Adige more clearly to Italy. The hotels would mostly be very simple places for walkers and for winter sports. There would be four types, with 22, 32, 44 and 50 rooms. The cable car system proved too ambitious and was never built, but the idea of the simple hotels in remote locations remained.

The Hotel Paradiso was a spin-off from the cable car project, with 100 rooms of various types. It was financed by the Italian Fascist Party, as a colonial enterprise to gain a foothold in the otherwise firmly Germanic countryside—Martell is today one of the few communes listed today as being 100 per cent German-speaking. Bährendt took other shots of the Martell area, showing tumbledown houses, with pitched roofs and timber outhouses, occupied by locals dressed in actual peasant costume and surrounded by large numbers of children.

This choice of location of the hotel was hardly pragmatic. The site was magnificent, not far from what had been the Italian border, with stunning views of the glaciers of Monte Venezia, but very remote and difficult to access, and with no cable car. Martell at the time had no paved road linking it back to the main valley, and it was 20km from the nearest railway station. Even when a road was constructed it was often blocked by snow and guests had to be transported on sledges (later it was even proposed to bring them in by helicopter). The construction of the hotel involved transporting building materials, and skilled workers, great distances. A strong element of fantasy lies behind the entire proposition, building a luxurious and specifically Italian project, for the most part visited by fascist party officials, financiers and businessmen, in an area which up to then had been inhabited only by German-speaking country folk. The construction of the hotel was opposed by the local population as purely suiting the Italians and not in keeping with the traditional building style of the area, but without success. The locals ended up carrying bags, cleaning rooms, piling up wood for the stoves for tourists who came, for the most part, from Italy.

However Ponti's hotel has considerable style and he was genuinely attempting to find a way of building in the mountains that was contemporary but not pretentious and irrelevant, which paid some attention to local tradition but was not either a rustic-style house or a Hapsburg recreation. The curved facade is elegant: the windows with the shutters, the long balconies, the ground level with its piles of timber and stacks of ski equipment, even the overhanging roof, all relate to local buildings, but reinterpreted. Inside, the floors were divided into the larger, more expensive rooms to the left and the smaller, cheaper rooms to the right, but this is hardly revealed on the facade.

Ponti was particularly interested in the use of colour. The facade was originally painted light green, relating to the woods, the snow and the sky, with the shutters in red forming an abstract pattern. While the rooms were very similar, as is typical in a hotel, they were each painted an individual colour, with the bedclothes and curtains in matching colours. The interlinking public rooms on the first floor were decorated with a complex design of contrasting colours, emphasising the views across the rooms. The rooms were carefully divided up for different three types of guest—those who were staying for a while, tourists, and day visitors—reflecting the class system of tourism of the period. The hotel accommodated a hair saloon, a sauna, a massage room, a post office, reading areas with English-style fireplaces, two kinds of restaurant. None of the rooms were particularly luxurious, with a simple style and furniture designed by Ponti in a modernist version of traditional Alpine furniture. All the rooms on the main facade received direct sunshine, and on the first floor a long terrace provided ample space for visitors to lounge in the sunshine, looking out to the south at the surrounding mountains.

The hotel had a short active lifespan. With the advent of the Second World War and Italy's alliance with the Nazis, tourism came to a sudden halt. In 1943, as the Italian army collapsed and the Germans assumed control of Südtirol–Alto Adige, the hotel became first an espionage centre—but spying on what is unclear—then a place of recuperation for military personnel, including the SS battalion Brandenburg, living in style while the war staggered to its end. In 1952 it was sold to a Venetian businessman who added two storeys and various other extensions and painted the facade an unsuitable Venetian red. But the venture was not a success and it was sold on to a Meran brewery firm, but never reopened. Today it is largely a ruin, beyond repair.

Paradiso del Cevedale, a fascinating documentary film by the director Carmen Tartarotti, born in Latsch near Martell, was made in 1993, long after the hotel closed, and shows the difference between the hotel guests and the local inhabitants, speaking in Italian, German and the local dialect. Voiceovers of those who actually experienced the hotel describe the life there, but the images show the ruin of the hotel and the local inhabitants, in their traditional farms, looking after their animals, growing their fruit and vegetables, continuing with lives that appear little different from 50 years before.

Tartarotti wrote of her film:

> My films neither wish to inform nor to teach, but to make something visible. When I watch a film, I wish to see and recognise something that I have not so far seen or recognised. That is uplifting.

And in a recent email:

> In my films I have always engaged with the land and its people and with their particular mix of *Frömmigkeit, Bodenständigkeit, Eigenwilligkeit und Autonomie* (piety, earthiness, individuality and autonomy)

Yes, there is a special quality to the land and the people. But somehow one has to look past what is already so well known to see what lies beyond it. Those four qualities can be positive, but they also have negative aspects. In Südtirol–Alto Adige everything has extreme surface charm, the mountains, the landscapes, the skies, even the people. It appears to be a land without problems. One is always confronted with the easily visible, and these qualities may be part of the essence of the place, but one has to scuttle sideways, to make jumps to find something more.

Is there any functioning Südtirol hotel that has the style and architectural quality of the Sporthotel Paradiso? Most of the province's newer hotels aspire to little more than a resemblance to pseudo-Alpine chalets or farmhouses. But down south of Bozen, on the way to Trentino, beside the Kalterersee, is the Ambach Seehotel (1973) by the Brixen architect Othmar Barth. Barth was the son of a joiner, from whom he learned a love of materials and of the way they are assembled. He studied in Graz, worked for a while in Rome and designed the late modernist Cusanus Akademie (1962), quiet, elegant, minimalist, with reinforced concrete frame and brick infill. He was invited to design the Ambach hotel by the owners of the site, the Ambach-Maran family, whose descendants still own the hotel today. The three-storey hotel sits near the lake, the mountains descend steeply nearby. The plan of the hotel is based around a long spine wall, and then two curves, one each side, the one in the front bounded by a curved wall containing the guestrooms, each a little different, and the other behind mainly service rooms. At the southern end of the spine is a triangular restaurant. In the interior another set of irregular curves define the corridor space. The geometry of the plan has a natural harmony, the curves and straight lines balance and remain in tension with one another. The curve of the front facade is broken up by the balconies and smaller projecting elements, so that the light is refracted both by the gradually changing orientation of the curve, and then also by the planes of the projecting elements. The interior spaces are very simple, much smaller than one assumes from photos, almost cramped—flamboyant architecture on a rather restricted budget—equipped with chairs and sofas by fashionable Italian designers.

The Seehotel was much criticised at the time of construction, seen as inappropriate to Südtirol, and compared to a sinking ship. It is full of contrasts, grand and diminutive, smooth and awkward, a potential film set for one of those hotel movies with stylish people, where nothing much happens. Paradiso, in splendid isolation on the upper slopes of the Martell valley, was always rougher, edgier. Down here the landscape is carefully choreographed, the hay tied in neat bundles, the fruit trees and vines well ordered, even the surrounding mountains seem to be in precisely the right place. The fierce mewling of a few wild cats emerging from the bushes suggests a less controlled nature. Barth himself in a 1977 interview warned: the general understanding of the landscape, even among well-meaning people, is mostly imprecise, not useable, a slogan (*Schlagwort*), even a stick for beating (*Schlagstock*). The landscape isn't just a view, as from the cable car, or a photograph, or a background, but a carefully manicured location.

But really, don't think, don't worry, lounge back in the designer chair thoughtfully placed by the lake, watch the ducks and swans swim by, consider the enormous grass carp and silver carp just under the surface in the waters of the lake, order a Negroni, or an over-sugary ice-cream, use one or other language.

The multiple languages of Südtirol–Alto Adige, and the complex mixture of peoples, create a rich mix of fact and fiction. A 2014 state survey states that 62.3 per cent of the population of Südtirol–Alto Adige are German-speaking, 23.4 per cent Italian-speaking, 4.1 per cent Ladin and a surprising 10.1 per cent, mainly recent immigrants, are registered as other. The German-speakers are principally in the countryside, small towns and villages. In Bozen–Bolzano, where Mussolini deliberately introduced large numbers of Italian workers to try to alter the population balance, and in several other smaller communities near the border to Trentino, there is an Italian majority. The Italians resident in Südtirol–Alto Adige tend to speak standardised Italian, since they gradually lose much of their connection to their place of origin and their kids learn standard Italian in school.

The double, sometimes triple, names of all towns and villages is just one of the many signs of the double and triple nature of life in the province. Which name anyone uses is an indication of their linguistic origin. Using a different name, usually without any hidden intent, can imply a different culture and a different history. Neutral arrivals from outside the province either cope with the rather tedious doubling of names, or succumb to using only one for the sake of an easy life. Francesca Melandri wrote that one should abandon both Südtirol and Alto Adige and settle for a cheerful Südtirolo.

There are of course certain linguistic areas where languages intermix, particularly when the subject matter is food. Another piece from Melandri's novel *Eva dorme*:

> The fish arrived from Chioggia at dawn on Fridays, in wooden crates covered with ice: cefali sardine, spigole, vongole. Hermann used the Italian names as he did with the fruit and vegetables, especially salads: radicchio, lettuga, valeriana, rucola, portaluca, crescione. On the other hand he used German for meat: Rinderfilet, Lammrippen, Schienbein, and also for desserts: Mohnstrudel, Roulade, Linzertorte, Spitzbuben. The only exception to this rule, almost an involuntary homage to Italian and German stereotypes, were potatoes ... everybody called them Kartoffeln. However when fried they would transcend Südtirol ethnic tensions, becoming Pommes Frites.

If the Mussolini policy of banning the German language had been successful then Südtirol–Alto Adige would by now have become much like Alsace, where the local German dialect is vanishing and the national language, French, is dominant. But the Südtirolers have stubbornly hung on to their language. Underground schools known as catacomb schools persisted in the fascist times to teach German. Families continued to speak the language at home. The Italian state was not so relentless as France in enforcing a standard language and, unlike in Alsace, the middle class remained for the most part German-speaking. Gradually in postwar times the situation became softer and fairer. Following a series of agreements from the 1970s onwards, all citizens of the province now have a right to use their own language in government business, schools are divided on linguistic lines, place names are in two, often three languages. Matters linguistic are based on the proportional make-up of the population. There is a wonderful eleven syllable German compound noun, *Sprachgruppenzugehörigkeitserklärung*, meaning something like declaration of adherence to a language group. Anyone who could master this word could presumably also master the German language. But the linguistic division into groups also creates a kind of Alpine apartheid, setting the inhabitants against one another.

In fact Südtirolers don't speak Hochdeutsch, official German, they speak in their own version of German, mostly derived from Bavarian. Or rather they speak in various versions of German, because the way of speaking varies from valley to valley. When the German-speakers talk to each other they speak their own way and understand at least enough of what the other is saying. The Italian-speakers have learned some standard German, but this doesn't help them a great deal in speaking with their neighbours; they can understand little of the German variations spoken in the streets, let alone up in the valleys. So the two linguistic groups tend to speak Italian together, as a form of lingua franca. Italian-speakers are however very gradually in decline. They often send their children to German-speaking schools, on the basis that these are better and open up the possibility of studying in Austrian and German universities. Meanwhile the Ladins in the southeast speak their own language with each other, and being sensible pragmatic people either standard German or standard Italian with everyone else as appropriate. They know nobody is going to learn to speak a minority language like Ladin. However Ladin, a language distantly derived from Latin, is related to various other regional languages, such as Friuli to the east and Rhaeto-Romansh in Switzerland, and even to Langue d'Oc in southern France. And the migrants? They speak of course their own languages, which for the most part nobody else understands, but they have by law to belong one of the three linguistic groups, the most useful of which is German, so they have to assume membership of an ethnic group to which they do not really belong and have a go at the *Sprachgruppenzugehörigkeitserklärung*. And in the meantime, just to complicate things, the German languages of the Südtirol are gradually being infected by Italian words, such as *magari* (maybe), *casino* (brothel, thus disorder), *tipo* (type), *patent* (driving licence).

All of which makes communication tricky, but also refreshing. Rather than the current depressing tendency towards a few global languages, Südtirol remains stubborn and individual, the specific and the local continue to fight successfully against the bland and the universal, but also adapt to survive.

Bisch koa Doige Madli oder?
Are you a local girl?
Woll, I bin a Tirolerin
Yes I am a Tirol woman.
Ja, ober halt nit va do.
But not from here.
Perfekt denk ich und renn
Perfect I think and run

The relations between Italians and Tirolers have been an evolving theme in postwar novels about Südtirol. These are of course fictions, but novels provide access into private worlds where official surveys cannot enter. They may depend for their attitudes on the origins of the writer, who may have a particular line to push, or who may also idealise, or demonise, one side or other.

One of the earliest novels on the theme of dual identity was *La casa sull'argine* (The house on the riverbank, 1965), by the Italian journalist Gianni Bianco, born in Capua but brought up in Bozen–Bolzano. The story is set in the 1950s. An Italian man from the town, Michele, lives a carefree life as a commercial agent, interested in bars, cars, women. He falls for a Südtirol woman, Marta, a teacher, living in the countryside, with her mother and an old man, in an inaccessible house by a river. It is the time of the separatist movement, terrorism, reprisals. They have a complicated, ambiguous relationship, the narrative revolves around violent events between Italians and her family at the end of the war, and an unsolved murder. As so often in these novels, the past determines the present and the book ends inconclusively.

A similar theme is taken up in Joseph Zoderer's *Die Walsche* (1982), in which a German-speaking woman, Olga, from up in the hills, moves in with an Italian boyfriend, Silvano. They run a bar in the Italian part of Bozen–Bolzano. *Walsche* is a derogatory word for the Italians, the German-speakers are the *Daitsche*. The woman returns to her home village for her father's funeral, but does not dare take her Italian partner with her. The inhabitants of the village are portrayed as rough and hostile, their connection to the exterior German world reduced to the tourism on which they are now dependent, and imagined memories of when things might have been better, when Germans were seen, or considered themselves, as punctual, disciplined, correct. They scorn Olga with her city ways, her dresses and high heels. But Olga is also confused, she feels comfortable in neither society:

> For a long time she didn't realise that she lived on the other side. The air had become yielding, softer and permeable, not just her office wall. She heard old phrases, which now sounded remarkably clear and hard: Idiot, Fool, *Sturheil, Bergheil, Siegheil.* Everything flowed like this: *Daitsche* and *Walsche.*

And later:

> How often had she felt, even if only for a moment, alone with Silvano, or more often with him and his noisy friends, suddenly strange and without belonging, certainly homeless, as though they, Silvano and herself, never came together, never could reach each other and bring their heads together through some separating wall. She had sometimes felt strange, really strange with him in the Italian quarter.

Silvano, her boyfriend, has in turn an idealised, almost colonial, view of the Tirolers as unspoiled mountain folk. He buys an antique peasant cupboard which she finds repulsive, and sings German traditional songs without understanding their fascist connections. Neither really understands the other, they have clichéd views of each other's background, but they care for one another enough to survive together. Zoderer himself came from an interesting family background. He was born in Meran, but his parents were *Optanten* who chose to leave the province in 1938 to become part of Hitler's Germany. They had returned after the war, but Zoderer was educated in Switzerland. He became for a while the best-known writer in Südtirol, very popular in Italy but often strongly criticised by German-speakers for his debunking of the myth of the idealised people of the land, living a pure life up in the hills, compared to the debased Italians in the city.

The German–Italian romantic–erotic relationship was taken up by Francesca Melandri in her already mentioned 2010 book, *Eva dorme*. Melandri relates a family saga running over the course of the twentieth century, interspersed with a journey made by Eva, the daughter of the main character, Gerda, from the Brenner Pass down through Italy to Sicily—the enclosed life in Südtirol set against the openness and variety of Italy. In the 1930s Gerda's Tirolean family live in poverty, and take up the Hitler Option of a life in Nazi Germany, again returning after the war. Gerda struggles to free herself from her family, works in a large hotel in Bozen–Bolzano, has her first sexual experience in a cable car, gives birth to her child Eva, falls in love with an Italian soldier. Their relationship seems to work, but her lover is told to leave by the Italian authorities since Italian soldiers are not permitted to cohabit with German-speakers. He returns to Sicily, where he is rediscovered and movingly reconciled with Eva years later. Francesca Melandri is actually Italian, born in Rome, but she spent many years in Südtirol–Alto Adige. Her saga includes characters representing all aspects of the province—peasants who get rich, tourists, gays, Italian soldiers, Tirolean bomb-makers. In the end the novel is optimistic. Eva, although brought up amongst German-speakers, comes to recognise the Italian side of her personality, awakes from her long sleep. The book was well received in both the Italian-Austrian and the German press.

Such novels may not offer a realist portrayal of life in Südtirol–Alto Adige, but they do show an imagination as to how this society could be, and give access to a life that would otherwise be concealed. Melandri went on to write novels about Italian terrorism in the *anni di piombo*, the years of lead, and about Italian colonialism in Ethiopia in the 1930s—in some ways parallel themes to the Italian colonisation of Südtirol–Alto Adige and the struggles between different sets of ethnic groups. It is no coincidence that the Victory Arch in Bozen–Bolzano has alongside it a column celebrating the Italian victories in Ethiopia. Melandri's novels show an unusual sympathy and understanding for the families of those who are usually portrayed as unacceptable, such as terrorists and colonialists, and for the unlikely love between very different kinds of people.

And finally—for now—there is Sabine Gruber's 2011 novel, *Stillbach oder die Sehnsucht*, which relates the stories, extending over several decades, of a sequence of three women from an imaginary Südtirol village called Stillbach who emigrate to Italy (the title of the novel is literally 'Stillbach or longing'). Relationships between the two linguistic groups remain problematic:

> —Married?
>
> —For the sixth time, and I have five children from four different men.
>
> —How come you speak such good Italian?
>
> —Four of my ex-husbands are Italian.
>
> —Good choice.
>
> —If so, then I would not have divorced them.

In the personal memory of the characters, Südtirol remains a lost paradise, a land of rural bliss, a victim of outside forces. Two young women, from different generations, go in turn to Rome, to work as chambermaids in hotels, as was customary at a time of poverty in the Südtirol countryside. A third woman writes the story. Each woman forms an attachment to an Italian man, but they are all to varying degrees uncommitted, longing for their homeland. Sabine Gruber, born in Meran–Merano to a family of book-binders, but now living in Vienna, writes in any number of forms (novels, plays, poems, essays, even a tourist guidebook) on fascist architecture and the divisions created by the Hitler Option. Grubner is interested not only in the romantic aspect of her story, but in the background of Nazi terror in Rome at the end of the war, and of the involvement of men from Südtirol–Alto Adige. Grubner's approach runs counter to the earlier novels, where Italians arrive in the North. Here, the Tirolers move to the South, and as ever find themselves trying to resolve their personal lives within the complexities of a much broader history.

None of these books is purely an attempt to describe the relationships between Italians and Tirolers, which is often as much background as foreground. Their time of writing spreads over half a century, attitudes change. Each has very different characters, but certain general lines can be set out as to the types of people who appear consistently, reflecting the linguistic division. Each of these novels question the usual clichéd version of Südtirol–Alto Adige as a land of rural innocence. The Italian men tend to be good-hearted and from an urban background, innocent, even naïve, gradually becoming detached from their background and getting involved with a woman from a society they don't really understand. Italian women hardly appear—there are few relationships described between Tirol men and Italian women. Südtirol tends to be a male-dominated society, and Tirol men are often portrayed as either uncultured or dodgy, with a family background in the Nazi period—take care! But Tirol women are always at the centre of the story. They emerge from a rural background from which they are determined to escape, they suffer and they make mistakes, they have big hearts and complicated psychologies and are often confused about their identity, hovering between their family, which they dislike, and their lover, who offers an uncertain sense of freedom. In order to move out of the narrow confines of their home they have to make a leap, take a risk, try something new. These stories aren't merely reduced to the fatal German-Italian duo, but reflect on the incompatibility of different kinds of people, from the land and the town, educated and uneducated, confident and shy—as in many other places. And the land itself, which at first seems so open and simple, a tourist idyll, is soon put in question and revealed—and not just because of binary ethnic differences, but because of any number of half-hidden factors—as complex, emotive, awkwardly loved, with dark corners, contradictory, and thus also all the more fascinating.

A small train, very clean and modern, runs west from the main Bozen–Bolzano station, through the sheds of the industrial suburbs to the south and along flat fields beside the river Adige. Step out at Ponte Adige–Sigmundskron station. Not much activity. Some cyclists pass by, wearing bright pink and yellow spandex, helmets, wraparound sunglasses, on smart mountain bikes, on the cycle route to the north. Beside the station bar a woman sits on a bench, looking up at the sky. Across the bridge and up the steep wooded slope from the river. Three skateboarders come down at great speed, swerving from side to side and occasionally leaping into the air, shouting to each other, followed by a large sports car, decorated with flowers, and containing a couple in bridal wear, he in a dark suit and felt hat, she in a white confection and wide white hat with trailing ribbons. They call out something as the car passes by.

The Südtirol architect Werner Tscholl, born in Latsch in the Vinschgautal, in a 2018 interview with Andrea Carloni and Carlotta Ferrati:

> The old remains old, the new becomes new and it speaks the language of this time. Nowadays it is difficult to speak a Baroque language, because the time has passed and we are no longer in that period. We cannot understand what the old is because it comes from a completely different society. The only way is to leave it where it is and try to interpret it. To leave it there as if it was something with a strong character, and put something of our period, or of our problems or society in front of it.

Through the old gate into the courtyard of Sigmundskron castle. To the left a rusted Corten steel wall with a bookshop. All the books are by or about the Südtirol champion mountaineer Reiner Messner.

> —Do you only have books about Reiner Messner, not about any other climbers?
>
> —Of course, only about Messner, for this is a Messner Mountain Museum.

Reiner Messner is the archetypal Südtirol hero, the mountaineer who climbed innumerable peaks in the Dolomites, climbed Mount Everest alone and without supplementary oxygen, crossed the Arctic and Greenland without packs of dogs or machines, who did things in the true way, the traditional Südtirol way, the heir of those mountaineers who used to climb Alpine peaks dressed in their loden jackets and hats with feathers, as though going out for an afternoon stroll. Messner was also for a while an MEP for the Italian Green party. Having injured himself (falling off a low wall at his Schloß Juval) he set up the Messner Mountain Museums, of which there are now six. Three—Sigmundskron, Schloß Juval and the ice museum on Ortles—lie to the west, and three to the east, in Ripa, also in an old Schloß, Corones, on a nearby mountain peak, and in an old WW1 fort on Monte Rite deep in the Dolomites. All these museums show aspects of mountain culture, paintings, photographs and equipment, together with Messner's collection of mementos from the Himalayas. The new buildings have all been designed to emphasise contemporary architecture within the Südtirol–Alto Adige landscape, using mainly Südtirol architects. These represent a kind of curation of mountaineering, where it is no longer a heroic outside activity, pursued by a few daring adventurers, but has in part become a mass tourist hobby, with mountaineers queuing up to take turns climbing peaks. The mountains of the Alps are always the backdrop to any activity in Südtirol, always present, visible behind the buildings of the towns, along the valleys, the roads, the rail lines. But in the Mountain Museums even the wild lonesome art of mountaineering is now shown as tamed, made accessible to all, hung on walls and set out in boxes.

The museum within the castle at Sigmundskron is the largest and is designed by Werner Tscholl. This is the same medieval castle where Silvius Magnano hosted the celebrated meeting calling for the independence of Südtirol in 1957. A place with special status in the formation of Südtirol identity, it has belonged to local lords, to the Austrians, to the Italians, and was even revealed to contain the mummified body of an Ice Age woman, a female equivalent to the ice man from the north. Because of the historic status of the castle, which means its original fabric cannot be altered, the large-scale insertions by Tscholl are designed to be removable. They are mostly built in Corten steel and form a kind of parallel architecture, hardly touching the old structure but ingeniously running up through, along and beside it, a second matching set of forms. There are spiral stairs and floors that rise through the towers, sets of long thin stairs placed beside the castle walls, with a theatrical air, showing off the visitors moving up and down, small buildings for the entry kiosk, and the cinema box, with a volume of gradually diminishing size, somehow propped up over a ditch beside the wall. There is a pleasant casualness about these constructions, which exist in a different timescale to the medieval castle. They are clearly modern, but the Corten steel gives them already a weathered and slightly battered, almost medieval appearance, Although large scale they have a temporary feel, as though they really might be dismantled and carried way.

Back down the slope to the station and continue on the train line to the north. Meran, once beloved by the Russian aristocracy, who stayed in villas around the town and built their own church. Before the Russian Revolution there was even a weekly direct train connection between Petersburg and Meran, linking, at least for the affluent, the Baltic to the Alps. But now is not the moment for Russians. Keep moving, along the line, change trains at the station onto the Meran to Mals line. This opened in 1906, closed down in the 1990s, but was recently restored and reopened. Many of the stations along the line now have minimal modernist designs by the architect Walter Dietl, flat roofs, coloured walls, bicycle sheds, all constructed in steel, concrete, larch. At Plaus the station name is written out in giant letters that hold up the station roof, combining, with casual humour, art, writing and architecture. The modernity of the stations contrasts with the greenness of the valley floor, where industrial-scale crop sprayers sprinkle water over the fruit trees, and with the daunting background of the mountains.

The line runs through the long east–west Vinschgautal–Val de Venota, a valley originally settled by tribes speaking Rhaeto-Romansch, a language still used in eastern Switzerland and related to Ladin. The descendants of these tribes belatedly became German-speakers in the nineteenth century. There is a certain irony in the Italian fascists then insisting these people were really Italian and should speak Italian. Even Ötzi the iceman is linked to Vinschgautal; certain kinds of moss that still grow in the valley have been identified in his clothing. It is only some 15km as the crow flies to where he was discovered besides the Similaun glacier, longer of course via the valleys. The Vinschgautal was historically agricultural and poor, cut off from the main North–South routes through Tirol. The climate is very particular, long hours of sunlight but little rain, so that the soil on the mountain slopes is barren and steppe-like. However the old glacier bed in the wide valley is very fertile and is now a successful area for growing fruit, apples, pears, apricots, and thus has grown affluent, a change reflected by the new architecture. Ah, the Vinschgau, highly individual with its particular light, its inhabitants, and then also with some of the best contemporary architecture in Südtirol—mostly by three local architects, Walter Dietl from Schlanders and the slightly younger Werner Tscholl from Latsch and Arnold Gapp from Mals.

The mountaineer Reiner Messner, who at one stage commented that he would rather have been an architect than a mountain adventurer, speaks of the valley in an expansive mood:

> ... I am not a native of the Vinschgautal, I come from Valle Arnico ... my character is I think different from that of a typical person from the Vinschgau, they tend to be very anarchic. In contrast to the people from Val Arnico they are Alemani, whereas we, the people of the North, are Bajuvars (Bavarians). These Alemani, who also have Ladin blood, are different to the other Tirolers, they are more creative, most of the artists of Südtirol come from here. The best architecture in Südtirol is found in the Vinschgau. In Vinschgau there is more light, which makes the people more spirited.

The Vinschgautal architects are both local, in that they work mostly in the area in which they were born and have great respect for the landscape, and also internationally minded, never provincial. The deep division of the 1930s, when the Italians proposed rationalism and the Tirolers clinged to tradition, has long since vanished. Until very recently, there was no architecture school in Südtirol–Alto Adige. Architects who came from the valleys and elsewhere in the province studied abroad, in Innsbruck, Vienna, Venice or Verona. Dietl studied in Innsbruck and Vienna, Gapp in Vienna, Tscholl in Florence. These architects have benefited from being in a multi-ethnic, multi-lingual society.

Along the valley are ancient castles and churches, but also large sheds for the fruit growers, a mix of old defensive and religious buildings and new rural industries. Just past Naturns–Naturno the line passes Schloß Juval, one of the Messner Mountain Museums, a typically irregular mass with a crenelated tower, sited on a hilltop, as a proper Tirol Schloß should be.

The small town of Latsch–Laces lies a few kilometres further down the line. Werner Tscholl's hometown. Tscholl has built all over Südtirol, in a wide variety of forms including hostels, wine depots, offices, those curious lookouts already mentioned up on the Austrian border, the interventions in Sigmundskron, even a glazed multi-coloured pop-up chapel. However many of his domestic buildings are located in or around his hometown and the nearby village of Morter, where his office is based. These private houses have passed through various styles as Tscholl's architectural ideas have evolved:

> Haus Knoll-Thulle (1996) in nearby Galsaun–Colsano is formed of an ingenious timber frame sitting like a classical temple on an ancient stone base, with a sliding terrace that moves horizontally to follow the path of the sun—and a strange 50m-long tunnel that leads into the interior of the nearby mountain.
>
> Haus Gruber (2002) and Haus Schöpf (2001) are geometrical, modernist, slightly staid but also playful; the Schöpf house has the feel of a pair of binoculars looking out over the landscape.
>
> Haus G&M (2016) is modish, a smallish space contained in a cranked shell, like an enlarged toy.
>
> Haus 22 (2017), Tscholl's own house, consists of two flat white horizontal planes, sandwiching a recessed glass wall, suspended over a white pier, floating above the landscape in the little village of Morter, somewhere between a sci-fi observation tower and a traditional Tirol castle perched on a rock. Perhaps Tscholl himself sits in this look-out, surveying his work in the surrounding landscape, plotting the next move.

Sometimes on larger projects the Tscholl office, which is deliberately kept small with only four employees, becomes too chic, too concerned with what it sees in magazines, but here in Latsch it is very much at home and these villas are a wonderful set of architectural forms, placed in the landscape like pieces in an ever-evolving game. On the edge of town the Selimex building (2000), providing offices for a firm distributing fruit and vegetables grown in the valley, is a large cube with square-gridded facades. In the daytime the grid is a darkish green and seems solid, but at night it becomes transparent, illuminated internally, moving from yellow to light blue to red and violet. From the exterior the building is much an art installation as an office; inside it is pragmatic and functional. And finally, there is the extension to the Latsch cemetery (2000). A long horizontal roof, slightly curved in plan, leads across the cemetery to finish a small chapel, shaped in plan like a domestic iron. In Latsch the architecture of Tscholl accompanies the residents through their comfortable lives and into the next world.

Another cable car conversation. Two men in brightly coloured shorts and shirts. Sunglasses, small bags, large cameras. One with unlit cigarillo. They appear nervous as the car rises steeply above the Vinschgau valley.

—Do you remember that scene in a James Bond film, on a cable car, where the man with iron teeth bites through the cable?

—Jaws.

—Yes Jaws.

—And then there is a fight on top of the cable car?

—Yes, it was Sean Connery.

—No surely it was Roger Moore.

—*The Spy who Loved Me*?

—Maybe *Moonraker*.

—Well that could never happen here. Not in the Vinschgau.

There is an awkward silence as the car pulls into the station. The cable car travels 1,000m to link Latsch to the otherwise hard to reach village of St Martin in Koffel–S Martino al Monte Koben. It serves both tourists and local residents, for whom the connection would otherwise be a long winding road. The upper cable car terminal in St Martin in Koffel (2002) is a wonderful machine building by Arnold Gapp. Usually the machinery is concealed, but here the large bright yellow wheels carrying the cables are set above a small glass box where the passengers wait to board the red cars. Metal bars sprout out horizontally to guide the arrival of the cars. The building has the edginess and slight sense of danger that a cable car needs, balanced on the side of the mountain. Standing in the glass box the visitor is cantilevered out over the steep slope, looking out into the mountains to the south. Beside the cable car station is a small pilgrim church, dedicated to St Martin, the interior filled with strange baroque paintings and sculpture of the life of the saint, with blue and orange woodwork. The two buildings balance one another, both dedicated to means of travelling away from the banality of life on solid earth.

Further on the rail line, always moving west. Sponding station, then a short bus trip into the mountains. The Messner Mountain Museum in Solda, Ortles, the ice museum, by Arnold Gapp, lies up a long road leading to the edge of a glacier. Ortles is the old Ladin name for the Ortler mountain range. A forest of larches, some green fields, and then the rocks of the mountains. The site is not far as the crow flies from the Hotel Paradiso, but separated by a mountain range. However, where the Paradiso shows itself off to the landscape, the Ortles is hidden away. The Gapp part of the museum is underground, entered through a doorway in a long rough zigzagging stone wall, and is lit from above, through a zigzagging slot that runs along the base of the wall. The feel is of being within an ice crystal, inside a glacier. On the walls are nineteenth-century paintings of ice in the mountains. The actual glacier is of course retreating as the climate changes. The ice world is vanishing, and but a memory remains in this room. This is the most modest of the Messner Museums.

Back on the train, as the line curves to the north. The carriages have emptied out. Some kids play video games on a laptop and chatter into their phones. A man in a smart suit also talks into his phone, reading out figures and prices:

> —Three hundred thousand? No, too much. Two hundred and fifty? You are joking. Do you think I'm an idiot? Two hundred thousand at the very most. Call me back when you've decided.

The conductor, in a neat grey uniform, arrives.

—Where are you travelling to?

—To the end of the line and then a bit further on foot.

—Well, the train runs every half hour in the daytime. And then there are buses. You just follow the road, up to the border with Austria and Switzerland.

—No, I'm only going to Marienberg.

—Aha, well that will certainly be good for your soul.

And from Anita Pichler's novel *Wie die Monate das Jahr*, a scene showing the strange mix of former peasant culture and new wealth.

> The farmhouse looks like all farmhouses: dwelling house, stable and barn in another building. Pointed roof, balcony, flowers. I recognise the type. The nearer I come, the more unusual it appears: a tennis court near the house, to the left, a swimming pool. The beggar from the town sits beside the pool. She is dressed differently. She winks. I go over to her, she points to the glass wall of the house. Inside eight men are sitting at a table playing cards. 'Do you want to go to them?', she says. They are waiting till summer, till the guests come.

Glass walls, tennis courts, swimming pools. Geometric shapes in the fields, machines on the hills. Waiting till summer. It is difficult to match the contemporary architecture with those Südtirol novels, which portray a regressive resentful rural world, mostly orientated to the past. Perhaps the Vinschgau was always special, different. Or more likely it has moved on, become wealthy, more open, more than a bit *bürgerlich*, self-satisfied. It has however avoided becoming Disneyfied, neo-Tirol, something individual and different has emerged. Messner is right, there is a certain anarchic spirit, but tempered by money.

The train pulls into Mals–Malles Venosta, the end of the line. Beside the tracks is a fine train shed by Walter Dietl, grey metal frame, grey metal panels, bright orange doors. Mals–Malles Venosta is a medieval town with several Romanesque towers. And in Bahnhofstraße is the Gamperheim, a student hostel with walls of reinforced concrete, small square windows with protruding concrete surrounds, 1980s brutalism transferred to the Alps, designed by the Bozen architect Helmut Mauer. Nothing here is quite as it should be, it all seems a little on edge. The sun shines. Little roads pass through some suburban housing. The fields stretch out along the valley. A little further north are the large artificial reservoirs, created by damming the valley, which generate hydroelectric power.

A young woman with two small children on skateboards and a fine brown cow:

—No, it's not so far, maybe an hour's walk, you can see the building across the fields and then always uphill, just follow the path.

Numerous angels dressed in white, brown and green robes and with brown wings. Faces open, eyes wide, brown curly hair. Sky very clear blue, dotted at regular intervals with bright white stars, small, with spiky protrusions, disturbingly reminiscent of coronavirus spheres.

Hares run across the fields, sometimes the large males stand up and fight with one another, punching with their front feet. An omen.

A group of young girls on bicycles sing with accented enthusiasm:

—Hartbrekkers gönna break, break, break, break, break
—And the fekers gönna fake, fake, fake, fake, fake
—Bäbi, I just gönna shake, shake, shake, shake, shake ...

They stop singing and argue furiously with each other about the words. One sits down and sulks.

At first the path runs across the fields, then it becomes much steeper and begins to zigzag. A sign says it is named Stunden Weg, path of hours, presumably relating to the old religious practice of reciting the hours. Soon a black onion dome comes into view, an unlikely apparition over the vineyards. Then two smaller pointed onion domes, like the decorative elements on an old bedhead or cupboard. Each of the domes is surmounted with a small gold cross. Below the domes is a massive white wall, perhaps 20m high, like a fortress, its upper part lined with three rows of windows. Below the wall are a series of small gardens, stepping down the slopes, with rows of vegetables immaculately laid out. The path turns back on itself and arrives beside an arched gateway.

This is the Marienberg Kloster, at 1,395m, just higher than the Brenner Pass, the highest Benedictine abbey in Europe. The abbey looks down over the valley, to the vineyards in the south and the larch forest to the north and west.

Paolo Rumiz, wanderer and writer originally from Trieste, writes in his recent book *Il filo infinito* about his visits to a series of Benedictine abbeys, including Marienberg. Rumiz, rather unexpectedly for a journalist who has covered some of the dodgiest zones on the continent, has a touching mix of faith and optimism, and suggests that the Benedictine order, with its monasteries all over Europe, is an international organisation, with one set of beliefs and mode of behaviour, acting for the common good at a time when Europe has little to hold it together. Rumiz also comments on the clockface on the main Marienberg tower, and its mechanism, constructed in the late nineteenth century:

> There is a mechanical noise, surprising for those who are accustomed to the silence of electronics. It comes from the cables which connect from the main motor to the other dials on the walls, 11 in total, distributed throughout the abbey; a Leonardo-like apparatus of rods and belts extending hundreds of metres, which are held in tension and which run through tunnels, tubes, junctions, gear and pulleys to connect in a network the interior of the building, corridor by corridor, horizontal and vertical, to unite in perfect synchrony the life of the monks.

The effects of this complex machinery in keeping the lives of the monks to one single time system do not extend to any longer notion of time. The monastery, which was founded in the twelfth century and has burned down and been rebuilt at least twice, is a baffling confusion of different periods. The wooden door of the entrance from the exterior world is opened by a man dressed in a dark medieval robe. Beyond is a long open courtyard, to the right a modern glass pavilion on which are biblical quotations in Latin—the architect naturally Werner Tscholl. A doorway further to the right, in a highly decorated painted facade, perhaps early Renaissance and including one of those eleven clock faces, leads into the church, white and a light baroque style. Through a small door to the right and into a cloister, with a pleasant medieval feel. Everything very clean, as yet no sense of the spiritual. Now there is a confusion of passages, small rooms, golden statues, some seventeenth-century figures holding up a model of the abbey, in which there is no doubt an even smaller model, a large blue stove, almost a building in its own right, maybe Dutch, a painting of the Last Supper with a real clockface, no doubt properly synchronised, a picture of bears, elephants and other beasts gazing upwards at the divinity, more saints, a strange rococo room, taken from another abbey and installed here, with elaborate decoration in blue, green and yellow, on the ceiling a painting of a vision of St Benedict, as though there was not vision enough already. And yet there is more: downstairs in the crypt are wonderful medieval frescos of angels, Byzantine in style, dressed in long robes and with large brown and gold flapping wings gazing at another divine appearance. Another paradise to add to those already found on the Rhine and along the Baltic coast. Saints stand in rows in similar spaces. The good Lord is on a central panel, holding a great book, also gazing outwards. Many of the frescoes are damaged, pieces are missing, the paintwork a bit tattered. These frescoes, painted in about 1160, were for many centuries covered over with plaster, until rediscovered and restored. Yes, the spirit may be here, underground, but in an artificial sky.

Up again and down another passage, a door into a pleasant garden. Fresh air. Some steps lead down again across a lawn, to a door in a tower, topped with another, rather flattened onion dome. It seems that the garden must be at ground level, but a stair leads down two storeys into the recently constructed library, also inevitably designed by the omnipresent Werner Tscholl.

The library is two storeys high, with walls of ancient stone and concrete and a collection of 13,000 volumes stacked on freestanding floor-to-ceiling steel shelving. It is simple and open, clean in the way of much Südtirol architecture. Nothing here is out of place, the books are all neatly organised. A memory surfaces of the library in Umberto Eco's novel *The Name of the Rose*, also set in a Benedictine monastery library in Italy, where there are a series of murders, and a monk detective who searches for the identity of the killer. The Eco library has an octagonal shape and a labyrinthine interior, which the narrator sees as a kind of being:

> Now I realised that not infrequently books speak of books: it is as if they spoke among themselves. In the light of this reflection, the library seemed all the more disturbing to me. It was then the place of a long, centuries-old murmuring, an imperceptible dialogue between one parchment and another, a living thing, a receptacle of powers not to be ruled by a human mind, a treasure of secrets emanated by many minds, surviving the death of those who had produced them or had been their conveyors.

At a desk sits a young man, rather smartly dressed, working at a laptop. He points out a small spiral staircase leading up into the former church of St Giles or Aegidius, an ancient ruin which Tscholl restored. It is now a reading room, with a long wall glazed with obscure glass, letting in a faint light. Some desks and chairs are occupied by silent figures. At the end of the room is a small window looking down into the valley. In the distance are cars, animals, a few figures, they seem to inhabit a very different world.

Ah but here it is all too underground, too quiet, too learned, and in spite of the wonderful luminous angels who point out the way to redemption, probably the wrong religion.

Away from the abbey, with its synchronised and also erratic time systems. A small path runs up the mountain, in amongst the larches, increasingly steep. If one followed this little path far enough one would arrive at one of the unmarked border crossings to Switzerland. Away to the northeast, 25km as the crow flies, is the Similaun glacier where the iceman was found, another 50km to the Brenner Pass, where this journey began, at 1,370m above sea level. After a long curving route down to Bolzen, up to Meran and along the Vinschgau, the journey has returned to the same altitude it started from. Even though here the eastern side of the mountains is moving into shadow, the sun still shines in the valley below. There is a curious bluish light, the whole area appears not to be high up, but low down, as though undersea, in a subaquatic world. where all the light comes from above—a vague memory perhaps of how many millions of years ago, before the Alps rose up, this area was all undersea.

A chairlift, unused at this time of year, runs up the slope. Just above the treeline there is a small lake. A little beyond, on a small bench sit a group of hikers, with rucksacks, hats, sunglasses, hiking boots. They are drinking red wine and eating large salami rolls. They cut the salami from a fat sausage, with large knives. Two small calico cats casually pick up the scraps. The hikers speak to each other in a language a little like Italian. They can manage a bit of German.

—Where are you hiking?

—We've been in the Swiss mountains but now we're on our way back.

—To where?

—To Trieste. We come from there. But we are Slovenes, we live on the border in Trieste.

—But that's so far, it must be hundreds of kilometres.

—Yes, it will probably take us a while. But it's mostly downhill and we have lots of time. And anyway, we'll take the train and the bus most of the way, we're not at all purists. We're on the way home and we know the way well. We like it here. Like Trieste it's in Italy but not really Italian....

A moment of silence.

—And you, why have you come here?

—I went to the monastery. There everything was so complicated. I thought maybe I'd just stroll up the mountain, but it looks a little high ...

We all sit for a while and chat. The bluish half-light fades slowly, so that we seem for a moment suspended in an uncertain place, time seems to have slowed right down, as though something is about to happen, as though we are about to move suddenly in a different direction to somewhere different. The little track leads up and along the mountain, sometimes following the contour line, sometimes winding back and forth. Keep moving. Zick zick zack zack.

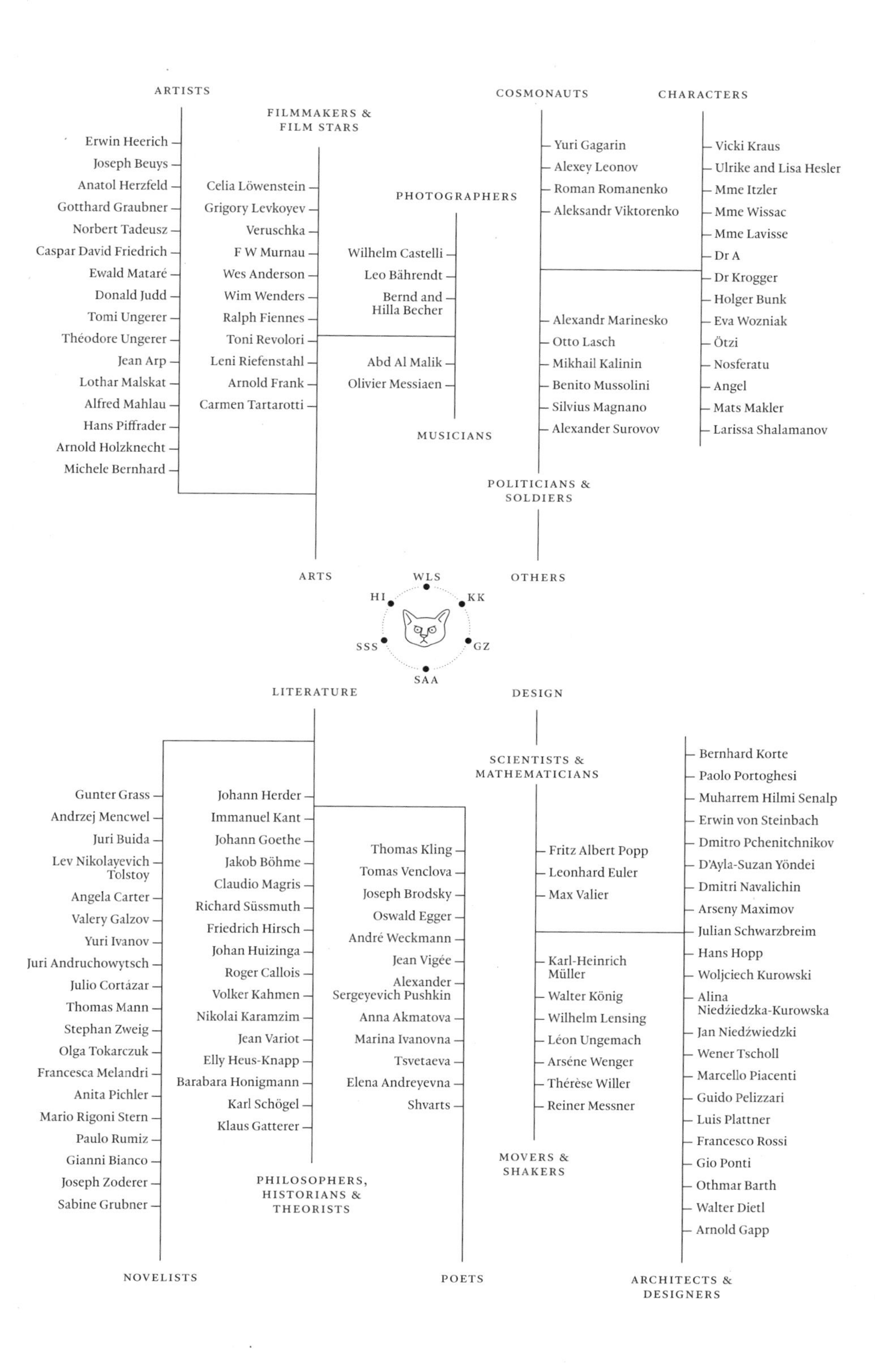
ARTISTS
Erwin Heerich
Joseph Beuys
Anatol Herzfeld
Gotthard Graubner
Norbert Tadeusz
Caspar David Friedrich
Ewald Mataré
Donald Judd
Tomi Ungerer
Théodore Ungerer
Jean Arp
Lothar Malskat
Alfred Mahlau
Hans Piffrader
Arnold Holzknecht
Michele Bernhard
FILMMAKERS & FILM STARS
Celia Löwenstein
Grigory Levkoyev
Veruschka
F W Murnau
Wes Anderson
Wim Wenders
Ralph Fiennes
Toni Revolori
Leni Riefenstahl
Arnold Frank
Carmen Tartarotti
PHOTOGRAPHERS
Wilhelm Castelli
Leo Bährendt
Bernd and Hilla Becher
Abd Al Malik
Olivier Messiaen
MUSICIANS
COSMONAUTS
Yuri Gagarin
Alexey Leonov
Roman Romanenko
Aleksandr Viktorenko
Alexandr Marinesko
Otto Lasch
Mikhail Kalinin
Benito Mussolini
Silvius Magnano
Alexander Surovov
POLITICIANS & SOLDIERS
CHARACTERS
Vicki Kraus
Ulrike and Lisa Hesler
Mme Itzler
Mme Wissac
Mme Lavisse
Dr A
Dr Krogger
Holger Bunk
Eva Wozniak
Ötzi
Nosferatu
Angel
Mats Makler
Larissa Shalamanov
ARTS
OTHERS
WLS
HI
KK
SSS
GZ
SAA
LITERATURE
DESIGN
Gunter Grass
Andrzej Mencwel
Juri Buida
Lev Nikolayevich Tolstoy
Angela Carter
Valery Galzov
Yuri Ivanov
Juri Andruchowytsch
Julio Cortázar
Thomas Mann
Stephan Zweig
Olga Tokarczuk
Francesca Melandri
Anita Pichler
Mario Rigoni Stern
Paulo Rumiz
Gianni Bianco
Joseph Zoderer
Sabine Grubner
NOVELISTS
Johann Herder
Immanuel Kant
Johann Goethe
Jakob Böhme
Claudio Magris
Richard Süssmuth
Friedrich Hirsch
Johan Huizinga
Roger Callois
Volker Kahmen
Nikolai Karamzim
Jean Variot
Elly Heus-Knapp
Barabara Honigmann
Karl Schögel
Klaus Gatterer
PHILOSOPHERS, HISTORIANS & THEORISTS
Thomas Kling
Tomas Venclova
Joseph Brodsky
Oswald Egger
André Weckmann
Jean Vigée
Alexander Sergeyevich Pushkin
Anna Akmatova
Marina Ivanovna
Tsvetaeva
Elena Andreyevna
Shvarts
POETS
SCIENTISTS & MATHEMATICIANS
Fritz Albert Popp
Leonhard Euler
Max Valier
Karl-Heinrich Müller
Walter König
Wilhelm Lensing
Léon Ungemach
Arséne Wenger
Thérèse Willer
Reiner Messner
MOVERS & SHAKERS
Bernhard Korte
Paolo Portoghesi
Muharrem Hilmi Senalp
Erwin von Steinbach
Dmitro Pchenitchnikov
D'Ayla-Suzan Yöndei
Dmitri Navalichin
Arseny Maximov
Julian Schwarzbreim
Hans Hopp
Woljciech Kurowski
Alina Niedźiedzka-Kurowska
Jan Niedźwiedzki
Wener Tscholl
Marcello Piacenti
Guido Pelizzari
Luis Plattner
Francesco Rossi
Gio Ponti
Othmar Barth
Walter Dietl
Arnold Gapp
ARCHITECTS & DESIGNERS

Bibliography

Until the Bretchellmann Speaks
Abd Al Malik, *Qu'Allah bénisse la France* (2004)
Adrien Fink, *Lire Claude Vigée* (1977)
Emma Grunz and André Weckmann, *Das Elsaß* (2001)
Kaoutar Harchi, *Comme nous existons* (2021)
Barbara Honigmann, *Chronik meiner Straße* (2016)
Hélène Meyer and Monique Halmos, *Jouets* (1993)
Tomi Ungerer, *Die Drei Räuber* (1961)
Tomi Ungerer, *Zerada's Ogre* (1967)
Tomi Ungerer, *No Kiss for Mother* (1973)
Tomi Ungerer, *Flix* (1997)
Tomi Ungerer, *The Beast of Monsieur Racine* (1972)
André Weckmann, *elsassischi gramatik oder ein Versuch die Sprache auszuloten* (1989)
Thérèse Willer, *Tomi Ungerer* (2008)

Now You Understand
Josef Brodsky, *Collected Poems* (1994)
Yuri Buida, *The Prussian Bride* (2002)
Frédèric Caubin *Cosmic Communist Constructions* (2011)
Valerij Gal'cov, *Der Krieg und Ostpreussen im Gedächtnis der Einwohner des Gebietes Kaliningrad* (2015)
Nicholas Grospierre, *Modern Forms: A Subjective Atlas of Twentieth-Century Architecture* (2016)
Bert Hoppe, *Auf den Trümmern von Königsberg* (2000)
Bert Hoppe, *Königsberg/Kaliningrad nach 1945 aus deutscher Sicht* (2015)
Juri Ivanov, *Von Kaliningrad nach Königsberg* (1991)
Baldur Köster, *Königsberg: Architektur aus deutscher Zeit* (2000)
Andrzej Mencwel, *Kaliningrad, mon amour* (2013)
Markus Podehl, *Architektura Kaliningrada* (2012)
Karl Schlögel, *Promenade in Jalta* (2001)
Gunnar Strunz, *Königsberg Kaliningrader Gebiet* (2021)
Tomas Venclova, *An Initiation to Europe* (2015)

Paradise on Erft
Oswald Egger, *Val di Non* (2017)
Volker Kahmen, *Erotic Art Today* (1972)
Volker Kahmen, *Art History Photography* (1974)

Joachim Peter Kastner, *Erwin Heerich* (1991)
Thomas Kling, *Sondagen* (2004)
Wolfgang Schepers, *Erwin Heerich: Plastische Modelle für Architektur und Skulptur* (1997)

Silesian Scenes
Friedrich Blau, *Görlitz* (2017)
Jakob Böhme, *De signatura rerum* (1682)
Uwe Gerig and Andreas Bednarek, *Görlitz* (1992)
Olga Tokarczuk, *House of Day, House of Night* (1998)
Matt Zoller Seitz, *The Wes Anderson Collection: The Grand Budapest Hotel* (2015)
Adam Zagajewski, *Dwa Miasta* (1991)

Hop Rayuela Backstein
Juri Andruchowytsch, *Die Stadt-schiff* (1999)
Robert Callois, *Les jeux et les hommes* (1958)
Julio Cortázar, *Rayuela* (1963)
Günter Grass, *Die Rättin* (1966)
Mannfred Hamm and Brunhilde Windoffe, *Backsteinbauten zwischen Lübeck und Stralsund* (1990)
Friedrich Hirsch, *Der Sonnwendbogen* (1965)
Thomas Mann, *Buddenbrooks* (1901)
Johan Huizinga, *Homo Ludens* (1938)
Werner Schäfke, *Deutsche Backstein-Architektur* (2008)

Olagaga in the Alps
Giovanni Bianco, *La casa sull'argine* (1965)
Reinhard Christanell, *L'alfabeto di Bolzano* (2018)
Giovanni Denti and Chiara Toscani, *Gio Ponti Albergo Paradiso* (2011)
Sabine Gruber, *Stillbach oder die Sehnsucht* (2004)
Lucio Giudiceandrea and Aldo Mazza, *Das Handwerk des Zusammenlebens* (2019)
Claudio Magris *Microcosmi* (1997)
Francesca Melandri, *Eva dorme* (2010)
Anita Pichler, *Wie die Monate das Jahr* (1989)
Anita Pichler, *Die Frauen aus Fanis* (1992)
Paul Preims, *Architektur in Südtirol* (1979)
Paolo Rumiz, *Il filo infinito* (2019)
Bettina Schlorhaufer *Neue Architektur in Südtirol* (2006)
Gunter Waibl, *Leo Bährendt Südtirol* (1992)
Joseph Zoderer, *Die Walsche* (1982)

Credits and Acknowledgements

The writing of this book has involved numerous conversations, travels, discussions and research based on a wide range of sources. I would particularly like to thank Thomas Weaver for his long-term and patient encouragement on the book and his many comments and advice on the text; to Pamela Johnston for her expert text editing; to John Morgan and Adrien Vasquez from the John Morgan studio for this design template and their generous assistance with the images, map and family tree; to Gabriela Bueno Gibbs, Matthew Abbate and Jay Martsi at the MIT Press; for assistance, conversations and suggestions: Thérèse Willer, Luc Berujeau, Cissi Itzler; Bert Hoppe, Markus Podehl, Aleksandr Popadin, Yulia Bardun, Svetlana Chekina; Frank Boehm, Ricarda Dick, Victor Kahmen, Uwe Pauschert, Irmgard Weiz, Anje Ewerling, Walter Dickmann, Walther and Franz König, Vicky Kreuels, Antonie von Schönfeld, Ute Langanky, Lisa and Ulrike Hesler, Dr Winfried Stöcker, Holger Bunk, Lena Kosecki, Felix Wozniak, Dr Andreas Bednarek; Tim Wray (specialist title advice); Prof Julian Krüger, Prof Adrian Forty, Prof Mark Dorrian; Prof Matthias Ludwig, Elise Michaels, Etti Harksen, Kati Sommer, Monika Maels-Strinner; Tilman Heller, Gabriele Oberkofler, Andrew Peckham, Ursa Rosner, Andrew Higgott. Among the many institutions that provided important resources, I would like to thank the staff of the London Library, GAKO Kaliningrad, Stiftung Insel Hombroich, Mediathek Bozen, Tomi Ungerer Museum Strasbourg, Silesian Museum Görlitz. Thanks for support and assistance to Sabine Kunze, Milo Firebrace Kunze and in particular Luky and Pippin.

Image titles and credits

Cover: Church, © William Firebrace

Auf dem Vorgipfel der Punta Taviela, photographer Otto Schob, From J J Schatz (ed), *Südtirol*, 1931

Tomi Ungerer, Dessin pour la campagne publicitaire d'Electricité de Strasbourg, Dépôt privé au Musée Tomi Ungerer—Centre International de l'Illustration, Strasbourg, © Diogenes Verlag, Zurich / Tomi Ungerer Estate

Tomi Ungerer, Dessin pour la campagne publicitaire d'Electricité de Strasbourg, 2000, Dépôt privé au Musée Tomi Ungerer—Centre International de l'Illustration Strasbourg, © Diogenes Verlag, Zurich / Tomi Ungerer Estate, 2000

Monument to the Heroes of Space Exploration (Leonov Monument), Kaliningrad, c 1988, © Kaliningrad Public Archive (GAKO)

Julian Schwarzbreim, *House of the Soviets*, photographer Nicolas Grospierre 2011, © Nicolas Grospierre

Erwin Heerich, *Turm* pavilion, 1985–88, Museum Insel Hombroich, photographer Tomas Riehle, © Tomas Riehle / Bildarchiv Foto Marburg

Erwin Heerich, *Archiv*, 1998–99, Museum Insel Hombroich, photographer Tomas Riehle, © Tomas Riehle / Bildarchiv Foto Marburg

Erwin Heerich, isometric sectional studies, 1982, photograph Dejan Saric

Hombroich Insel, c 1910, photographer Wilhelm Lensing, © Vicki Kreuls Estate

Görlitz seen from the Gerhardt Hauptmann Theatre, with the Reichenback tower in the distance, 1959, photographer Lowe, © Bundesarchiv Berlin/ Bild 183-63751-0001

Wes Anderson, *The Grand Budapest Hotel*, poster, 2014, courtesy Wes Anderson

Marienkirche, Lübeck, drawing Insoo Hwang, © William Firebrace / Petrikirche, Lübeck, drawing Insoo Hwang, © William Firebrace / Dom, Lübeck, drawing Insoo Hwang, © William Firebrace / Nikolaikirche, Lübeck, drawing Insoo Hwang, © William Firebrace

Dom, Lübeck, photographer Wilhelm Castelli, copyright unknown

Burggräfler Trächten (Meraner Gegend), photographer S Schöner, from J J Schatz (ed), *Südtirol*, 1931 / Schutzhütte Schöne Aussicht gegen Finialspitze, photographer Leo Bährendt, © Amt für Film und Medien, Autonome Provinz Bozen-Südtirol

Sporthotel Valmartello, publicity poster, c 1936, © Archivio Ponti / Werner Tscholl, Haus 22, Morter, 2017, © Werner Tscholl Architekten

Tomi Ungerer, illustration from *No Kisses for Mother*, 1973, Dépôt privé au Musée Tomi Ungerer—Centre International de L'Illustration, Strasbourg, © Diogenes Verlag, Zurich / Tomi Ungerer Estate

Text credits

For text permissions I would like to thank SALDE, Éditions Albin Michel, Wylie Agency, Suhrkamp Verlag. All translations by the author except where indicated.

Every effort has been made to trace copyright holders and to obtain their permission for the use of copyright material. The publisher apologises for any errors or omissions in the above lists and would be grateful if notified of any corrections that should be incorporated in future reprints or editions of this book.

Five chapters in *Zickzack* are based on previously published articles, now extensively rethought and revised: 'Until the Bretchellmann Speaks' is based on an article in *Raritan* Winter 2020, edited by Stephanie Volmer, many thanks for kind permission to use these extracts; 'Now You Understand' is based on an article in *AA Files* 74 (2017), 'Paradise on Erft' in *AA Files* 71 (2016), 'Silesian Scenes' in *AA Files* 69 (2014), and 'Hop Rayuela Backstein' in *AA Files* 64 (2012), all four edited by Thomas Weaver with the assistance of Pamela Johnston and Sarah Handelman. Many thanks to the Architectural Association for kind permission to use extracts.

Zickzack William Firebrace

© 2022 Massachusetts Institute of Technology

All rights reserved. No part of this book may be reproduced in any form by any electronic or mechanical means (including photocopying, recording, or information storage and retrieval) without permission in writing from the publisher.

The MIT Press would like to thank the anonymous peer reviewers who provided comments on drafts of this book. The generous work of academic experts is essential for establishing the authority and quality of our publications. We acknowledge with gratitude the contributions of these otherwise uncredited readers.

This book was set in Haultin by the MIT Press. Printed and bound in Canada.

Library of Congress Cataloging-in-Publication Data
Names: Firebrace, William, author.
Title: Zickzack / William Firebrace.
Description: Cambridge, Massachusetts : The MIT Press, [2022] | Includes bibliographical references.
Identifiers: LCCN 2021052080 | ISBN 9780262544061 (paperback)
Subjects: LCSH: Borderlands—Germany—Civilization. | Europe, German-speaking—Civilization.
Classification: LCC DD61.8 .F57 2022 | DDC 320.1/20943—dc23/eng/20211123
LC record available at https://lccn.loc.gov/2021052080

10 9 8 7 6 5 4 3 2 1